Cinema, Black Suffering, and Theodicy

Cinema, Black Suffering, and Theodicy

Modern God

Shayne Lee

LEXINGTON BOOKS
Lanham • Boulder • New York • London

Published by Lexington Books
An imprint of The Rowman & Littlefield Publishing Group, Inc.
4501 Forbes Boulevard, Suite 200, Lanham, Maryland 20706
www.rowman.com

86-90 Paul Street, London EC2A 4NE, United Kingdom

Copyright © 2022 by The Rowman & Littlefield Publishing Group, Inc.

All rights reserved. No part of this book may be reproduced in any form or by any electronic or mechanical means, including information storage and retrieval systems, without written permission from the publisher, except by a reviewer who may quote passages in a review.

British Library Cataloguing in Publication Information Available

Library of Congress Cataloging-in-Publication Data

Names: Lee, Shayne, author.
Title: Cinema, Black suffering, and theodicy : modern God / Shayne Lee.
Description: Lanham : Lexington Books, [2022]. | Includes bibliographical references and index. | Summary: "This book analyzes how films depict God when black characters experience suffering and tragedy to elucidate how cinema often portrays a God that is considered supportive, yet who does little to mitigate suffering. This sparks theodical contemplation on the role of divinity in protecting people from the consequences of human depravity"—Provided by publisher.
Identifiers: LCCN 2021049087 (print) | LCCN 2021049088 (ebook) | ISBN 9781666904215 (cloth) | ISBN 9781666904239 (paperback) | ISBN 9781666904222 (epub)
Subjects: LCSH: African Americans in motion pictures. | God in motion pictures. | Theodicy in motion pictures. | Race in motion pictures. | Motion pictures—United States—History and criticism.
Classification: LCC PN1995.9.B585 L44 2022 (print) | LCC PN1995.9.B585 (ebook) | DDC 791.43/652996073—dc23/eng/20211027
LC record available at https://lccn.loc.gov/2021049087
LC ebook record available at https://lccn.loc.gov/2021049088

Contents

Introduction	1
Chapter 1: Theodical Secularity	19
Chapter 2: Tactical Deists: Black Liberation Theology and Cinema	49
Chapter 3: Cinema and American Slavery	79
Chapter 4: Ousmane Sembène: Toward a New and Modern Africa	113
Chapter 5: Contemporary African American Films	141
Epilogue: Africa: The New Cinematic Holocaust	173
Filmography	207
References	211
Index	231
About the Author	235

Introduction

Two decades ago, I was an overworked graduate student at Northwestern University with no time on my hands to attend Cornel West's guest lecture. When I quizzed my friend Dorcas for highlights, she griped that West tackled a topic no one had heard of called theodicy. Her frustration surprised me since I did not see theodicy as an unfamiliar term. A year later the same difference in familiarity resurfaced when I told a professor that my paper will assess Max Weber's treatment of theodicy in *Economy and Society*. Intrigued by my topic, the professor asked if Weber had anything cool to say about *The Iliad*. I smiled and walked away, reminding myself not to presume that people understand what is meant when one utters the word theodicy. Notwithstanding its susceptibility to Homeric misplacement, theodicy is too relevant an issue to ignore.

Weber (1978) delineates theodicy's main objective as to reconcile God's perfection against the end products of human injustice, unrighteousness, and sin. But skeptics often allude to heartbreak and misfortune to reject the notion of divine providence or cast aspersions on God's credibility. Enjoying no decisive rallying point, theodical discourses explicate evil and suffering from varying theoretical (and theological) perspectives. So when a person stands face to face with the dreadful scowl of tragedy, whether she defends divine justice, cries out to Yahweh for comfort, bemoans Allah's silence, or announces God's death, she ostensibly engages in theodical discourse as she attempts to make sense of calamity. And it need not be a real person to partake in theodical ponderings. Dramatic works, from Voltaire's (1759) philosophical tale *Candide* to contemporary hip-hop lyrics, feature protagonists grappling with the vagaries of misfortune from shifting theodical vantages.

Recognizing cinema as one of the most overlooked artistic domains of theodical reflection, this book investigates how films, set in multiple countries, contexts, and cultures, reference God when black characters endure slavery, wars, famines, genocides, poverty, prison abuse, sickness, sexual assault, homophobia, or other upsetting circumstances. Its findings reveal how theodical tactics in cinema often affirm God's existence while insinuating rational limitations on God's interventionist capacities. Cinema's preferred theodical perspective is easily summed up in the parlance of sport: God coaches from the sidelines and humans make all the plays in the game of life.

In addition to assessing cinema's sidelined sovereign, this study also explores how filmic treatments of theodicy exert hermeneutic handiness toward the social construction of evil and suffering. The chapters catalog how theodical films: code and narrate historical processes that undergird dysfunctional systems and maladjusted people; demarcate clear lines of distinction between victims and perpetrators; clarify the social dynamics driving inequality and oppression; humanize sufferers; and transform individual episodes of suffering into collective and memorialized identities of trauma—all while incubating modern liberal values reflecting a wide range of emotions. This work ultimately concludes that cinematic theodicy is in the construction business, that is, the business of meaning construction. However, before exploring how films situate God's instruction or support into the backdrop of tragic events while concomitantly divesting divine proclivities of supernatural efficacy and contextualizing malevolence and misfortune within modern structures of meaning, we should consider how questions about the nature of evil and human suffering in relation to providence had been broached long before Gottfried Leibniz (1710) introduced theodicy as an apologetic enterprise to address those inquiries.

THE JANUS FACE OF THEODICY

The Epic of Gilgamesh (Foster 2001) goes back to the third millennium B.C.E. and is one of the oldest texts to negotiate grief and death as unavoidable outcomes of the human condition. After mourning the passing of his friend Enkidu, the protagonist Gilgamesh finally accepts the limits of humanity in contrast to the immortality of the gods. Similarly, the tragedians created characters that navigate the crossroads of divine fate and human choice in relation to evil and suffering. For example, in the last line of Sophocles's (2007) play *Women of Trachis* (written around 420 B.C.E.), the character Hyllus attributes familial misfortune to the hands of Zeus even though the tragic chain of events that led to the death of his parents had obvious links to human actions.

Perhaps no sentence encapsulates theodicy's essential quandary better than the evocative question, "Why does God let bad things happen to good people?" The Old Testament book of Job is feasibly the best-known example of literature to grapple with that query after Job suffers terrible losses when God grants permission for Satan to harm his children, livestock, and health. As his friends theorize about the nature of his afflictions, Job continues to bet on God's trustworthiness. Job's perspective on divine providence precludes him from attributing the deluge of misfortunes to a malevolent god, as one could do when subscribing to the dualism of a religion like Zoroastrianism which, as Weber points out, sacrifices God's omnipotence for a world in which "the powers of light and truth, purity and goodness coexist and conflict with the powers of darkness and falsehood, impurity and evil" (1958a: 358). Ethical monotheists like Job believe that perfect justice and morality emanate out of the one true God in whom they place their faith. Hence, Job has more at stake in terms of explaining tragedy in a way that preserves God's righteousness than dualists, polytheists, and skeptics who can trace tribulation back to an evil deity, ignore God altogether, or credit divine indifference for the extensiveness of human misery.

While discourses on evil and suffering carry considerable credence in ancient literatures and medieval apologetics, they evince even more magnitude in a modern world that increasingly emphasizes individualism and the burden of choice. Accordingly, Gottfried Leibniz (1710) coined theodicy during a time when the rapidly changing social climate of Western Europe created new epistemological challenges that impelled ethical monotheists to tackle the problem of evil and suffering head on. For Leibniz, theodicy's function is to demonstrate through logical deductions how a world created and ruled by God, despite its flaws and gestations of tragedy and suffering, is the best of all possible worlds. Leibniz's theodical defense of the rational acceptability of theism in an imperfect world provides the foundation for the freewill defense that Alvin Plantinga (1967, 1977) would later employ to resolve the logical problem of evil. However, while philosophers now recognize, largely due to Plantinga's efforts, how evil and God can logically coexist, a recalcitrant skeptic might claim that cracking the logical problem of evil does nothing to increase the probability of divine governance coinciding with genocide, war, infanticide, rape, and other gratuitous atrocities.

Such theodical cynicism owes a debt to Voltaire (1759) whose philosophical tale *Candide* satirized Leibniz's apologetic proposal so effectively that it helped broaden theodicy's connotative scaffolding to include what some scholars frame as anti-theodicies. Consequently, scholars now designate both the biblical story of Job and Voltaire's *Candide* as classic theodical texts even though they constitute divergent theological aims: the former, a salutation to God's supremacy considering Job's misfortunes; the latter, a scornful weaponizing of evil and suffering to subvert the very notion of divine intervention. A glance over contemporary treatments of theodicy confirms how Leibniz's neologism evolved to encompass conceptual elasticity and a capacity for valence.

W. S. F. Pickering (1980: 65) recognizes that theodicy "gives rise to a variety of responses, from science and technology at one extreme, to prayer and ritual at the other," while claiming that within such a theodical spectrum are assorted arrangements of political emancipation including reform and revolution. Similarly, David Burrell (2008) reveals what the biblical story of Job contributes to theodicy beyond Leibniz's preoccupation with an explanation of God's justice or human suffering. Jill Hernandez (2016) discloses theodical arguments that are unique to modern theists who venture far beyond the original borders Leibniz established. D. Z. Phillips (2001) acknowledges that even when an antitheist like J. L. Mackie articulates his opposition to theism on grounds that point to evil, Mackie does so through a theodical framework. Zachary Braiterman (1998) admits that his use of theodicy throughout his analysis of post-Holocaust intellectuals is intentionally indefinite so as to incorporate both theists (who affirm Leibniz's approach) and Jewish thinkers who reject the very project of theodicy. And rather than defending God's righteousness, John Roth's (2001) theodicy of protest interrogates God for allowing vexing manifestations of evil, suffering, and death to exist.

So not every theodical project promotes divine benevolence or prioritizes providence in the grand scheme of human suffering, as secular conceptualizations proliferate in multiple academic disciplines. Four years before Ernest Becker (1968) designates sociology as the ideal intellectual domain to retool theodicy with a nontheistic focus, Milton Mays (1964) posits that Mary Shelley's classic novel *Frankenstein* offers a dark theodicy in how its treatment of evil raises questions about the relationship between humans and nature and challenges the notion of universal justice. Kathleen Higgins (1987) argues that Friedrich Nietzsche proposes a secular theodicy through his doctrine of eternal recurrence. Francis Fukuyama (1992) uncovers and critiques the widespread belief that a universal history must function as a secular theodicy to account for Nazism and Stalinism. D. Christopher Kayes (2006) appropriates the problem of theodicy toward the task of explaining organizational corruption as the attempt to clarify incongruity between experience and normative anticipation. Tara Burton (2020: 176) describes the social justice movement's revisionist take on American history in response to the election of Donald Trump as "a profound and powerful theodicy capable of explaining the evils of 2016 with recourse to a still wickeder past."

Secular theodicies also address black suffering. Stacey Floyd-Thomas's (2008) theodical project dispenses with God as a possible solution to what she refers to as the existential crisis of black female embodiment, instead choosing to rely on writings of the victims themselves, black female scholars who have overcome such oppressive conditions. So theodicy for Floyd-Thomas is not a way of questioning God's presence in the overall index of suffering that black women endure but ignores God altogether when articulating prescriptive measures for those very same sufferers to survive racist misogyny. Emilie Townes (2006) explores evil as cultural production to shed light on how particular discourses reflect and support systems of inequality and social oppression. Townes never contemplates God's role in the perpetuation (or elimination) of evil structures of inequality against black women. Michael Lackey (2007) studies black artists and intellectuals of the twentieth century who offer scathing critiques against religion and remove God entirely from the equation of addressing the problem of evil and black suffering. Craig Prentiss (2014) assesses how traditional theistic approaches to theodicy are incommensurate with mid-twentieth-century black anti-lynching dramas called "theodicy plays," some of which go so far as to question God's existence. Anthony Pinn asserts that segments of African American religious history are conversant with alternating theodicies including those brokered by atheists (2002), while Pinn himself recommends nontheological humanism to replace theistic theodicies when addressing the complexities of black suffering (1995, 2012). Kurt Buhring (2008) illuminates humanist responses to the problem of theodicy which turn their gaze from explaining why God allows evil, toward focusing on human freedom and how humans can resist evil. Judylyn Ryan's (2005) assessment of theodicy in Toni Morrison's (1987) classic novel *Beloved* reveals how the character Baby Suggs interrogates the strength and breadth of evil against the backdrop of her own waning faith and sense of agency, ultimately attributing harmful interventionist dimensions to white people for targeted acts and systems of violence against black people. Accordingly, Baby Suggs's contemplation on white excess functions as what Ryan calls a "liberating theodicy" because such reflection makes sense of white aggression while empowering Baby Suggs to continue in the path of righteousness. Josiah Young (2007) shows how Toni Morrison broaches theodicy in her earliest novel *The Bluest Eye* (1970) through a pedophile's ruminations on evil and wickedness.

In contrast to theodical projects that ignore divinity, theocentric conceptualizations can generate theodical valence, which implies a spectrum of positive and negative propositions about God's relationship to evil and suffering. For example, Robert Wuthnow (2012: 120) clarifies how conventional questions of theodicy ask: "Is God in control? If so, how can a powerful and merciful God allow such suffering? Is God punishing the wicked? Teaching humans a lesson? Are there evil forces in the world that God cannot control?" Each of Wuthnow's inquiries can trigger answers that endorse God or answers that challenge divine efficacy. Similarly, J. Deotis Roberts insinuates theodical valence while triangulating Leibniz's concept with hermeneutics and teleology:

> All philosophies of Black experience must tackle the question of meaning. Not only the question: Who am I?, but the question of purpose or teleology must be raised and dealt with. If the philosophy of the Black experience takes a religious turn, the problem of theodicy arises. The question: why there is so much

unmerited suffering in a world in which the One said to be in charge is lovingly just? (1989: 255)

Here we see Roberts not only tacitly cosign Max Weber's (1958b) position on the exegetical import of theodicy, but also classify theodicy as a natural consequence of a marginalized group questioning the teleological presumptions behind and existential meaning of its oppression. Like Wuthnow, Roberts offers theodicy as a deliberative process that can elicit both affirmations and denials of God's justice.

The above studies and numerous more demonstrate how theodicy functions as a discursive weapons system for a variety of theological and nontheistic confrontations. Perhaps a less bellicose simile is to think of theodicy as a brewing stew containing broths and fixings endorsing the logical compatibility of divine justice and evil (Leibniz 1710; Hick 1963; 1966; Plantinga 1977) simmering alongside spicy ingredients undermining the notion of theistic intervention (Rubenstein 1966; Cohen 1993). This culinary simile is useful toward clarifying how what Leibniz intends as a defense of God's justice, what David Blumenthal (1993) constitutes as theology of protest, what Richard Swinburne (1977) and Zachary Braiterman (1998) classify as antitheodicies, what John Roth (2001) modifies as theodicy of protest, what Susan Neiman (2002) organizes as modern theodicies, and what Jared Hickman (2017) establishes as modern anthropotheodicy, all belong in the zesty gumbo of theodical discourse.

This study owes analytical debts to Gottfried Leibniz (1710) for establishing theodicy as a modern intellectual enterprise, Voltaire (1759) for unwittingly expanding theodicy's framework so that it now encompasses anxieties about God's silence and inactivity in a precarious world of evil and injustice, Max Weber (1958b, 1978) for introducing theodicy's sociological relevance, and Charles Taylor (2007) for reconceptualizing secularity in a manner that stimulates my interest in theodical connections to the boundary work of secularity. What differentiates this present study from other approaches is its interest in cinema and its inquisitiveness toward exegeting how theodical "God-talk" (how people talk to and about God) incorporates boundary imputations on divine attributes in ways that illuminate cultural configurations of modern identities. Whereas many theodical projects defend, castigate, or de-center God-talk, this study retains God-talk as the focal point of theodical analysis, while indicating the ways in which it suggests rational boundaries on divine intervention. Accordingly, this present study reveals how modern theodicy need not function as a binary that either campaigns for God or condemns God; that theodicy can also entail theocentric nuance that affirms God's existence and importance while sidelining God's supernatural activity.

And thus, this work juxtaposes God-talk and the cultural work of secularity within shifting interpolations of modern identities.

This synergistic relationship between theodical discourse and symbolic boundaries underscores how those antebellum slaves who questioned God's silence in response to the severities of their subjugation (Cone 2011) did not need to employ Leibniz's best-of-all-possible-worlds stratagem or Alvin Plantinga's (1977) freewill defense of divine benevolence in order for their inquiries to be classified as theodical; their mere decision to ask the question, "How is God responding to our plight?" constitutes the problem of theodicy (Pinn 1995). And the fact that some slaves' answers to the latter question cast doubt on God's willingness to intervene is unsurprising when considering that even the most devoted theist will struggle to detect teleological designs undergirding the architecture of the so-called peculiar institution of slavery. Hence, there may be no better theodical base from which to assess boundary ascriptions to God than the institution of slavery, and no better artistic starting point from which to commence assessments of slavery's peculiar representations than the mini-series *Roots*, a television adaptation of Alex Haley's (1976) novel that continues to affect (and afflict) American consciousness long after it first aired to a record-breaking viewership in 1977. As a small-screen warmup for the slavery films we will assess in chapter 3, the mini-series depicts various stations of the transnational slave trade: captivity in Africa, degrading conditions on the slave ship, disorienting transition from free beings to dehumanized servants in the Americas, and abusive treatment by American slave masters, as each episode questions the meaning and merits of this organized system of human exploitation and God's ability to change it.

ROOTS, ART, AND CINEMA

Theodical God-talk in *Roots* emerges early when an exasperated young African fighter named Kunta Kinte reminds his elder tribesman Wrestler, "I am a man, a warrior!" Wrestler responds, "Kunta, we have been chained in the white man's canoe house for many days now. Allah sees, He understands, He knows you are a man." After hearing Wrestler's reassurance, Kunta appeals, "Allah the merciful, Allah the all-powerful, Allah the compassionate, please hear my prayers! Allah, Allah please!" As they endure the misery of the Middle Passage voyage, Wrestler's confidence in Allah seems to diminish. When they conspire to take over the ship and Wrestler reassures Kunta, "We will kill the white man and we will go home," Kunta confidently responds, "It is in Allah's hands," and Wrestler interjects, "It is in our hands. Allah made us warriors." Here we see Wrester pivot from Allah's intervention to their own combative efforts as the solution to their tragic plight. And when their mutiny unfolds, the crewmen's gunpowder, not Allah's hands, casts the decisive blow, thus confirming Wrestler's deistic hunch. If Kunta's earlier prayer was hopeful, his invocation following their crushed rebellion is suicidal: "Allah the merciful, Allah the compassionate, take this man to paradise. Let him see Muhammad the prophet. Let him taste joys of the faithful."

Once Kunta and his captured comrades reach the United States, they are auctioned off to the highest bidders. When they reach their new residences, his friend Fanta is promptly subjected to sexual assault and Kunta suffers a vicious whipping by the slave breaker Mr. Ames under the authority of Massa who calmly reads his Bible while each lash shreds deeper layers of Kunta's skin. Witnessing the brutal beating is an older slave named Fiddler who utters, "Lord God, help that boy." But the same God who does nothing to avert Fanta's debasement, does nothing to prevent Kunta's flesh-torn rite of passage from brave African warrior to submissive slave renamed Toby. *Roots'* most explicit theodical exchange occurs decades later when the master's daughter Missy Ann explains to Toby's daughter Kizzy that blacks serving whites in slavery "is the natural way of things." Missy Ann corroborates this racial order by insisting that "white folks are just naturally smarter than Niggers." Kizzy responds with an inquiry, "You mean, that's the way God made it?" Missy Ann replies, "Exactly. So if it wasn't right why He'd change it, wouldn't He?" Immediately after Missy Ann issues God's sovereign stamp on racial hierarchy and slave labor, Kizzy steers their conversation from God to abolitionists who do in fact want to change the presumed natural order of things and do away with slavery. So instead of engaging in a debate on the teleological underpinnings of her bondage, Kizzy throws her white counterpart a humanist curveball. Upon hearing the mere mention of those dreadful abolitionists, Missy Ann is aghast and rhetorically defeated by her slave's cunning pivot.

Like other cinematic treatments of slavery, *Roots* features black sufferers who believe in a God who can't be counted on to disrupt their mounting vulnerabilities. For example, when Kizzy's love interest Noah escapes the plantation, Kizzy cries out, "Protect him sweet Jesus. Protect him from the patrollers and the slave catchers." Despite Kizzy's prayer of protection, the patrollers bring Noah back to the plantation dirty, bloody, and in chains. When Kizzy's master learns she forged documents to help Noah escape, he sells her to the menacing slaveowner Tom Moore as retribution. So not only does Kizzy's prayer go unanswered but subsequently she has to endure the trauma of embracing her parents and the man she loves for the very last time. Ripped apart from her family and Noah, the young virgin quickly learns what Fanta discovered shortly after leaving the auction block: that sexual assault is part of the tragic defenselessness of being a female slave. Tom Moore rapes Kizzy the first night she arrives on his land. In a later episode, the mini-series unveils the nation's post–Civil War iteration of racial terrorism: white Southerners riding in at night shooting pistols, burning equipment, destroying crops, and breaking windows of the homes of newly freed blacks. Ironically, one of these night raids interrupts the former slaves while they are singing spiritual songs, as if the mini-series is bent toward driving home the point that evil prevails even when vulnerable black people are worshipping God.

If *Roots* constitutes television's first theodical showcase of slavery, we must return to Voltaire's (1759) *Candide* to consider the world's first artistic amalgamation of slavery and theodicy. While much of Voltaire's philosophical tale is centered in Europe, a crucial sequence in Surinam features Candide and his traveling companion Cacambo encountering a black slave's heartbreaking testimony of abuse and deformity. Voltaire's inclusion of this slave's sad story is designed to implicate a world in which Africans are abducted and exported to a Dutch colony in South America as a world that undoubtedly lacks God's intervening hand. The Surinam encounter complements the philosophical tale's plentiful episodes of rape, exploitation, genocide, and disaster to ridicule Leibniz's claim that humans occupy the best of all possible worlds that God could create and maintain.

If Voltaire's masterwork is the first published theodical deployment of black suffering, Ahmadou Kourouma's (2006) novel *Allah Is Not Obliged* can be styled as *Candide*'s twenty-first century remake, shifting the focus from European aggression to black-on-black crimes in African countries. Set in the 1990s with a precocious twelve-year-old "retired" child soldier named Birahima as narrator, the novel revisits atrocities Birahima encountered in Liberia and Sierra Leone, while the young raconteur lampoons Allah's condoning nod to each event. Not unlike *Candide*, sexual assault is a recurrent transgression in Birahima's stories which include how young Sita was raped and decapitated and her body parts recovered from three labor camps, and how twelve-year-old Mirta was gang-raped at a cacao plantation. Birahima arrives in Sierra Leone at the same time a freedom fighter named Foday Ankoh conducts a widespread practice of amputating the arms of citizens to obstruct the election process, presuming that citizens with no arms cannot vote. *Allah Is Not Obliged* mimics *Candide* in how its tales of heinous infringements and unimaginable suffering express deep-seated contempt against the very notion of divine providence.

Within the timespan between the publications of Voltaire's and Kourouma's provocative texts exists more than two hundred years of artistic contemplation on God and black suffering broaching a wide range of theodical inclinations. While some certify unwavering trust in God's faithfulness, others sympathize with *Roots'* sidelined God and *Allah Is Not Obliged*'s unregulated world of mayhem and misery. Some slave songs pose tension between a God of justice and the toll of suffering (Jones 1987), and a considerable proportion of black plays written between 1916 and 1941 use the historical tragedy of lynching as a framework to challenge the notion of divine sovereignty (Prentiss 2014). The blues and Negro spirituals often serve as repositories of black faith traditions (Douglas 2012), but at times they also express frustration at God's passivity concerning the poverty and hardship African Americans endure in their communities (Cone 1992; Pinn 1995, 2002). By the same token, literary artists of multiple generations grapple with the challenges of understanding black oppression against the backdrop of sacred texts and religious promises of divine intervention (Whitted 2009).

Treatments of black suffering in hip-hop are no less amenable to theodical disputation, as exemplified by: Tupac's treatise "Only God Can Judge Me," which ponders whether the Lord cares about the cries of thugs; Silk the Shocker's "Ghetto Tears," which questions if the redemptive reach of divine power extends to black people in the ghetto; Jay-Z's on-the-ground grassroots theodicy as assessed in Michael Eric Dyson's popular course titled "Sociology of Hip Hop—Urban Theodicy of Jay-Z" (Dyson 2015); and Anthony Pinn's (1995, 2015) perceptive insights on how progressive strands of hip-hop can inform interrogations of the problem of evil from a black humanist perspective. What remains overlooked within the analysis of theodicy and black misery is how countless films propose worlds where black characters make sense of their tragic plight by ultimately (or inadvertently) conceding that the laws of nature are final, humans are free to commit evil deeds and create oppressive systems, and God is sequestered to the sidelines of human sufferings, never to exert divine energy toward the removal of said sufferings.

This study fills in the void by revealing how filmic representations of black suffering and God-talk infer rational limitations on divine intervention. In the context of evil and suffering, cinema often showcases the same passive divinity represented in *Roots*: the God who sees, hears, and understands human pain and abhors evil—but does little to set situations straight, enforce justice, or remove tragedy. Rather than removing God altogether from the equation, cinema often keeps divinity in play by renegotiating God's governing contract from sovereign ruler to cosmic coach. Simply put, evil and suffering persist because God is on the sidelines and humans alone step on the field to conquer evil or mitigate suffering.

This work presents filmic treatments of theodicy as modern rituals in the manner in which their vivid depictions of evil and suffering can moralize, memorialize, and mobilize audiences around a wide range of spiritual, symbolic, political, and emotional touchstones. In other words, filmic treatments of theodicy enjoy all the markings of a modern tribal dance. If face-to-face encounters in traditional rituals work to collate a general stock of knowledge while shaping group sentiments and enhancing social cohesion (Collins 2004;

Alexander 2010), then cinematic theodicy operates as a souped-up village ceremony, embodying both deliberative and affective mechanisms that have the potential to generate new forms of political consciousness and intercontinental solidarity. As ritualistic performances, their plotlines, conflicts, and boundary ascriptions offer tutorials on liberal humanist ways to negotiate God's role in the modern world.

Most of the numerous films assessed in this tome are short on the kind of dazzling supernatural displays one finds in ancient mythic traditions, as representations of God in realist dramas are almost exclusively closed off by rational borders. Occasional celluloid displays of magic and allure simply remind us that the cinematic world respects a clear line of demarcation between fantasy and reality and its realist forays into black suffering predictably cast God as concerned but also uninvolved in human outcomes. But the fact that divine representation and God-talk still emerge in realist filmic representations of black tragedy is a noteworthy pattern that should challenge scholars to rethink their own conceptual controlments of secularity. If meddlesome deities are relics of ancient imaginations or enchanted medieval mindsets, then cinema gives God an immanent upgrade.

Since films were birthed during an inimitable period of Western transformation, perhaps they are innately insulated to absorb the shocks and flow of modern momentum (Gunning 2006; Lee 2015). Over the past few decades, scholars have shown increasing curiosity concerning cinema's intersections with modernity, uncovering how films: stimulate religious transformations and globalizing African cultural forms (Hackett and Soares 2015); are accurate and meaningful modes of historical narration (Davis 2000); have great social import (Nichols 2010); reflect present-day perspectives and concerns (Cooper and Skrade 1970); illuminate broad social, economic, and cultural innovations (Charney and Schwartz 1995; Robinson 2007); collapse the difference between religious and secular functions in modern society (Lyden 2003); serve as storehouses of theological significance (Deacy 2007; Garrett 2007); facilitate dialogues with Christian theology (Jewett 1993, 1999; Marsh 1997; Detweiler 2008); extend intellectual resources that can help existing religions extirpate ideological baggage from earlier civilizations and cultures (Hurley 1970); exhibit and shape modern perceptions of race and ethnicity (Leab 1975; Cripps 1996; Watkins 1998; Yearwood 2000; Massood 2003; Dunn 2008); and mediate representations of black modern identities (Stewart 2005; Sotiropoulos 2006; Weisenfeld 2007; Field 2015; Lee 2015). But what remains entirely overlooked in scholarly discussions of cinema is how films convey the ways in which modern presuppositions about the world require new theodical strategies that help to refine people's understanding of secular boundaries. This work corrects this oversight by exploring how cinematic theodicy's representations of God and God-talk are themselves metrics and mechanisms of modern identities.

Treating filmmakers as modern exegetes who recalibrate divine attributes to the cadences and cultural tastes of their contemporaries, this book reimagines films as scaled-up modern rituals in light of their socializing potential to shape public perceptions, elicit emotional responses, promote liberal humanist values, disseminate interpretive frameworks for evil and suffering, and generate intercontinental solidarity. Moreover, it introduces and establishes the study of cinematic theodicy as an archeological mission in search of celluloid fossils that inform how meaning-making mindsets operate in the modern world. But before scouting new terrain, I would encourage present and future excavators to be mindful of how the mining of theodical sites almost inevitably uncovers inconceivable concentrations of human carnage. Fittingly, if viewers of films can be vicariously traumatized (Kaplan 2005), we should assume that viewers can also be vicariously "theodicized." Modern representations of tragedy and trauma may not only shock and outrage some viewers, but also press them to contemplate the problem of evil in distressing ways, just as literary works like *Candide* and *Allah Is Not Obliged* ostensibly bait bibliophiles into questioning the prospect of divine intervention. We can extrapolate this principle of vicarious theodicy to presume that perusing a study such as this, replete with collocations of human suffering and God-talk, comes with the hazard of vicarious distress and indignation at the human capacity to inflict evil and God's unwillingness to stop it. Such an intense engagement with the macabre side of humanity requires that both excavators and onlookers alike expose themselves to artifacts of genocide, rape, and numerous other atrocities. Consequently, this inaugural expedition and future diggings into theodical topographies require an obligatory note of caution: archeological discretion is advised. Trigger warning aside, it may very well be that cinematic theodicy's propensity toward shock and awe is what makes it such fertile terrain for excavation. I imagine few people can scrutinize dramatizations of the cruelty slaves experienced on the Middle Passage or watch vivid depictions of the unprecedented density of death endured during the Rwandan genocide and remain untouched by cinema's signifying proficiency. Hence, this study encourages scholars to devote more attentiveness to cinematic theodicy's ability to keep viewers affectively stimulated and cognitively attentive. More than offering audiences creative contexts for artistic contemplation, filmic treatments of theodicy construct evil and suffering in calculated ways that connect specific acts, actions, and institutions to greater structures of meaning.

OVERVIEW

While some scholars specify essential elements in "black theodicy" that distinguish it from other theodical discussions (Jones 1973; Jackson 2009; Key 2011), affirm the notion of a black or Afro-Americanized conception of God (Jones 1987; Lloyd 2018), or treat blackness as an ontological reality (Cone 1969, 1970; Sinclair 2013), this work veers away from naturalistic claims or insinuations regarding racial authenticity. As such, my choice of black suffering does not specify any fundamental racial or ethnic identity contention concerning cinema's penchant for sidelining God. Conversely, this study engages a diverse array of films set in different countries, cultures, and contexts to steer clear of any semblance of an authoritative vantage point of black suffering. And thus each chapter quite intentionally consists of works by filmmakers of various racial and ethnic backgrounds to dismiss the presumption that writers and directors of a particular hue or ethnicity enjoy representational entitlement over black experiences and pains. If Martians made compelling offerings on black suffering then I would have included some of their films under the belief that filmic representation of black life is fair game to all sentient beings. Fittingly, while my chapter on American slavery contains no extraterrestrial offerings, it does cover an eclectic swath of movies that include a mainstream production like *Amistad* (1997, Steven Spielberg), a radical drama like *Sankofa* (1993, Haile Gerima), and a satirical documentary like *Goodbye Uncle Tom* (1971, Gualtiero Jacopetti and Franco Prosperi), directed by a Jewish American, an Ethiopian American, and two Italian filmmakers, respectively. Even when films under analysis depict race, ethnicity, or national identity in realist or naturalistic ways, my intention as an interpretive aesthetician is to assess the implications of those significations while my own analyses fly above the essentialist fray.

Chapter 1 introduces a fluid relationship between theodicy and secularity that elucidates how people negotiate tragedy and trauma by adjusting divine characteristics to the cadences of modern identities. It points out an important compromise that Max Weber and other scholars missed because they predicted the imminent demise of theodicy and God-talk under the soul-crushing influence of modernization. The chapter introduces a new sense of secularity to challenge the old presumption that modernizing forces, like pluralism, urbanization, the formation of political centers, collapsing plausibility structures, scientific-technological advances, capitalism, consumerism, and globalization, generate necessary declines in religious belief, practice, presence, or import and nullify the need for theodicy in a world in which God and religious ideas no longer have a lingering presence or impact in society. If the miscalculation of sociologists and secularization theorists was to assume the dissolution of religion and theodicy in a highly technological, advanced capitalist age of plurality, Nancy Ammerman's (2014b) and Robert Wuthnow's (2012) studies of American believers, along with my assessments of cinematic juxtapositions of black suffering and divine representation, suggest that society can function as a complex balancing act between secular and spiritual resources and that modern theists, just like modern theologians, and filmmakers, are quite adept at triangulating rationality, faith, and tragedy. The chapter concludes with an important discussion of sacred/secular mutuality as a hallmark of theodical secularity as well as contemporary modern identities.

Chapter 2 engages black liberation theology, positioning its leading proponents as scholarly complements to filmmakers in how they remove God's interventionist capacity from the durability of black suffering. Like the sample of liberationist films discussed in the chapter, proponents of liberation theology rarely if ever allude to Satan, demons, or dark powers as causal forces undergirding tragic outcomes, but rather choose to translate evil in modern sociopolitical language, while engaging in complex intellectual interrogations on inequality, discrimination, racism, sexism, and systems of exploitation. Like filmmakers, liberation theologians offer modern liberal frameworks through which to perceive evil systems and suffering people. While advocates of black liberation theology extend perfunctory claims on God's preference for and presence among black people, their significant talking points never proffer a direct role for God in punishing oppressors and liberating victims. In other words, the God of black liberation theology, like the God of cinema, cannot be counted on to protect the vulnerable nor alleviate vast levels of oppression and inequality that black people face disproportionately. In God's place, humans must make all of the big plays toward ensuring justice. Hence, chapter 2 presents black liberation theology as a deistic analogue to cinematic theodicy for the many ways in which it sidelines God in the context of black suffering.

Most intellectual expeditions into black suffering will in due course come ashore the domain of American slavery. As humanity's only time machine, cinema is uniquely prepared to afford current and future generations of Americans creative opportunities to revisit the pain and suffering of slavery. Chapter 3 explores cinematic representations of black bodies chained and packed together like sardines in slave ships, poked and prodded in auctions, and primed to endure inhumane treatment in plantation life to reveal how slavery films generate pressing questions about God's role in chattel servitude. Most relevant is the refusal of slavery films to afford a more active role for God beyond cosmic coach or cheerleader of vulnerable slaves. And in those scenes where slaves place trust in divine intervention, the plots ultimately sideline God or expose the complexities and contradictions that come with the notion of divine jurisdiction over humans against the cruel technologies of chattel slavery. The chapter also unveils how aforementioned radical slavery films like *Sankofa* and *Goodbye Uncle Tom* allege a nexus between religious adherence and the dehumanization of slaves to suggest that religion and God not only lack mechanisms to hold societal forms of evil accountable, but also function as impelling forces (or manipulatable pawns) behind the perpetuation of black suffering. Chapter 3 brings to light how cinematic theodicy signifies slavery as part of a pernicious system of human exploitation, while it deploys modern liberal discourses to defend the dignity of human life. In narrating oppressive conditions, while documenting God's inefficacy at alleviating those conditions and the ways religion and God were deployed to endorse exploitation and brutality, slavery films accentuate modern reinterpretations of God and slave societies in ways that draw attention to the socially constructed nature of evil and morality.

Chapter 4 evaluates the classic works of Africa's first black filmmaker, Ousmane Sembène, which present postcolonial challenges and tragedies as contexts to contemplate divine representation in African history and contemporary cultures, sometimes depicting the gods of African traditional religion as unnecessary distractions, and other times presenting the God of major world religions as an albatross of African suffering. But Sembène's films also explicate the social meaning of suffering in ways that draw on lingering grievances and emotions from slavery, colonization, and postcolonial traumas he believes still resonate with his black African audiences (and world audiences). Sembène refuses to let African tradition off the hook, revealing how it sometimes serves as a propagative component of social suffering. The chapter illuminates how, later in his career, when Sembène is less bent toward a socialist revolution and more open to a peaceful merger between God and the prospect of a thriving African future, the aging filmmaker reduces God's relevance to that of an unobtrusive and inclusive cultural marker in a new modern Africa, while drawing upon modern liberal values as solutions toward disabusing evil and black suffering. In general, Sembène's revolutionary works recommend God and religion to remain on the sidelines of African progression, while confronting, coding, and memorializing continental traumas.

Chapter 5 studies theodical themes in contemporary films featuring African American protagonists. It begins with two of Tyler Perry's works, *Meet the Browns* (2008) and *Daddy's Little Girls* (2007), focusing on the ways in which their plots credit the role of human talent, grit, and instinct as solutions to problems that earlier sequences alleged to have required divine intervention. In the battle between humanist and theological interpretations of and solutions to black suffering, God is sidelined in both films so that agentive capacities can rise to the occasion to provide swift resolutions. The chapter turns to *Red Hook Summer* (2012) to explore how Spike Lee's film generates questions concerning why God allows depressing levels of inequality and oppression to persist within black urban environs and why God would allow a vulnerable young boy to suffer trauma at the hands of a trusted cleric. The chapter then tackles theodical tensions and nuances in *Eve's Bayou* (1997), *Civil Brand* (2002), *Woman Thou Art Loosed: On the 7th Day* (2012), *Taken From Me* (2011), and other contemporary films that display African American characters negotiating pain and contemplating their futures in a world where God often seems afar off.

The epilogue reveals how the deistic tremors first detonated in Sembène's influential oeuvre continue to reverberate throughout more recent cinematic intersections of Africa and black suffering. It covers films recounting the Hutu killing spree in Rwanda, the cruel contours of South African apartheid, the hostile regions of Central Africa, and other ethnic cleansings and continental tragedies, to show how films set in Africa pose pressing challenges against divine intervention while converting specific episodes of black suffering into collective identities of traumas. Their signifying functions set discursive lines of demarcation between oppressors and victims, heroes and perpetrators, while almost uniformly epitomizing black African suffering as contingent, episodic, and gratuitous. The epilogue devotes particular attention to the manner in which Nigerian contributions, known as Nollywood films, exhibit a modified deistic dualism where lower-level powers, magical spells, and hexes appear as the only efficacious forces in the cosmic realm while the supreme God of the universe remains stunningly passive and detached from tragic outcomes and individual suffering. The epilogue also engages documentaries set in Africa that offer claims on God's interventionist capacities in ways that elicit questions about divine inscrutability.

The large sample of films assessed in this study includes works covering multiple genres and time periods, works embodying both small and large-scale production capacities including a few notable television films, and works exemplifying numerous ethnic identities to disentangle common threads in modern cinema when treatments of black suffering, God-talk, and religious representations are at play. By casting my methodological net so wide as to select a broad range of filmic contributions, I divert from the prevailing mode of cinematic analysis categorized by granularity. Whereas most aestheticians of cinema focus their studies on a small sample of contributions which fall under particulate genres or are distinguished by specific countries of origin, my approach offers a birds-eye view of filmic treatments of theodicy and black suffering. But such methodological munificence need not normalize selection criteria for future studies on the subject. With any luck, my "forest" approach will encourage future scholars to implement more intensive examinations of specific "trees" within cinematic theodicy's breathtaking timberlands.

Some readers might appreciate how my forest approach generates the most expansive assessment of black filmic representations to date. And yet others might perceive such a broad scope as an overreaction to Jonathan Haynes's (2016) playful reminder that one cannot adequately assess the splendor of Carnival by standing in one place. Admittedly, such prolificacy does come with drawbacks, namely, the necessity to balance perspicacity with parsimony by targeting (sometimes with a sniper's precision) how each film reflects the book's overall themes. In other words, such a large snapshot of modern cinema compels me to jump to the chase without submitting elaborate background information on each film, as is the luxury of scholars who deploy methods of analytical granularity and put forward book-length treatments of only a handful of films. Hopefully this work's rich findings will convince readers that the benefits of gaining a comprehensive look at cinematic theodicy outweigh the pesky costs of unrequited particularities, and that my manifold filmic allusions do not require the reader to be acclimated to the intricacies of every scene and background detail to appreciate how each film functions as a secularizing and signifying force.

Along these lines, I hope readers will come to understand how filmic treatments of theodicy not only resemble other ritualistic ceremonies that memorialize collective traumas, but also share much in common with ancient religions and myths as artifacts and architects of greater structures of meaning. If social facts themselves are reticent without representation (Alexander 2011), then cinematic representations of today's social facts can do much to illuminate future historians' understandings of how present-day humans perpetrate and endure inequities, atrocities, and traumas. I speculate that future historians perusing through the celluloid remains of our day will assess and tally how many of today's filmmakers circumvent the challenges and conundrums of theodicy with the same tactic that allows many of today's theologians and everyday Americans to sidestep its absurdities: by constructing a modern God.

Chapter 1

Theodical Secularity

If Max Weber came back to life in the twenty-first century, films could provide contexts to assess earlier convictions about modern society. Presuming theological touchstones by now would have diminished, Weber might acquiesce to cinema's sidelined sovereign as a more cogent instantiation of disenchantment than his previous predictions of divinity's ultimate dissolution. Hence, cinematic juxtapositions of God-talk and human suffering could teach our resurrected theorist a crucial lesson on secularity: that in a rationalizing, bureaucratizing, increasingly mechanistic world, God need not be dead, only modernized.

Weber's new insight alleges synergistic links between theodicy, God-talk, and secularity, a symbiosis henceforth conceptualized in this study as "theodical secularity" to encompass exegetical strategies people employ to keep God alive and meaningful while making sense of tragedy and misfortune. Theodical secularity's interdependence between God-talk and boundary ascriptions challenges conventional thinking alleging modernization causes secularization which, in turn, nullifies the need for God-talk and theodicy altogether (Berger 1967; Weber 1978) or removes God-talk from theodical discourse (Becker 1968; Pinn 2012). Conversely, this study envisions God's sustained meaning and relevance as collaborative with secular boundary work, positing that "in the historical process of secularization, the religious and the secular are inextricably bound together and mutually condition each other" (Casanova 2006: 21). When considering how traditional understandings of secularity are inattentive to boundary ascriptions to God, one can comprehend why sociologists and scholars devote little attention to studying how both the God-talk of contemporary believers and the theodical discourses of cinema and art can function as exegetical windows onto modern identities. Theodical secularity's interpretive curiosity can inspire a new generation of sociologists, film scholars, and aestheticians to study how fictional depictions of God-talk are retrofitted for a modern global audience in ways not unlike how the gods depicted in *The Epic of Gilgamesh* and

The Enuma Elish were reified to the sociocultural specs of ancient minds in Mesopotamia.

As the latest shock wave of a seismic shift in the study of religion and society, theodical secularity builds on emergent interpretive frameworks that: challenge longstanding assumptions about the effects of modernization on religious belief, practice, and social influence (Casanova 1994; Lee and Sinitiere 2009; Dillon 2018); clarify how "Secular and religious arguments play an equal and generally also interconnected role within the complex social structure of religious communities" (Reder and Schmidt 2010: 44); distinguish secularity as a descriptive category from secularism as a normative doctrine, while rejecting the latter and reimagining the former (Connolly 1999; Asad 2003; Taylor 2007); expose modernity's theological roots and integrations (Taylor 1989; Salvatore 2007; Gillespie 2008; Sorkin 2008); detect religion's functional contributions to replicate and sustain societally desirable motivations and attitudes (Taylor 1999; Habermas 2006, 2011; Dillon 2018); acknowledge how "religion is holding its own in an increasingly secular environment" and that "religious fellowships will continue to exist for the foreseeable future" (Habermas 2006: 46).

Theodical secularity diverts sociological attentiveness from dying mainline churches and privatizing macro structures to discursive negotiations of God's function (or lack thereof) behind mitigating evil and relieving human suffering. This pivot from large-scale surveys and macro structures to discourse analysis and "God-talk" not only revives hermeneutic connectivity between religious ideas and social theory that once dominated early-twentieth-century intellectual thought, but also proffers critical discernments on the cultural dimensions of secularity that cannot be observed in quantitative studies on religious belief. Thus, in addition to introducing a new understanding of what it means to be secular, this book-length treatment of cinematic theodicy challenges cultural scholars to become more inquisitive about the ways in which "vertical" boundaries, the ones people ascribe to God, offer insights toward understanding modern identities.

Cultural theorists who study boundary work cover a broad range of symbolic distinctions that "mark the difference between inside and outside, strange and familiar, relatives and non-relatives, friends and enemies, culture and nature, enlightenment and barbarism" (Giesen 1998: 13). Their focus is almost exclusively on "horizontal" boundaries, the ones people ascribe to social phenomena to clarify how mental maps, symbolic classifications, and cultural codes shape group perceptions, identities, and religious practices (Lamont and Thevenot 2000). Notable contributions to boundary work include how: scientists publicly brand their work as science while segregating their research plans from non-scientific intellectual pursuits through rhetorical strategies (Gieryn 1983); a young nation integrates symbolic binaries between orthodoxy and modernity as part of a strategic process to establish a national identity (Katz and Gurevitch 1976); politicians attempt to align themselves on the right side (while positioning their opponents on the wrong side) of the moral dichotomies of American democracy and civil society (Alexander 2010; Mast 2013); people create borderlines between their home life and their workplace (Nippert-Eng 2008), between their neighborhood environments and their religious communities (Lamont 2000), and between themselves and those of different classes as a means to discern their own identity, worth, and status (DiMaggio 1992; Lamont 1992, 2000); mental maps shape French and American publishers' judgments on the quality of books (Weber 2000) and people's overall perceptions of their environments (Zerubavel 1997); modern musical genres emerge and evolve (Lena and Peterson 2008) and reflect tastes and racial attitudes that reinforce cultural exclusion and racial boundaries (Bryson 1996); and discursive strategies on racial authenticity or regional distinctiveness produce collective identities and intra-racial divisions (Binder 1999; Robinson 2014).

While the above studies increase our awareness of the complex ways collective dimensions of memory and sociocultural differentiation make modern life meaningful and manageable, they overlook how boundaries ascribed to God correspondingly shed insight on the meaning-making capacities of modern mindsets. Challenging cultural sociology's limited focus on horizontal boundaries, theodical secularity indicates the various ways people negotiate evil and suffering by divesting from God's arsenal those pesky supernatural attributes that don't jibe so well with modern sensibilities. Nancy Ammerman's (2014b) groundbreaking study on American believers unwittingly displays the exegetical promise of theodical secularity. Chapter 1 discusses Ammerman's participants in conjunction with a sample of filmic exemplars to highlight this new sense of secularity that is observable when real life Americans and their fictional counterparts attempt to make sense of tragedy and misfortune by calibrating divine attributes to the specifications of modern identities.

But first we must pause to revisit sociological precursors whose understandings of the exegetical merits of theodicy anticipate my interest in God-talk as a dance partner of secularity. And at the start of this journey we will stumble upon a remarkable irony: that the same classical theorist who claimed the rigorous rationalism of Protestant reformers provided symbolic resources toward the development of modern society, and who explained how monotheism birthed the early and crucial components of secularization (Weber 1920, 1978), could not foresee theodical discourses adapting to more modern contexts and perspectives without jettisoning theistic convictions. But Max Weber's oversight does not give us a pass to overlook his crucial function as theodicy's first exegete. Weber's interpretive framework set the ball rolling for future scholars to examine how the questions and disputes of theodicy speak to the necessity and vitality of religions to construct meaning out of evil and suffering.

THE ODYSSEY: FROM WEBER TO BERGER

While theodicy is often docketed as a prescriptive platform for philosophers, theologians, religion scholars, and lay theists to debate God's existence, benevolence, or sovereignty, sociologists tackling the subject are more preoccupied with theodicy's hermeneutic significance. Emile Durkheim (2004) in his philosophy lectures of 1883 became the first sociologist to cite Gottfried Leibniz's name and neologism, but Max Weber was the first to prioritize theodicy's interpretive relevance. But unlike how Ernest Becker (1968) and his successors ignored or removed God and God-talk from their theodical projects, Weber's (1958b, 1978) conceptualization of theodicy stays closer to Gottfried Leibniz's (1710) original intent. Like Leibniz, he frames theodicy as the pressing need for humans to reconcile incongruity between a transcendental and omnipotent God and the noticeable imperfection of the world over which God presides (Weber 1978). But whereas Leibniz engages in theodical disputation as an apologist of ethical monotheism, Weber has no theological horse in the race and thus assesses religious methods to redemption as the means by which to assuage the harrowing problems of theodicy, as Jeffrey Alexander (2013: 34) explains:

> Weber created the crosscutting ideal types of his religious sociology in order to explain the approaches to salvation—the theodicies—that had evolved in the course of world history. With the typologies mysticism/asceticism and this-worldly/otherworldly, he sought to describe the degree of emotionality as opposed to control that theodicies allowed, and the degree to which the religious organization of thought and emotion was directed towards world transformation or away from it.

Echoing Friedrich Nietzsche (1887), Weber proposes a more practical and selfish responsibility for religious thought than an ethical monotheist like Leibniz could ever endorse, an assignment which "provides the theodicy of good fortune for those who are fortunate" while also offering collective religious arrangements for individual suffering (Weber 1958b: 271). In true Nietzschean fashion, Weber points out how the concept of sin can be manipulated by the powerful to explain away suffering and maneuvered by the weak in a manner drenched with resentment. Moreover, Weber sees in theodicy a rational hermeneutic technique in which sacred values certify social stratification, empowering the rich to reject misgivings about wealth and power, and the poor to embrace a rigorous asceticism that positions their sufferings as part of a divinely inspired mission. He believes religion in general, not just ethical monotheism, offers psychological functions that rationalize power and oppression within a preordained proposal of redemption.

Weber's interpretive approach treats theodicy as a conceptual apparatus that is deeply concerned with the believer's perspective on God's place in the vicissitudes of the human condition. Notwithstanding his interpretive hijacking of Leibniz's neologism, Weber's presumptions about increasing disenchantment of modernizing societies precluded him from offering prescient alternatives to what he could only foresee as theodicy and God-talk's eventual and inescapable decline in social relevance. Whereas he does explain how magical theodicies over time were replaced by the more rational theodicies of Hinduism, Zoroastrian dualism, Judaism, and Christianity (1958b), Weber never considers how the latter theodicies could undergo further adjustments to remain relevant as the forces of modernization gain increasing compulsion. Hence, Weber couldn't foresee what theodical secularity brings to light: how the human desire for salvation and the religious nature of morality can survive the relentless forces of rationalization, more specifically, how future theists can negotiate theodical disenchantment by reinventing, rather than merely replacing, God.

This omission is rooted in Weber's perspective of modernity as an inexorable train headed toward a destination where the problem of theodicy will eventually require no resolution because, trapped in the train's steely compartment of instrumentality and bureaucratic efficiency, people will no longer have use for God. So while Max Weber understands the exegetical import of theodicy, he cannot foresee theodicy ever becoming an integrative feature of secularity because he does not believe that modern identities could survive ongoing rationalizing, bureaucratizing, and instrumentalizing processes with the requisite improvisational capacities intact to reinvent theodical strategies that jibe well with those very same modern sensibilities. He also underestimates religion's facility for mediating integrative functions of core values within the structure of modernizing societies, which is an ironic miscalculation when considering his seminal theory on the emergence of capitalism depends on such reasoning (Weber 1920). And thus, Weber unwittingly inspires a successive generation of secularization theorists to take the next logical step and hypothesize a linear relationship between modernization and the decline of religion and theodicy in society.

In contrast to Weber's diminishing role for theodicy in an advanced modern world, Ernest Becker (1968) keeps theodicy as a relevant exegetical enterprise and instead calls for the removal of God (and thus God-talk) from theodicy as a necessary concession to the new secular age. Unlike Weber, who comprehends theodicy and God-talk as conjugal, Becker perceives in the transition from medieval cosmology to scientific rationality the seeds of a theodical viewpoint that no longer looks to God and nature for clues concerning human morality and destiny. Becker traces the tentacles of his secular theodicy back to Francis Bacon's and Isaac Newton's seventeenth-century scientific revolutions and envisions its proliferation in various sectors of society to construct a moral compass that interprets evil entirely from a nontheological perspective (requiring the death of God-talk). If Weber's forecast of theodicy's diminishing function is fatalistic, Becker's retooling of theodicy is pragmatic because he wants to maintain theodicy's utility as an industrial-strength adhesive for moral solidarity. Like Weber, Becker detects the instrumental rhythms of an increasingly modernizing world, but Becker's solution is to rid theodicy of all theological nuances and teleological underpinnings so that theodical proponents can march to the beat of a more rational drummer. Becker's retooled theodicy is motivated by "the guidance of imagination and vision, of planning and control, purposive experimental manipulation and reasoned intervention" (1968: 32) and can be summed up with a triad of pragmatic values: progress, liberty, and the moral ideal.

It is worth noting how Becker's call for God (and God-talk's) expiration date opens the door for successive sociologists to depart from Weber's (and Leibniz's) theistic approaches to theodicy. Accordingly, many scholars since Becker remove God entirely to assess how sociology as a discipline can: function as a secularizing theodicy in its attempts to explain human suffering (Pickering 1980; Meldau and Knapp 2013); calculate how theodicies adapt to the existential effects of human suffering against the backdrop of modern anticipations of social progress (Morgan and Wilkinson 2001); elucidate how Karl Marx's prescriptive vision of a post-revolutionary paradise in which evil is conquered through the final erasure of class conflicts serves as an implicit theodicy to mitigate the disorientation of present struggles with evil and suffering (Pickering 1980); incorporate cumulative interpretations and sympathies with regard to modernity and the Holocaust toward a general theory of morality (Bauman 1989); explicate links between the rational processes of the regulation of bodies as a result of secularization and human embodiment, while specifying their relation to human suffering (Turner 1992); adopt a Jewish social philosopher's contributions toward developing a theodicy of culture (Urban 2012); and provide the theoretical grounding for a cultural understanding of evil (Alexander 2001, 2003, 2013). These studies offer only modest fulfillment of Becker's lofty vision for sociology to reprioritize its orientation toward the removal of theodicy's theistic impulses.

Notwithstanding their divergent conceptualizations, it should be clear how Becker and Weber are both oblivious or resistant to God-talk that simultaneously situates divinity in the midst of human struggles and sidelines its interventionist capacity as a crucial feature of secularity. For even as no sociologist before him better understood how the changing social climate of the scientific age raises new questions and temperaments for theodicy, Ernest Becker's only adjustment from Weber is to omit God and religion altogether, and so, like Weber, he fails to consider the alternative possibility (and hermeneutic potential) of modern theists recalibrating theodical perspectives toward what they perceive as more reasonable specifications without ditching God and religious sentiments. And so it is Talcott Parsons, not Becker, who takes a closer step toward discerning how religious belief and practice can persist while adapting to changes in advanced societies.

Resembling Weber and successive sociologists who broach the topic, Parsons (1952: 296) upholds the hermeneutic necessity of theodicy, contending, "good fortune and suffering must always, to cultural man, be endowed with meaning," while offering a useful construction of theodicy's sociological import:

> The religious problem par excellence in the more generalized sense is the justification of the ways of God to man, is making sense out of the totality of the human situation, both in the cognitive sense of a theory in which the discrepancies and the established order can be brought within a single view, and in emotional adequacy so that man can adjust to his own fate and that of the societies with which he is identified. (1952: 298)

Here we can detect Nietzsche's (by way of Weber's) influence on Parsons with his contention that God helps people attune themselves to predicaments that cause strain in their life situations. Parsons adds the Durkheimian dictum that religion is implicated in the profoundest intricacies of human experience. Unlike Weber, Parsons is careful to spell out how sociologists miscalculate when they predict the imminent decline of religion as collateral damage in an increasingly modern society. To the proponents of such a position, Parsons posits:

> Like the historian, the sociologist can now say unequivocally that the fairly recent popular positivistic view that religion was essentially grounded in the ignorance and superstition of a prescientific age, and could be expected rapidly to disappear in our era, is definitely in error. The proponent of this view is the victim of his own ignorance and counter-superstition. (1952: 335)

While Parsons (1974) documents how a modern society can adjust to rationalization without completely jettisoning religious beliefs, his focus on cultural systems and corporate entities precludes him from discerning the creative ways that individual theists can resolve theodical tensions by reimagining instead of abandoning God. Peter Berger's interpretive approach makes him a more suitable candidate to elucidate a richer understanding of the ways that people renegotiate religion and God in advanced industrial societies.

Berger (1967) is interested in how the problem of evil immediately distresses the individual in his tangible engagements with his social order, and how religious legitimations help toward the task of maintaining meaning under the anomic stress of suffering. While Berger borrows from Weber and Parsons (and Nietzsche) when he specifies how theodicies give credence to the predominant disparities of power and privilege, he innovates by introducing the masochistic attitude as a critical motif within the construction of all theodicies, regardless of one's social location or economic status. Whether it be the biblical story of Job, the fatalism of the Protestant reformer John Calvin, or the total capitulation to Allah's will in Islam, Berger clarifies how the sovereignty of God and the cancellation of humans reach their absurd climax in theodicy when religious adherents are liberated through losing their sense of self. What interests Berger is the incongruity of religion's alienating capabilities juxtaposed with religion's crucial hermeneutic role in legitimating meaning and order for humans. For Berger, theodicy quite paradoxically dehumanizes via its attempts to humanize through masochistic liberation.

But Berger (ibid) does sound much like Weber when he contends that as the winds of modern change come crashing against the plausibility structures of religious theodicies, humans lack adequate hermeneutic strategies to cope with evil and suffering. Hence, some might perceive Berger less as a precursor to theodical secularity and more as the posterchild for Talcott Parson's aforesaid reprimand against scholars who overstate the demise of religion in secular society. But it's helpful to point out how Berger's notion of a sacred canopy that will crumble under the compression of opposing religious perspectives is ironically the first edifice of his secularization theory to collapse (Ammerman 2014a). And only a decade later, Berger concedes that he and some of his colleagues "have overestimated both the degree and the irreversibility of secularization" (1977: 160) and later rejects secularization theory (Berger and Zijderveld 2009), while attributing his deconversion not to a new philosophical perspective, but rather to daunting empirical evidence proving religion remains alive and well in many modern countries (Berger 2014). For his penance, Berger joins a growing list of scholars to replace secularization with a new focus on religious plurality as the upshot of modernization: "Modernization produces plurality. And plurality increases the individual's ability to make choices between and among worldviews. Where secularization theory went wrong was in the assumption that these choices were likely to be secular. In fact, they may very well be religious" (Berger and Zijderveld 2009: 18). The latter statement reflects an important conviction of Charles

Taylor's (2007) new sense of secularity that informs and anticipates theodical secularity.

But even before renouncing secularization theory, Berger recognized different ways people can approach their religious traditions and practices in a modern world without necessarily succumbing to pluralistic threats. At this ambivalent phase of his career, Berger shared Weber's concern about modern pluralism undermining religious authority and yet, unlike Weber, appreciated how different societies and people derive actionable strategies to cling to their faith. Hence, where Berger is particularly impactful for theodical secularity is not in his earlier support and later rejection of the secularization thesis, nor in his once staunch (and later withdrawn) insistence on plurality's deleterious effect on religious authority, but rather in his mid-career contemplation of the diverse ways modern religious minds can respond to pluralistic threats against their traditions.

Berger (1979) offers three broad options for people to maintain the authority or worthwhileness of their religious tradition and to survive the forces of rationalization and what he then perceived as the crisis of modern pluralism. The first is perhaps the most obvious: that people can stubbornly endorse the authority of their religious tradition and rebel against challenges to it. The second and more inventive option captures exactly what Parsons' focus on macro structures ignored: the ways in which individual believers can adjust or even rationalize their religious tradition. His third option involves believers extrapolating from their own experiences to intuit the experiences that are inherent in their religious tradition. Although Berger prioritizes his third option (which explains why he would later replace secularization with religious plurality as a consequence of modernization), what most directly informs and anticipates the exegetical promise of theodical secularity is found in Berger's second option: for believers to retool their religious tradition. Theodical secularity as a framework builds on Berger's second option with its focus on how modern believers modify traditional ways of perceiving God and how those adjustments come in the form of boundary ascriptions in theodical discourses. This new understanding suggests that secular people are not solely those who reject God but the distinction also includes those who believe in God, worship God, and ascribe boundaries to God's attributes and governing responsibilities. In other words, even the most ardent believers are citizens of a secular age (Taylor 2007).

A NEW MODE OF SECULARITY

Charles Taylor's (2007) three modes of secularity consolidate the competing ways scholars measure and theorize how societies have responded to modernizing processes evolving at rapid speeds for centuries. They are helpful toward situating how theodical secularity rejects some assumptions of the first two modes that are consistent with traditional secularization theories, is indebted to Taylor's third-mode reconceptualization of secularity, and yet calls for a new mode of secularity (inspired by Peter Berger's second option) that emphasizes how people respond to suffering and tragedy by modifying God's attributes and responsibilities on Earth in ways that fit the needs and tastes of modern identities.

Taylor's first mode covers theories that understand secularity as involving the removal of God and religion from the public sphere. This sense of secularity assesses how social structures no longer depend on validation from God or religion, and its proponents subsequently predict religion will become less socially dominant in modern societies and will retreat to privatized sectors of a competitive religious economy. The underlying logic that drives first-mode theorizing is that as modern society becomes less traditional and less monolithic (or in a Durkheimian sense, less "mechanical"), social structures and cultural options become more functionally differentiated and pluralistic (or in a Durkheimian sense, more "organic"). The first-mode perspective notes how modern processes of urbanization, capitalism, increased communication, and media saturation expose alternative meanings that compete with and gradually erode privileged plausibility structures, leaving religious traditions and rituals fated to diminished capacities in public social life. In other words, when religious authority faces competition in a modern pluralistic society, it becomes increasingly questioned and replaced by more rational alternatives. This line of reasoning does not suggest that religion is voiceless in society, but rather that it is privatized and no longer looms large over non-religious spheres of public life because functional differentiation now looms larger, allowing modern institutions to incubate rational standards and values calibrated to their optimal performance and success.

Peter Berger's (1967) classic tome *The Sacred Canopy: Elements of a Sociological Theory of Religion* is perhaps the most noted and sophisticated presentation of first-mode theorizing. Asserting the triumph of modern differentiation over traditional mechanisms of socialization, which of course include religious monopolies, Berger contends that dominant Christian narratives for explaining evil and suffering are becoming increasingly antiquated, resulting in a crisis of plausibility for Christian theodicies in advanced societies. In another work, Berger estimates that American Protestantism is in various respects already secularized in both social function and disposition (1977). Similarly, Talcott Parsons (1974) believes the key to understanding the complexities of secularization lies at the societal level with the privatization of religion and the disintegration of traditional religious organization. Parsons points to American Protestantism's individualistic trajectory, voluntaristic membership, religious toleration, and denominational plurality as signs of its increasing secularity even as he warns against hasty forecasts of religion's demise. Thomas Luckmann concludes that religion and morality have already become increasingly privatized and centered around the individual person: "As the reach of religious institutions diminished, the obligatory social and intersubjectively compelling evaluation of human conduct by reference to a transcendent reality became weaker. Morals and religion, structurally privatized, took a definitive inner turn in the form of conscience and faith" (1996: 79). Luckmann's vision of a growing modern religious marketplace characterized by individualism and chaotic bricolage is partially realized in a more recent study of religious reorganization in the United States, which demonstrates how secularization leads to new kinds of "remixed" religious configurations involving selective integrations of various traditions to fit individual needs and tastes (Burton 2020). From the vantage point of first-mode theories, secularization does not necessarily replace religion, it only transforms religious choices by offering an array of privatized forms of community that emerge out of new technologies like the Internet.

José Casanova's contention that a global movement representing the "deprivatization" of religion compels scholars to have second thoughts about such first-mode predictions:

> Religions throughout the world are entering the public sphere and the arena of political contestation not only to defend their traditional turf, as they have done in the past, but also to participate in the very struggles to define and set the modern boundaries between the private and public spheres, between system and life-world, between legality and morality, between individual and society, between family, civil society, and state, between nations, states, civilizations, and the world system. (1994: 6)

While Casanova agrees that modernity's differentiating structures provide the public sphere with some degree of manumission from religious institutional controls and norms, he ultimately concludes that public religions in countries worldwide still exert the kind of political, social, and economic influence that disconfirms expectations of religion's inauspicious retreat from public life. Likewise, Judith Butler (2011: 71) claims that "some religions are not only already 'inside' the public sphere, but they help to establish a set of criteria that delimit the public from the private." And while Michele Dillon (2018) acknowledges how the separation of church and state confirms the state's established secular status, she also highlights religion's continued presence and relevance within functionally differentiated domains.

Whereas Taylor's first mode speaks to religion's retreat from the public sphere, the second mode of secularity relates to a decline in religious belief and practice. Like the first, the second mode presupposes causal links between modernization and secularization, but instead of studying religious institutions, proponents of second-mode theories point to statistical markers of a rise in disbelief or a decline in church attendance in modern countries (Wilson 1982; Brown 1992; Bruce 1996; 2011) and more creative indicators such as the increasing number of prominent church buildings in Great Britain that are sold and transformed into pubs, discos, apartment complexes, and laundromats (Zuckerman, Galen, and Pasquale 2016). But with the rise of Islamic and Christian fundamentalism, Pentecostalism, and other religious expressions in recent decades, scholars have reconsidered this once presumed correlation between modernity and declines in religious belief and practice (Berger 2014; Dillon 2018). The continued European and worldwide presence of ascribed religious identities and traditions, which make up what Slavica Jakelic (2016) calls collectivistic religions, poses additional challenges to second-mode presumptions, while the Internet-driven "remixed" religious progressions of modern societies may render conventional metrics for measuring religiosity such as church attendance and religious affiliation less trustworthy (Burton 2020).

Like Tara Burton (ibid) and a growing coterie of scholars, Charles Taylor (2007) understands that modern people are finding new ways to be religious and are participating in new forms of religious community that can be easily overlooked by conventional methods utilized to assess declines in religious belief and participation. Hence, Taylor challenges both the naturalistic underpinnings and descriptive reliability of scholarly instantiations of the first two modes of secularity. In response, Taylor introduces and endorses a third mode of secularity that more specifically relates to a shift in Western society's horizon of meaning whereby belief in God is no longer taken for granted but rather exists within a competitive constellation of theological (and anti-theological) options. Taylor's third mode offers an interpretive reformulation of secularity as a mélange of diverse perspectives and identities that are upshots of the same immanent frame. Thus, he does not perceive religion's lingering presence in advanced modern societies as disconfirmation of a secular age. Taylor's retooled notion of secularity not only fashions what he portends to be a more plausible descriptive account of the pluralistic theological harvests that grow in modern pastures but, when put alongside his earlier work, unleashes a prescriptive charge that endorses universal rights and humanist values while assigning an important role to religious faith as the teleological rudder and engine to direct and drive human flourishing in a free pluralistic society.

Challenging his fellow Catholics who dismiss the gains of human rights culture as carnal compromises, Taylor (1999) explicates how the demise of Christendom's despotic reign over Western Europe created strategic opportunities for social forces outside of Catholic hegemony to cultivate political freedom and universal equality in ways that endorse much of Jesus's teachings in the Gospels. And challenging antitheists who fetishize secularization and see no room for religion in a flourishing liberal democratic state, Taylor (ibid) insists on the notion of divine love and his own modified understanding of religious transcendence as necessary components to hold human rights culture accountable. From Taylor's perspective, we all live in a secular age, and the greatest capacity for human flourishing comes via dialectical integrations of sacred and secular discursive resources.

There are intriguing analogues to Taylor's third-mode understanding of a new age of sacred/secular mutuality. First off, the fact that both the popular French Enlightenment mantra, "freedom from belief" and its American counterpart, "freedom to believe," emerged out of the same eighteenth-century modern progressive mindset (Berger, Davie, and Fokas 2008) can be interpreted as a conformation (and confirmation) of a new horizon of meaning that projects both sacred and secular perspectives. Correspondingly, as discussed above, Peter Berger's new focus on religious plurality unwittingly corroborates the descriptive merits of Taylor's refitted sense of secularity: "There is indeed a modern reality of secularity. But the United States provides a vibrant case of a society that is both thoroughly modern and strangely religious. This has interesting implications far beyond the Western world" (Berger 2007: viii). And Tara Burton (2020) lends empirical weight behind Taylor's third mode of secularity by delineating how people mix and match religious traditions and formulate new kinds of religious identities around secular rallying points. Burton's remarkable study should inspire sociologists of religion to become more inquisitive about how new technologies reshape existential compartments and geographic configurations of religious identity and community.

Aptly titled *The Secular Relevance of the Church*, Gayraud Wilmore's (1962) earliest tome anticipates (and fits nicely within) Taylor's understanding of secularity for the way it challenges American Protestantism to reject its conservative, individualistic focus to formulate a unified front and effectual church mission in a technologically savvy, organizationally complex modern society. Wilmore recognizes a "holy secularity" that operates outside of the confines of the church, while living out Christ's liberationist mission in the world through humanist rationalism. He contends that such an authentic secularism (as opposed to what he calls a spurious secularism) is paradoxically more in line with authentic Christianity than American Protestantism, which Wilmore sees as a middleclass, individualistic, soul-saving reworking of Christianity that is out of step with the rigorous challenges of an increasingly complex world. Wilmore explains how Protestant individualism prevents many Christians from understanding the true communal message and mission of Christ for social justice and freedom and perceives secular voices outside of Protestant Christianity as equally inclined to function as divine instruments to change society and correct the church and humanity from wayward individualism.

And there is great continuity (and contiguity) between Taylor's third mode of secularity and Jürgen Habermas's conciliation for religion to function as a democratizing asset in the public sphere. In Habermas's (2006) postsecular compromise, public religion is divested of metaphysical claims, intolerance, and dogmatic constraints, while modern mentalities, in turn, recognize religion's functional contributions toward facilitating the propagation of incentives and dispositions that are societally advantageous. Michele Dillon (2018: 7) clarifies Habermas's pronouncement of the need and vitality of religion in the public sphere:

> Thus Habermas argues, the realities of Western modernity require a change in public consciousness and an appreciation of religion, what he calls a postsecular consciousness. A postsecular consciousness recognizes that while secularization is the settled reality, religion has public relevance and culturally useful resources for addressing contemporary societal ills. Thus postsecularity does not mean that we have moved beyond secularism or that secularization has not occurred. And nor does it denote the return of religion, as religion never, in fact, disappeared from Western society. Rather, postsecularity requires appreciation of the mutual relevance and intertwined pull of the religious and the secular.

Unlike how Max Weber (1920: 96) offers a binary relationship between (and less optimistic outlook for) religion and modernity, perceiving modernization as a juggernaut leading the world toward a last stage of cultural development ruled by "specialists without spirit, sensualists without heart," Habermas (like Taylor) concludes that the transition from ascetic rationality to humanistic rationality need not be a zero-sum game but that post-metaphysical religion and a more accommodating communal form of rationality could peacefully coexist as part of the discourse of modernity. He writes:

> In the postsecular society, there is an increasing consensus that certain phases of the "modernization of the public consciousness" involve the assimilation and the reflexive transformation of both religious and secular mentalities. If both sides agree to understand the secularization of society as a complementary learning process, then they will also have cognitive reasons to take seriously each other's contributions to controversial subjects in the public debate. (2006: 46–47)

Conceding "there is a ready audience for the theory that the remorseful modern age can find its way out of the blind alley only by means of the religious orientation to a transcendent point of reference" (2006: 37), Habermas prescribes an integrative form of democratic discourse undertaken by secular and religious citizens engaged in discursive networks within the public sphere to "spur deliberative politics in a pluralistic society and lead to the recovery of semantic potentials from religious traditions for the wider political culture" (2011: 28). Even as we acknowledge that Habermas's primary concern is the maximization of rational capacities of communicative action rather than a quest for theological clarity (1984, 1987, 2002), his new urgency to include religious contributions within those rational capacities as crucial symbolic assets of civil discourse promotes the potential for mutually achievable aims in an open modern society in a way that strongly resembles Taylor's prescription for human flourishing in a secular age.

Whereas Habermas's proposed cooperation between religion and secularity comes rather reluctantly as a repented secularist (and committed atheist) making prescient concessions to religion's unrelenting presence in the public sphere, and through his equally perceptive recognition of religion's underrated utility toward enhancing normative integration, group cohesion, and mitigating conflict, Charles Taylor's refurbishment of secularity comes as a Catholic scholar whose own faith and social vision exemplify an intriguing extenuation of sacred and secular cultural resources. Yet despite traveling from divergent spiritual paths and assigning different names to their desired end points, Habermas and Taylor arrive at the same theoretical destination: a late modern epoch of sacred/secular mutuality. Fittingly, in his last published tome, Peter Berger (2014) calls for what Habermas's compromise, Taylor's third mode, and this present study's interest in theodical secularity endorse: a new paradigm for modernity that negotiates exegetical interdependence between religious and secular discourses. While Berger, Taylor, and Habermas contribute thinking that both informs and anticipates theodical secularity, they overlook how discursive boundary ascriptions to God's legislative functions on Earth serve as important indicators of secularity.

Accordingly, this present study introduces theodical secularity as a fourth mode of secularity that incorporates vertical boundaries into its analysis, while presupposing (what Taylor's third mode clarifies) how those same boundary imputations to God indicate modern identities as exegetical (and existential) upshots of the immanent frame. Like Taylor's third mode, theodical secularity makes no linear or mechanistic claims on the effect of modernization on the presence of religion in the public sphere, nor calculates diminishing attendance and membership rolls in local churches. It substitutes quantitative analysis with an interpretive focus on how God-talk epitomizes modern tweaks and alterations of premodern religious traditions. Such an approach clarifies how not all secular people are irreligious, that many secular people believe in God and serve God while renegotiating God's governing attributes to fit rational sensibilities. Nancy Ammerman's (2014b) study is a timely exemplar of the promise of theodical secularity through its use of in-depth interviews, oral diaries, and discourse analysis to uncover how contemporary Americans talk about God in the context of various capacities of human suffering.

AMERICAN BELIEVERS AND CINEMA

Philosopher Mary Litch states: "One of the most difficult intellectual problems facing those who believe in an all-powerful, wholly good God is reconciling that belief with the existence of so much pain and suffering in the world" (2010: 188). Participants of Nancy Ammerman's (2014b) study negotiate this theodical challenge by ascribing boundaries to God's activity on Earth. "Even among the most spiritually aware people, daily physical complaints are simply not God's problem," Ammerman explains, as most of her participants do not anticipate supernatural intervention even though they often allude to spirituality, faith, and religion in their discussions of health, illness, and death (2014b: 260). Rare exceptions include what Ammerman calls "foxhole" prayers in reference to a few participants hoping that God will make their crisis disappear. But by and large, in the process of suffering with AIDS, neurological problems, severe chronic pain, cancer, cardiac distress, depression, and other physical and mental ordeals, Ammerman's participants turn to God for support and comfort rather than for healing.

Hank Matthews prays with his dying mother as a coping mechanism, just as Charlotte McKenna prays to endure nine months of pain from an injury. And although Grace Shoemaker visits a Charismatic healing service and receives a prayer from the minister that leaves her feeling relaxed and serene (without being healed from her condition), she often encounters God's presence and communication during her daily health rituals to mitigate the vagaries of muscular dystrophy. Grace recalls one occasion when the pain is unbearable and God instructs her to lay down, take some Tylenol, and rest. Grace does not find such practical instructions coming from an omnipotent God as counterintuitive because, as she records in her oral diary, she is not looking for a miracle. In this regard, Grace is quite like other participants, as Ammerman confirms:

> Many people told us that what got them through their difficult times was their faith, but faith rarely came with a definitive road map. It was more likely to include holistic practices of spiritual healing—including prayer—than the expectation of a physical miracle cure. For most people, faith meant a sense of divine presence, a willingness to depend on a higher power and to expect that power to provide comfort and assurance of one's inner well-being. (272)

This instrumental use of faith and prayer characterizes how, in contrast to ancient expectations of God's supernatural activity to improve world conditions, Ammerman's participants perceive God as a comforting (rather than a healing) deity. And in cases where Ammerman's participants do credit God's intervening hand, such divine mediation comes by way of modern medical procedures rather than supernatural dynamism.

Ammerman's participants keep God as the center point of their existential identity, while they believe God responds to their prayers and concerns in natural ways. If the result of them turning to God is spiritual growth or this-worldly coping, either outcome is theodical because, as Ammerman explains, "Theodicy in both cases means trusting God to have a plan, whether or not the contours of that plan are immediately apparent" (270). We see this trust blossom in Jessica who is initially leery about using a drug to relieve her chronic bouts of depression until she concludes that "God created medicine," and so "we should be smart enough to use it when we need to" (265). Jessica's resolution reflects a nexus of science and faith that many of Ammerman's participants affirm. Theodical secularity interprets these women and men as part of an age of sacred/secular fluidity in which believers relate to modern science and technology in a way that makes God meaningful to (or makes meaning out of God's place in) their struggles and pains without violating laws of nature. They impute God's presence in the medical interventions and perceive successful procedures as divinely orchestrated phenomena.

I imagine many sociologists would consider the critical role a friend's niece plays in helping Liz secure entrée to one of the best bone doctors in New England as a perquisite of Liz's social capital. But her husband William perceives the unanticipated mediation that led to Liz's successful back surgery as miraculous. Once again, secularity is still at play because God "fixes" Liz's condition via a surgical procedure rather than supernatural intervention, but, from William's perspective, God was responsible for Liz getting the best treatment available. Whereas from an Old Testament prophet like Elijah's perspective it makes sense to call down fire from heaven as a demonstration of God's power (1 Kings 18:36–38), from William's modern perspective it makes perfect sense that God respects the laws of nature and works through human hands and institutions like the medical industry to relieve a believer's suffering.

In a similar vein, after Jen Jackson spends the night in the emergency room hoping and praying God would take care of her sick newborn, she distinguishes the pediatrician's heady intervention that brings a positive outcome as choreographed by God, "cause He's the only one who could have spared my child's life" (275). Jen was not even remotely bothered by God's roundabout way of ensuring a positive outcome after her night of panic because she already takes it for granted that God works through human hands.

Ammerman clarifies how even though Jen still relies on the medical system to help her newborn convalesce, the successful medical intervention is very much a story affirming Jen's relationship with God. "Like William Pullinger, she does not blame God for the suffering, but she does believe that God is present in the process of healing" (275).

Theodical secularity accounts for how Jen and William are ascribing boundaries to God's activity on Earth even as they prioritize God's role in providing the solutions to their problems. In this way, Grace's aforementioned message from God to rest and take Tylenol reflects a new kind of God and a new kind of interventionism that adjusts religious tradition to the contours of modern medicine. William, Jen, Grace, and many other participants in Ammerman's study secularize their religious tradition by casting "miracle" status on carnal medical mediations (and the perks of social capital accompanying them). Whereas premodern miracles defy the laws of nature, modern miracles are mediated by rational parameters and professional institutions. This rebranding of miracles is reminiscent of Peter Berger's early quip that the theologian who affirms supernaturalism "more and more resembles a witch doctor stranded among logical positivists" (1969: 10). When God provides solutions for Ammerman's participants, it is mostly through modern interventions and human mediators.

Robert Wuthnow's (2012) discourse analysis of American believers provides added confirmation of the hermeneutic potential of theodical secularity by revealing how modern theists acknowledge God's existence and importance while limiting God's interventionist capacities in the context of suffering. Wuthnow reflects on the theodical connotations of his interviewees' boundary ascriptions to God:

> On the surface, it would seem that a God who has so little impact on the world is not much of a God at all. Yet it is clear from people's comments about their faith that God is quite real to them, they entertain few doubts about this God, and they find it meaningful to talk to God and about God. They largely avoid talking about miracles in the old-fashioned sense of divine intervention and instead use the word to mean something that can be identified after the fact as a rare and favorable outcome in a problematic situation. (2012: 143)

Wuthnow's interviewees integrate God in their struggles in ways that maintain God's existence and utility without sacrificing their own rational sensibilities. They come across as thoughtful people of faith who question God—and admit that they sometimes do not even like God—when trying to understand pain and suffering. They even wrestle with God only to end their protests by rationalizing God's non-intervention in ways that preserve their faith. Wuthnow explains how some of them resolve the theodicy problem "by implicitly denying that God purposively plans—and in this sense causes—specific events, especially bad ones that might be interpreted as wrathful or punishing," treating God as an incomprehensible "kind of CEO who keeps the universe under control but lets people make their own decisions for good or for ill" (ibid). Other interviewees deploy creative strategies to negotiate how God can both be in charge of what happens on Earth while remaining detached from tragic events. Like Ammerman's participants, Wuthnow's subjects naturalize miracles and sideline God and in doing so share much in common with the following filmic characters whose God-talk reveals similar synergistic links between theodicy and secularity.

George C. Wolfe's *Lackawanna Blues* (2005) presents a character named Nanny who in a reflective moment admits to her mentee Rueben that she doubted God after her only child died from pneumonia. Nanny eventually resolved her pain by realizing that God filled the empty void in her heart with surrogate children to love, including Rueben himself. Nanny's secularity comes into play by renegotiating God's non-intervention with a teleological appraisal of her mentorship to Rueben and others. Nanny exegetes her child's death as indication of God's greater plan to give her many more "children" to love in a similar fashion to how two of Ammerman's participants—Vicky Johnson and Marjorie Buckley—were certain that God would use their heart surgeries toward a greater purpose. Not unlike many believers, Nanny does not dwell on counterfactuals, like the prospect of a supernatural God both healing her only child and giving her more people to love, because Nanny has already made peace with God's redefined role as cosmic coach.

Vertical boundary work as a theodical strategy is even more prominent in Edward Zwick's biopic *Glory* (1989). This Civil War drama follows a white commanding officer and his black brigade as they prepare and eventually fight for the Union army. *Glory*'s theodical crescendo manifests during the brigade's campfire worship service the night before its dangerous mission to lead Union sieges against Fort Wagner. Along with their praise and singing to God, the combatants engage in a communal form of supplication in which a soldier prays while his comrades hum in solidarity. The first to pray is the regiment's sharpshooter Private Jupiter Sharts: "Tomorrow we go into battle, so Lordie, let me fight with the rifle in one hand and the Good Book in the other. That if I should die at the muzzle of the rifle, die on water or on land, I may know that you, Blessed Jesus Almighty, are with me. And I have no fear. Amen!" Rather than beseeching the heavens for help to conquer the Confederate stronghold, Sharts only petitions God for sentimental support. Sergeant John Rawlings follows with an equally passive prayer requesting nothing of God except to notify surviving family members of their courage. Private Silas Trip is the third and last soldier up and his prayer fails to even mention God. One can infer from the lack of optimism in all three prayers that the soldiers comprehend God as a mere spectator of military conflict and presciently perceive tomorrow's prefatory siege against Fort Wagner as a suicide mission. While the black brigade's lively worship and prayers verify that the pain and suffering they endured as slaves and racist treatment they bore as Union soldiers did not drive many of them to lose faith in God's existence and importance, their pessimistic prayers exemplify a valuable lesson about theodical discourse in a modern world: that secularity and doubt come in many forms, one of which does not necessitate the rejection of divine existence, just low expectations of supernatural interference. *Glory*'s praying soldiers demonstrate how people can simultaneously believe in God and modify divine capabilities toward the more rational specifications of modern identities.

While *Glory*'s brave soldiers faced tragedy with composure, some black filmic characters in other films respond to harrowing circumstances by issuing diatribes against God. A prime example of this erupts in a crucial scene in *The River Niger* (1976, Krishna Shah). Johnny reacts to news of his wife's cancer by yelling out to God, "Son of a bitch! Why do you keep fucking with me? What do you want from me you bastard?" Mattie scolds her husband for discharging such blasphemous sentiments, which does nothing to stop Johnny from uttering more irreverence: "You know what I'm gonna do on Judgment Day? Ima grab that motherfucker by the throat and I'm going to squeeze and squeeze till I get an answer." The fact that Johnny responds to God so angrily and alludes to the eschatological notion of a day of final judgment confirms his biblical worldview and belief in God's existence remain intact, even as he doubts God's willingness to do anything to resolve Mattie's condition. Similarly despairing but less sacrilegious is how characters in Mahamat-Saleh Haroun's film *A Screaming Man* (2010) mull over God's noninterference in the aftermath of losing their longtime means of employment. David tells Adam, "Our problem is that we put our destiny in God's hands," rather than in proactive planning, which made them vulnerable to unexpected misfortune. With their country engrossed in a brutal civil war, Adam asks David, "Do you believe God really exists?" to which David responds, "I do believe in God but I'm beginning to lose faith in him." And later Adam tells his wife, "Heaven won't help us, Miriam." In both *The River Niger* and *A Screaming Man*, secularity is expressed with characters' realization that God cannot be counted on as a solution to their problems.

In Tina Mabry's film *Mississippi Damned* (2009), when Junior exhorts his wife to be thankful to God for surviving cancer, Delores responds, "You know what? When you get one of your titties cut off, then you can start preaching to me about thankin' God. Till then, shut up talkin' that mess to me!" Delores credits the surgeon's scalpel for ridding her body of cancerous cells, whereas Junior (like Ammerman's participant William Pullinger) credits God for the medical mediation on behalf of his wife. Later when her doctor finds new tumors, Delores once again endures expensive procedures that leave the poor couple in straits even more dire. When their daughter Kari realizes their financial desperation and offers her college fund to defray the costs of medical bills, Junior initially declines, claiming, "The Lord's gonna make a way," but reverses his position after Kari sums up her parents' gloomy prospects: no money, no medical insurance, and no sign of mercy. Perhaps Kari's own trust in divine intervention expired in younger years when her cousin raped her. Battling the vicissitudes of poverty, malignancy, and sexual assault, characters in *Mississippi Damned* acknowledge God's existence, but ultimately (and in Junior's case eventually) display a lack of trust in divine intervention to relieve their suffering. Religious discourses and tragic circumstances capture a common point of reference in cinematic theodicy where God remains on the sidelines while humans accept their fate with resignation and on rare occasions protest.

But we should briefly go off course to consider how filmic treatments of theodicy manifest secularity not only in sidelining God, but also in the manner in which they signify evil and suffering. *Mississippi Damned* imposes a sociological framework that relates individual suffering to larger structures of inequality, while pushing viewers to infer how systemic forces affect the lives of poor people around the world in parallel ways. Such an approach articulates structural rather than spiritual diagnoses of and solutions to suffering and oppression. Similarly, Edward Zwick's aforementioned film *Glory* (1989) not only sidelines God with soldiers' pessimistic prayers, but also signifies the Civil War as a painful correction to American history, situates slavery as a pernicious system of human exploitation and abuse, and distinguishes Confederates as artifacts of a racist society and black soldiers as oppressed victims fighting for freedom. And Mahamat-Saleh Haroun's aforementioned film *A Screaming Man* (2010) balances poignant reflections on God's passivity with a sociological understanding of evil as the symbolic underpinnings of war and the soul-crushing effects of corporate downsizing in terms of economic and existential costs to vulnerable individuals and families. Many more films throughout this book will demonstrate cinema's sociological explanations of evil and suffering, while positing solutions to the problem of theodicy with a willingness to delimit God's interventionist capacities. But the mere fact that God-talk and divine representation remain important touchstones of cinematic faith, hope, and ethical accountability demonstrate the fluid partnership of theodicy and secularity, one we see similarly manifested in the lives of Nancy Ammerman's and Robert Wuthnow's subjects.

In this way, the theodical God-talk of everyday Americans and cinematic characters is indicative of a new age of sacred/secular mutuality in which theists refashion divine attributes utilizing modern interpretive resources. If Peter Berger's (1961a) earliest tome hints at what he then perceived as a curious paradox in Western society where religious institutions thrive while exploiting secular resources, then we might presume that citizens of that paradox are quite adept at drawing secular and spiritual devices from the same cultural toolkit. Future historians can download Ammerman's testimonies about "lived religion," or filmic treatments of black suffering to discover how today's modern sojourners keep God and religion as symbolic resources while maintaining a sociological understanding of evil and suffering and a rationalistic outlook that denies the prospect of supernatural activity. Fittingly, this chapter on theodical secularity concludes with the sentiments of philosophers, theologians, sociologists, anthropologists, religious intellectuals, activists, filmmakers, and musicians who similarly comprehend that modern society thrives from the inevitable and dynamic synergies between religious faith and secularity.

POSTSCRIPT: SACRED/SECULAR MUTUALITY

Fifty years prior to the writing of this chapter, Kenneth Burke (1970) makes synergistic claims on how the rhetoric of religion offers secular analogues to illuminate the dynamic nature of language. Coincidentally in the same year, John Cooper and Carl Skrade's edited volume *Celluloid and Symbols* uses cinema to establish a necessary dialogue between contemporary faith and American secularity, and Neil Hurley composes a compelling case that modern cinema can be exploited as a sociological, anthropological, and aesthetic apparatus toward generating interfaith bonds among global communities. Not only does Hurley refuse to see secularization as "intrinsically evil or dispassionately neutral," but he also considers it a vital social development in pluralistic societies for humans to conquer debilitating forces such as "total institutionalization, political, cultural and social ideologies, economic subservience, and religious dogmatism" (Hurley 1970: 25–26). Hurley represents a growing list of scholars who understand how religion is obliged to conform to both "the modern principle of structural differentiation of the secular spheres" (Casanova 1994: 212) and hermeneutic constraints of the immanent frame (Taylor 2007), while appreciating how the very notion of modernity incorporates critical functions of religion and theology (Gillespie 2008; Sorkin 2008).

So even as the Apostle Paul classifies the carnal mind as death and hatred against God (Romans 8:6–7), while instructing believers to guard their spiritual mindsets from being contaminated by worldly patterns (Romans 12:2), Richard Niebuhr (1951: 236) ponders the changes Christianity must endure, as it exists in and relates to a modern world two thousand years after Christ walked the Earth, admonishing believers to consider how "Christians in an industrial culture cannot think and act as if they lived in feudal society." Mark C. Taylor (1998, 2007) avows that to claim modernization overrides or negates religion is to overlook religion's influences on modernity itself, while also noting that it is impossible to comprehend the contemporary world without understanding the intricate interplay of religion and secularity. Mark C. Taylor's attitude matches Neil Hurley's (1970: 14) assertion that "with the increase of secularization, the conditions of both psychological freedom and religious commitment are inescapably linked to urban technological forces." And more recently, an intellectual conversation emanating out of Harvard University's Hauser Center inspired a coterie of distinguished scholars to propose "that social service work and policy debates are often both religious and secular at the same time" (Ammerman 2014a: 100).

In the same year that Gibson Winter (1963) insists that secularization is an outgrowth of the liberating freedom that comes from the gospel, Paul van Buren (1963) promotes secular Christianity and his "this-worldly" understanding of that same gospel. Within the same timeframe, the Second Vatican Council recognized the legitimacy of modernity after centuries of resisting it (Casanova 1994), conceded to the separation of Church and state, and collapsed the binary between Catholic believers' sacred and secular roles (Dillon 2018), while aspiring to be a public and modern Church that refuses to allow religion and morality to be consigned to private spaces (Casanova 2006). In the post-Vatican II era, a growing number of Catholics integrated modern outlooks into their personal experiences and advocacy for doctrinal modifications, as "religion is maintained, in part, because those who are moderately religious push for the sorts of institutional changes that would make the Church more palatable to a secular sensibility" (Dillon 2018: 24).

As a self-professed bluesman, Cornel West (2011) asserts that democratic fitness thrives on secularists and religious adherents becoming more "musical" with each other's worldview. West's appeal unwittingly anticipates Saba Mahmood's (2015) ethnographic insights on the kinds of threats to political freedoms and interreligious conflicts that can escalate in the Middle East when secular domains become unmusical with the discordant outcries of religious minorities. And those Occidentals who blithely dismiss all Middle-Eastern Muslims as foes of modernity should consider, among numerous disconfirmations, the radical Islamic discourse of Ali Shariati and his followers that critiques and expands progressive modern projects around the globe (Saffari 2017), along with Lila Abu-Lughod's description of a new feminist archetype in Middle-Eastern societies:

> She quotes fluently from the Qur'an, is familiar with Islamic law, invokes precedents from early Muslim history, writes sophisticated articles on the UN Convention on the Elimination of All Forms of Discrimination against Women

(CEDAW), arranges conferences on Google Calendar, conducts online surveys, and draws from a wide range of experiences of organizing for change. (Abu-Lughod 2013: 201–202)

Along these lines, Lara Deeb's (2006) ethnographic work rejects the lazy branding of Muslims as intrinsically resistant to modern culture, raises questions about the merits of a universalizing notion of modernity by which to assess whether particular Muslim communities measure up to Western standards, and appreciates the intriguing ways contemporary Islamic societies facilitate and celebrate sacred/secular fluidity, while concluding, "the continued importance of the intersection of piety and modernity also underscores the inseparability of religion, politics, and social responsibility" (2006: 231). Thus we see how Ali Shariati's emancipatory Islamic political discourse, Lila Abu-Lughod's notion of "Islamic feminism," and Lara Deeb's discussion of enchanted modern Muslims collectively fulfill Robert Bellah's (1970) contention that Islam as a meaning-making system contributes to the conciliations that Muslim societies make between the religious and the secular when negotiating pressing problems of modernity.

Emil Fackenheim (1968: 301) clarifies how even conservative theologians bear the effects of secularity, contending that "whatever questions may be asked about the positivism of Karl Barth's neoorthodoxy, it does not ignore secularism but arises from self-exposure to it." Quite paradoxical but equally synergistic is the way: radical theology can't shake the unmistakable influence of Barth's conservative theology (Cooper 1967); Henlee Barnette (1967) perceives in radical theology the aim to reclaim Christianity for an age of secularity; Karl Barth (1978: 38) declares the greatest challenge of a new generation of evangelical leadership is "to derive the knowledge of the humanity of God from the knowledge of His deity" (1978: 38); many Protestant theologians after World War II affirmed secularization as the fulfillment of crucial Christian motifs (Berger 1967); Don Cupitt (1976) contends secularity reawakens Christian faith with an infusion of self-awareness; Gianni Vattimo (1999) claims secularity rids Christianity of impurities; and Armando Salvatore reveals how "Efforts at reforming and remolding faith into an increasingly secular trust proved to be crucial to the modernization of the public sphere" (2007: 216).

David Bentley Hart (2013) reminds us that the sacred impulse continues to invigorate Western intellects, imaginations, laws, and cultural revolutions and that world history offers no such thing as a genuinely secular civilization. Johannes Metz (1969: 16) goes a step further by asserting, "The task of theology is to show that the historically irreversible process of secularization does not mean that Christianity is disappearing, but that it has become truly historically effective." If Metz here contradicts Saint Paul's contention that

Christianity fails when it becomes too congenial with the world, Metz's sentiment nonetheless illuminates four captivating assertions of four sociologists: that Durkheimian notions about aboriginal religious practices can translate into concepts which clarify aspects of urban secular living, suggesting "this secular world is not so irreligious as we might think" (Goffman 1967: 95); that Protestant theologians have progressively participated in a contest whose rubrics are calculated by their secular antagonists (Berger 1969); that "Modern science is an outgrowth of the secularization of Christendom" (Fuller 2006: 131); and that contemporary Americans negotiate the rigors of everyday life with assessments incorporating sacred and secular sensibilities (Ammerman 2014b).

Jürgen Moltmann (1967, 1999) concedes that the upsurge of bourgeois society and the structural demands of industry and commerce have long since freed modern society from the classical concept of religion and divinity, and thus the German theologian endorses a notion of God uniquely calibrated for a secular society. We already discussed how a younger German Jürgen imagines modern society as a symphony of religious and secular syncopations (Habermas 2006; 2011). And if Habermas's peaceful nexus of religious and societal rational capacities has a familiar ring, it is because it reiterates Immanuel Kant's (1793) similarly hopeful perspective on the liberating effects of modernity when religion is calibrated within the limits of reason alone. If the above voices belt out too many Continental melodies, we can also listen to American slaves (who presumably never read Kant) sing sacred/secular harmonies of liberation (Glaude 2000). Not only slaves, but a host of early-twentieth-century black artists were posing new secular ideas in relation to preexisting impressions of Christianity (Lackey 2007), and promoting "humanistic or post-Christian perspectives, while challenging styles of Christian faith and practice judged to be counterproductive to progress" (Prentiss 2014: 74).

Decades before Harvey Cox (1965) fused the kingdom of God and the secular city, and William Hutchison (1976) identified the modernist impulse in American Protestantism, black social thinkers (see Sorett 2016) and musicians (see Reed 2003) were exhibiting varieties of sacred/secular fluidity. W. E. B. Du Bois personifies a confluence of secular and religious modalities (Blum 2007; Kahn 2009), tackles the function of religion in the modern world with remarkable clarity (Blum and Young 2009), works as an important facilitator of modern theology (Hopkins 2009), and is one of the principal predecessors to black theology and womanist theology (Blum 2007), while remaining staunchly uncompromising in his anticlerical attitudes, suspicion of religious tradition and dogmatism, renunciation of religious affiliation, and doubts about supernatural claims (Blum 2007; Evans 2008; Kahn 2009). Benjamin Mays, another educator and towering figure of the black social gospel movement (Wilmore 1989; Dorrien 2015), not only serves as an important bridge connecting American liberal theology to the progressive struggle against segregation and oppression (Jelks 2012), but also offers an early racial critique that serves as a viaduct to James Cone's black theology, as Ronald Neal confirms:

> Through his oratory and literary output, Mays was a pioneer in bringing a theological critique to American racism. Anticipating the efforts of James H. Cone and black liberation theology, Mays argued that American racism, including legal and de facto segregation, was unchristian and a betrayal of the gospel of Jesus Christ. (2012: 31)

Neal alludes to the parameters of Mays's secularity: "He wished to make religion sensible, accessible, and applicable to modern societies that were affected by rational forces such as science and technology and by urban forces such as corporations, crime, and slums" (2012: 27). And much can be said about the deployment of sacred/secular integrations by Mays's mentee Martin Luther King Jr., whose theodicy equips black churches and communities to confront societal manifestations of suffering (Edmondson 2017) to spark a civil rights mission that is as theological in its assertions as it is political in its fight for racial justice (Jelks 2012).

Occupying multiple sites of leadership as a religiously oriented educator, political advisor, and activist, Mary McLeod Bethune presses black religious institutions to effectuate change by marshaling spiritual and political resources, unveiling the new shapes that secular perspectives and pragmatic leadership can take when infused with religious cultural resources (Savage 2008). C. L. Franklin's widespread popularity as a mid-twentieth-century preacher partially derives from his titillating interface of spirituality, social activism, and secularity (Salvatore 2005). J. Saunders Redding (1951) proposes a secularized Christianity that is divorced from mysticism and otherworldliness, as a promising cure to the American sickness of racism. Aldon Morris (1984) explores the critical role of black churches in organizing boycotts and collective protests throughout the civil rights movement. Mary Pattillo (1998) delineates the potency of church rituals as cultural tools for facilitating local organizing and activism among African Americans, and Fredrick Harris (1999) displays how these cultural tools operate as political resources in the process of mobilization by legitimizing political goals. Marla Frederick (2003: 179) reveals how churches create alternative public spaces and "serve as meeting places for the NAACP, community groups, the Black Caucus, and a host of other civic/political organizations that work on behalf of African American citizens."

I imagine Barbara Savage (2008) might insist that we involve Zora Neale Hurston in any discussion of sacred/secular mutuality, while Wallace Best (2005) would compel us to include an artistic genre like gospel music and its most innovative composer Thomas Dorsey. By the same token, I speculate Judith Weisenfeld (2007) would enlist celluloid pioneers like Spencer Williams and Eloyce and James Gist for producing films that assess the social location of religion in the fabric of modern urban American life. And one could add Oscar Micheaux as another filmic exegete of the place for God and religion in an increasingly secular society, as his masterwork *Within Our Gates* (1920) favors a secularized brand of progressive religious activism (Lee 2015). Ebony Utley (2012) could point to gangsta rappers who deploy theological resources toward explicating the tragic murders, economic displacement, and corrupt social relations pervading their environments. Leigh Schmidt (2006) might select Oprah, while scholars and patrons of neo-soul music and style could anoint Erykah Badu as archbishop of mutuality.

But we should pause to consider how lurking in the shadows of sacred/secular symposia is the most hallowed symbol of theodical secularity: a sidelined sovereign. For nowhere in the analyses, political missions, or artistic visions of the abovementioned artisans of sacred/secular fluidity will you find any detailed explanation of God acting in time and space to mediate suffering or directly hold humans accountable for the pain and misery they often inflict on others. In modern domains, divinity's contributions to human flourishing only come through human hands. So in the process of fortifying humanist values with the teleological grounding of God's love and religious accountability, divine efficacy is clipped and curbed by the same rampant currents that faith and spiritual power are alleged to curtail; those raging winds of modern momentum that propelled Phil Zuckerman's (2008) Scandinavian subjects to engage in Christian practices while discounting Christianity's supernatural claims; and drove a lifelong Lutheran like Peter Berger (2004) toward Friedrich Schleiermacher's liberal Protestantism because it exemplified for him the appropriate equilibrium between skepticism and affirmation to maintain belief without drifting from rationality. Hence, prophets of Enlightenment who forecast God being crushed under the weight of a complex and increasingly mechanized modern world overlooked a sexy alternative via God's demotion from supernatural ruler to sidelined coach, a cosmic contract renegotiation presumably cosigned by many readers of this present book who recognize that "once you let modernity into religion, you cannot then forestall its implications" (Dillon 2018: 17).

If anyone pines for a theological analogue to theodical secularity that captures the ways in which modern cinema, modern scholars, and modern everyday believers transform the supernatural subject of religious faith into an immanent object of ethical accountability and solidarity, one viable option is Isabel Carter Heyward's (2010) relational ontology in which God is reborn through human engagement, mutuality, and communal spaces. Heyward offers a reshaping of God through human understandings of justice and love, thus adapting God to emergent existential needs and social problems. Relational ontology is another way of expressing a theological option that reinvents God via the appropriation of Saint Paul's concept of kenosis (Vattimo 1999), a term that connotes the humiliation God endured when disposing of divine attributes to become a human nailed on a cross (Philippians 2:7–8). Like Heyward's relational ontology, Gianni Vattimo's adaptation of kenosis empties the contemporary God of retributive violence and all intervening capacities, allowing for a kinder and gentler God to function as the object of human contemplation. Vattimo writes:

> If it is true that the whole relationship between God and the world must be seen from the perspective of kenosis, that is, of the dilution, weakening and denial of what the natural religious mentality believed to be God, then the Christian vision of God and humanity can face the process of demythification without fear of its essential content being disfigured or lost. (1999: 58)

Responding to Vattimo's recapitulation of the Pauline metaphor, Richard Rorty (2005: 40) mocks kenosis as God simply moving from "being our master to being our friend." But even in jest, Rorty must have grasped how his good friend Vattimo's modern remix on incarnation explains God's inaction during the bloodiest century in world history.

Vattimo's retrofitted understanding of kenosis, not unlike Heyward's relational ontology, vindicates a God who stood by and watched over a million lives decimated or displaced by Turkish genocidal activity against the Armenians, watched thousands of sexual assaults and murders against Chinese citizens go unpunished during Japan's invasion of Nanking, watched tens of millions of civilians crushed under Allied and Nazi bombings of cities, starved to death, or massacred in World War II, only years later to watch tens of millions more civilians eliminated in Communist revolutions in Russia and China. While some antitheists may consider these vulgar integers of human waste as symbolizing insurmountable evidence of God's death, many theists appreciate how a God, emptied of metaphysical dynamism, is also drained of blame for allowing grotesque gradations of human death and anguish to occur on His watch. I imagine some detractors might claim that they could teach divinity a thing or two about how to run the world in a manner that constrains gratuitous evil. But from the vantage point of everyday believers in Ammerman's and Wuthnow's studies, the black liberation theologians assessed in the next chapter, and scores of cinematic characters featured throughout this book, the practice of ascribing rational boundaries to divine efficacy is a more constructive theodical response to tragedy and misfortune than a Nietzschean call for divine expiry. Emile Durkheim (1912) did inform us that we can learn much about society from its deity. Modern people appreciate their modern God.

Chapter 2

Tactical Deists

Black Liberation Theology and Cinema

Cornel West begins his tribute essay for the thirtieth anniversary of James Cone's (1969) *Black Theology and Black Power* with a reference to Voltaire's (1759) philosophical tale *Candide*, calling it "one of the first towering texts of modernity to wrestle with the question of what it means to be human in the face of death" (West 1999: 11). West believes Voltaire's treatment of the Lisbon earthquake's blow to European optimism bears semblance to Cone's handling of disenfranchised black life. But West omits *Candide*'s momentous allusion to slavery (which I briefly discussed in the introduction) and in doing so relinquishes an opportunity to contrast Voltaire's and Cone's theodical deployments of black suffering as indicators of (or litmus tests for) their overarching theological aims. Such a juxtaposition would reveal how, in stark contrast to Cone's reverential affinity between black suffering and divine kinship, Voltaire's inclusion of black suffering serves an explicitly cynical agenda.

Published four years after Europe's greatest natural disaster, *Candide* unfolds unnerving accounts not only of the Lisbon earthquake but also of murder, gang rape, butchery, torture, theft, and deceit to challenge Gottfried Leibniz's (1710) claim that the world is the best one God could have possibly created. In a surprising sequence, Voltaire brings black suffering to the fore when the protagonist Candide and his traveling companion Cacambo reach the outskirts of the Dutch colony of Surinam and encounter a deformed half-naked black man who explains to Candide that his missing right hand and missing left leg are the results of slavery: "When we work at the sugar-canes, and the mill snatches hold of a finger, they cut off the hand; and when we attempt to run away, they cut off the leg; both cases have happened to me. This is the price at which you eat sugar in Europe" (Voltaire 1759: 48).

After alluding to his familial origins on the coast of Guinea, the place where he was sold into the transatlantic trade, the slave sums up his life of toil: "Dogs, monkeys, and parrots are a thousand times less wretched than I" (1759: 49). This exchange between a European traveler and a mutilated slave extends Voltaire's potent challenge against Leibniz's theodicy, presuming that the systematic exploitation of black bodies in the slave trade cannot be part of the best of all possible worlds. Voltaire construes black suffering as evidence of an ungoverned world; a glaring divergence from James Cone's depiction of black suffering as the navigational aid to locate God's identity and mission.

So one might consider Cornel West's comparison of these two seminal works quite puzzling when bearing in mind the conflicting theological aims driving each text. *Black Theology and Black Power* insists that God is attentive to human arrangements and shows partiality to oppressed people, whereas *Candide* assigns divine indifference to all human affairs. But despite variance concerning God's place in and awareness of human history, West's theological connection between the classic works of Voltaire and Cone does have merit—but for a different reason than West intended. What Voltaire and Cone do share in common is that, while proceeding from different directions, they both find God in the same deistic destination: the sidelines of human suffering. James Cone pays homage to God's liberating presence and periodically alleges divine support to oppressed people, but an overall assessment of his distinguished tome and canon reveals a God who is no less remote than the absentee deity of *Candide*. The difference is that Voltaire's deism is more upfront and makes God oblivious to all human concerns, while Cone and other progenitors of black liberation theology subscribe to a tactical deism that allows God to exist in time and space to coach and comfort black sufferers from the sidelines, leaving it up to humans to do all the heavy lifting. So, notwithstanding small divergences, black liberation theology is quite "Voltairean" in how it makes humans, rather than God, responsible to accomplish all confrontations against evil, inequality, and oppression. In this way, black liberation theology is no different than its Latin American analogue in how proponents of each offer perfunctory allusions to God's liberating presence and give lip service to God's allegiance to the poor and oppressed, while ultimately setting aside God's interventionist hand as a relic of the pre-modern past.

LIBERATION THEOLOGY AND CINEMA

Liberation theology emerges in the late 1950s among Latin American theologians and priests first as a theoretical perspective and later as a political mission that combines structural analysis of oppression with Catholic salvific interest in social justice. That Catholicism would play such an integral role in liberation theology is unsurprising when considering the Church's longstanding emphasis on solidarity with and concern for the poor and its mobilized activism against economic inequality (Dillon 2018). Whereas many theoretical approaches to theodicy discuss evil and suffering abstractly (Adams 1999), liberation theologians concern themselves with material sources of evil and concrete struggles for justice, drawing much from social theories like Marxism that assess structural disparities (Chopp 1986; Damico 1987). This interest in the material (rather than the demonic) mechanisms and manifestations of evil and social suffering makes liberation theology quite the modern outlook. José Miguez Bonino affirms the this-world focus of liberationist activity, acknowledging that the theological movement resonates with the advance of sociological theory in Latin America:

> Theology, as here conceived, is not an effort to give a correct understanding of God's attributes or actions but an effort to articulate the action of faith, the shape of praxis conceived and realized in obedience. As philosophy in Marx's famous dictum, theology has to stop explaining the world and to start transforming it. Orthopraxis, rather than orthodoxy, becomes the criterion for theology. (Bonino 1975: 81)

While Bonino here claims that liberation theology does not attempt to clarify divine attributes, its theological default mode is set to vertical boundaries. In other words, by focusing on human responsibility, its theological understanding of God is clearly defined as sidelined. Likewise, the Peruvian theologian and priest Gustavo Gutierrez, widely regarded as one of the prime movers of liberation theology, has many compelling things to say on matters concerning the God of justice against the backdrop of the sufferings of the poor (Gutierrez 1973, 1987, 1999; Gutierrez and Muller 2015), but only promotes human solutions toward addressing and removing oppression, never specifying how supernatural intervention will help suffering victims. Liberation theologians like Bonino and Gutierrez challenge the resignation and despair in Latin American popular religion by conveying God as keenly attuned to the voices of suffering people, while stopping short of presenting God as a supernatural solution to Latin American oppression and injustice (Sands 1994).

Andres Guerrero (1993) articulates a theology of liberation to address the oppression of Chicanos but makes God more like a social advocate than a governor of the universe. Likewise, Ada Maria Isasi-Diaz's (1996, 2004) mujerista theology creates a liberationist voice and method for Latinas in the United States to fight against oppression and inequality, making Latinas' struggle for survival the critical lens through which to view theology, while never stating the possibility of God intervening to reverse the disproportionate struggles and inequities Latinas face. Ruben Rodriguez (2008) infuses insights and metaphors from Latinx theology toward a transcultural theology of human liberation that emphasizes the role of the Holy Spirit as a symbolic representation (and motivation) for Christian solidarity without offering God a more active role in directly ameliorating racism, sexism, and classicism. Rodriguez joins the abovementioned projects in making humans the active doers of liberationist activities and God the inspirational coach wholly dependent on human performances to fight oppression. In a similar way, Nestor Medina (2013: 77) delineates five basic principles for cultivating a Latina/o–Canadian liberation theology:

> highlight the constitution and reality of Latinas/os in Canada; engage in a careful self-reflective analysis of the ideological and sociocultural dynamics at work in these communities; identify the concerns and challenges of Latina/o–Canadians as part of a larger set of concerns in the immigrant communities of Canada; interrogate the myth of Canada as a kind and welcoming country; and recognize that issues of social, political, ethnocultural and racialized injustice, oppression, discrimination, and marginalization are not separate from questions of religious plurality.

Notice how none of Medina's five principles have anything to do with divine efficacy and how each principle can be advocated and administered by a social worker or concerned citizen without a theological background. While Medina concludes his discussion with a vague reference to Latinx faith as a coping mechanism and source of hope, he never alludes to any direct activity from God to alleviate the struggles of Canadian Latinx people. This chapter later assesses more thoroughly how black liberation theology countersigns a similarly deistic outlook.

Cinematic representations of liberationist ideals predate liberation theology's emergence as a movement. Perhaps the earliest filmic depiction unfolds in the radical activity of Don Pietro Pellegrini in Roberto Rossellini's *Rome, Open City* (1945). Don Pietro believes his duty as a Catholic priest is to do more than pray for the sanctity of his people, so he collaborates with underground Communist fighters to resist Fascists and Nazis in Rome. He also provides refuge and false documents to Italians plotting to attack Nazi soldiers and quite bravely transports crucial funds to insurgents. After the Nazis capture the priest, the Gestapo commander Major Bergman asks Don Pietro why a man of God would support the efforts of Communist atheists. Don Pietro responds with feasibly the first and finest filmic formulation of liberation theology: "I am a Catholic priest. I believe that anyone fighting for justice and liberty walks in the ways of the Lord. And the ways of the Lord are infinite." Thus, the Italian priest makes justice and freedom core elements of his clerical mission and in doing so foreshadows future generations of liberation theologians in Latin America, such as Archbishop Oscar Romero who would place the onus on Christians to fight for justice and freedom as if doing so is aligning oneself with God's mission on Earth. But Don Pietro gets caught by the Nazis and dies a martyr, and so a pressing theodical inquiry for the film ponders why at no juncture do we see God intervene to help Don Pietro and suffering Italians. In one scene we even see a Catholic woman gratuitously gunned down in the street by Nazis. As is true of divinity's function for liberation theologians, Don Pietro's God is more of an idea than a force (or source) of liberation.

While *Rome, Open City* and other films insinuate liberationist ideals, Carlos Carrera's *The Crime of Padre Amaro* (2002) is one of a few that actually employs the term liberation theology. In a small Mexican town called Los Reyes, religious leadership appears ruthless and calculating, as priests engage in sexual dalliances and shady financial dealings. Ironically, the only cleric to be punished is Padre Natalio, the most heroic character in the film, who advocates for the poor and tries to protect his congregants from the corruptive reach of a drug lord. Padre Natalio's bishop excommunicates him under the charges of propagating liberation theology. While he was falsely accused of supporting guerilla warfare, Padre Natalio's concentration on relieving the oppression of his people makes him the consummate liberation theologian. But in the context of theodicy, Carrera's film (like *Rome, Open City*) mocks the notion of divine intervention, as the innocent are exploited and punished while corrupt men are empowered under the sanctuary (and sanctimony) of clerical leadership. Evil, in multiple ways, prevails over good and God appears as a passive bystander in a matrix of political power plays.

The most compelling filmic testimonial on liberation theology comes in the biopic *Romero* (1989), which unfolds how Cardinal Oscar Romero converts from a conservative Salvadoran priest into the highest-ranking clerical advocate of liberation theology in the world. *Romero* can be viewed as a filmic apology for liberation theology as well as a cautionary tale concerning its sidelined God. As corrupt Salvadoran powers start to recognize liberation theology as a threat and Archbishop Romero as too prominent a proponent to ignore, they respond by persecuting, torturing, and murdering Catholic leaders and lay liberationists. At the film's conclusion, governmental assassins kill Cardinal Romero while he is holding mass, showing no respect for God or the sanctity of religious experience. Hence, while the film offers Romero's theological transition to liberation theology, it proposes no indication of divine protection or support undergirding such a fight for the poor and the oppressed.

Summing up the archbishop's turn to political activism, *Romero*'s producer, Father Ellwood Kieser, offers comments in the "Behind the Scenes" section of the DVD that postulate the fundamental principles of liberation theology:

> I think he made the essential transition that the entire Catholic Church has to make, that society in Latin America and throughout the world has to make. I think he saw the essential truth that God is present in a unique way in the poor, that in the struggle to help the poor live with dignity and to acquire justice, that the affluent and the rich of the world will save their souls.

Projecting humanity's potential to effect change, liberationists, both in theology and cinema, neglect to clarify God's role in the removal of suffering and oppression. Hence, while varying strains of liberation theology situate the problem of theodicy as a concrete concern, they all execute a move reminiscent of the cinematic depictions we have discussed—the archbishop's political resistance in *Romero*, Padre Natalio's advocacy for the poor in *The Crime of Padre Amaro*, and Don Pietro's collaboration with Communist partisans in *Rome, Open City*—by situating God strategically as absent or above the fray, while funneling all focus on humans as change agents.

Some liberationist films not only leave no role for divine intervention, but add insult to injury by featuring malefactors acting in the name of God to instigate anguish. A distressing example is *Submission* (2004), a short drama that triggered the assassination of its director Theo Van Gogh not long after it was broadcast in the Netherlands. Written and narrated by black activist Ayaan Hirsi Ali, *Submission* presents disturbing testimonies and optics of battered Muslim women. One victim's uncle repeatedly raped her and another was forced to marry a man she despised. The film's violent antagonists accomplished their cruel deeds while affirming fidelity to Allah. *Submission* ends with a victim's suicidal prayer likening Allah's reticence in the midst of her suffering to the silent grave for which she longs. Other films bring to light how earthly stand-ins for God generate trauma for victims. In Abderrahmane Sissako's film *Timbuktu* (2014), Muslim jihadists make life miserable for a village in Mali by imposing violence, forced marriages, merciless death sentences, draconian laws, and great humiliation upon its inhabitants. Oliver Schmitz's *Life, Above All* (2010) discloses how Christians ostracize AIDS victims in South Africa. Rigid interpretations of what it means to live in service to Allah perpetuate Tariq's physical abuse at a Muslim boarding school in Qasim Basir's film *Mooz-Lum* (2010).

Predictably, sexuality often makes a person vulnerable to holy arrows of condemnation. The liberationist documentary *God Loves Uganda* (2013) includes sermonic excerpts from some of Uganda's most popular pastors and energetic street preachers communicating vitriol against homosexuals in the name of God. The film exposes how Christians contribute to a hostile and intolerant climate that eventually engenders and condones the violent murder of David Kato, Uganda's first and most vocal gay activist. An earlier film, *Call Me Kucho* (2012), offers a closer look at the activist's life, including the events that took place at David Kato's funeral where Pastor Thomas Musoke turns an invitation to pay his respects into an anti-gay tirade:

> May the Lord be with you. I have seen these people grow, as we all grew up here in this village. I was informed of Kato's death. But I wasn't aware of the work he was doing. Kato is gone! He can't repent, he can't change. The Lord is telling you to change! Sexual immorality is too much! The prayer we pray is for the total destruction of your group! Completely! Completely!

Pastor Musoke's admonition inspires rowdy Christians to harass gay funeral attendees who are already heartbroken by the death of their leader. But the film also showcases noted liberationist leader Bishop Senyonjo offering comforting words at David Kato's burial:

> I know people have been discouraged, even not going to church because they are being abused, as I have found today—people abusing them. Please don't be discouraged. God created you. God is on your side. This is the gospel I am preaching. And my church was not happy with what I said. Because they wanted me to condemn. But God showed me no, no no. I am free because I know the truth! And I will stand for that truth! So please, we pray for the soul of David Kato. I have known him. I have respected him, and his love for the human race. And that is the best thing God left us. God loves you Kato. He knows you. He brought you into the world. And you have done your work so rest in peace.

Bishop Senyonjo receives a letter from his archbishop expressing profound shock at Senyonjo's support of homosexuals and renouncing his right to exercise the office of bishop. *Call Me Kucho* (like *God Loves Uganda*) presents Christians causing pain and suffering to Uganda's homosexual community.

Faith Trimel's drama *Family* (2008) features a suffering black lesbian in confrontation with Christian ideals. Sabrina struggles with accepting her sexual identity because she worries about punishments involving fire and brimstone promised to homosexuals. She attends Messiah Baptist Church where the pastor offers an incendiary spiritual indictment in one of his sermons: "We need to take the drugs out of our neighborhoods, the gangs out of our neighborhoods, the prostitution, the homosexuality! That's right. The right to marry? They stand before God, expose their blasphemous union when they ought to be hiding. It ain't natural! And ain't no court gonna make it natural." Her pastor's comments fan the flames of Sabrina's turmoil about her love for women. Supportive friends step in, as one of the friends, Kemp, expresses disdain for homophobic clerics and another, Monifa, mocks a different preacher's claim that black lesbians are an epidemic and national emergency. When Sabrina expresses trepidation about going to hell as a result of God's judgment, Monifa responds incredulously, "Hell for what? Loving someone?" and Kemp chimes in, "Seems like you in hell now!" Monifa later adds that "God is not worried about who is in my bed," while Kemp expresses satisfaction with being a good person and "living my life like it's golden." Eventually Sabrina does find peace in acceptance of her orientation as Faith Trimel's film replaces religion and God with supportive friendships and humanist self-acceptance.

Dee Rees's film *Pariah* (2011) is the coming-of-age story of a black teen named Alike who must negotiate her sexual identity while enduring persecution from her mother Audrey, whose Christian faith fuels the fires of homophobic antagonism. Audrey gives her daughter a bloody beating after Alike confesses she is a lesbian. The film ends with Alike heading off to college on the opposite coast to be far away from her Christian mother's condemning voice and to start a new self-affirming life. In Arnold Laven's *Anna Lucasta* (1959), Joe thinks he speaks for God but patriarchal codes about female respectability motivate the slut-shaming he engages in against his daughter. In Rodney Evans's film *Brother to Brother* (2004), a homophobic subway preacher verbally attacks the gay protagonist Perry. Adaora Nwandu's drama *Rag Tag* (2006) includes an important scene with the protagonist's father quoting passages from Leviticus to inform his son that God hates his gay lifestyle. Kareem Mortimer's romantic drama *Children of God* (2010) presents Christian clerics and their followers as rabid homophobes. Like liberationist movements in theology, the above films are noteworthy for cataloging and resisting the ways in which political, economic, and sexual processes and systems reproduce inequality and injustice, and also for how they put God and religious conservatism under the microscope of modern liberal values.

Perhaps the best segue into our discussion of black liberation theology is a notable contrast to the above celluloid masterworks encompassing liberationist sentiments in the context of various forms of suffering. For no one can accuse Ralph Ziman's dark drama *Gangster Paradise: Jerusalema* (2008) of promoting liberationist ideals and yet its takeaway message resembles the tactical deism of James Cone and his successors. The film covers the late teen and early adult years of Lucky Kunene; a poor and smart South African who turns to a life of crime shortly after his acceptance to college comes without a desperately needed scholarship. Lucky gleans insights from an ex-guerilla fighter and criminal named Nazareth who informs the teen, "I may be a communist, but I believe that God helps those who help themselves," a theme Lucky appropriates in his early career of hijacking cars and in his later years as a criminal entrepreneur. Eventually Lucky's corrupt real estate activities make him a millionaire and his ill-gotten gains support his younger siblings and devout Christian mother. But his underworld dealings eventually catch up to him and he is arrested for murder and various other charges. Lucky beats the system once again by escaping from prison and heading toward the African coast to start a new business enterprise. Throughout the film, his mother's Christian faith produces little by way of materiality and sustenance, while Lucky's criminal enterprises meet the financial needs of his mother and younger siblings. Like Nazareth, Lucky truly learns what black liberation theology mastered from its inception: to see divine blessing as directly proportional to the human's own ability to harness his environment. Black liberation theologians resemble Latin American and filmic counterparts in requiring humans to confront evil and stave off suffering while holding no expectations of divine interference in the process. The God of black theology and womanist theology (predominant subsets of black liberation theology) is just as passive in the context of black suffering as God appears to be in many films.

BLACK THEOLOGY

Noted religious historian Gayraud Wilmore (1989: 173) reveals that black theology emerged "like a gentle earthquake undulating across the theological landscape from 1958–1970, loosening subterranean connections between African American Christianity and the old evangelicalism." Black theology not only has tentacles extending back to an earlier black social gospel movement which informally encompassed a variety of progressive intellectuals like W. E. B. Du Bois, radical preachers like Henry McNeal Turner, and social reformers and educators like Benjamin E. Mays (Wilmore 1989; Dorrien 2015), but also was in many ways a response to (and successor of) the larger American social gospel movement. But some proponents perceive black theology less as an extension of the social gospel (or Latin American liberation theology) and more as traceable to distinctive black religious experiences and the civil rights and black power movements (Cone 1969, 1970; Roberts 1971; Evans 1987; Hopkins 2000).

Black theology calls for the partnering of the distinctive concerns of black racism and oppression with theological commitments and analyses to address those concerns. "Within the classic formulation of black theology," Juan Floyd-Thomas contends, "liberation is focused upon the relationship between the black experience and a faith in God as an emancipatory force in the course of human affairs" (2014: 200). Black theology reflects an attempt to comprehend God through the prism of black oppression, alleging "the fundamental claim of black theology is that God is black" (Lloyd 2018: 10), and that "White Christian brothers and sisters worship a God who is essentially White" (Jones 1987: viii). But the specifics behind what God accomplishes on behalf of suffering black victims are left unstated in black theology's seminal texts. And thus, while black theology lays claim to black religion as its spiritual source (Evans 1987; Hopkins 2001), its sidelined God pales in comparison to the supernatural cosmic ruler of black religious traditions. More concretely, the God of black theology does nothing to remove black suffering and oppressive structures.

As black theology's architect and most prominent proponent, James Cone requires no tangible activity from God to enact change on behalf of suffering humans. Perhaps the greatest indicator of his anthropological emphasis is how he frames black theology as an earthly theology in contrast to what he perceives as the otherworldliness of some facets of black religion (Cone 1969). If Cone's earthly theology is at all theological, it is in the way he codes direct human confrontation against oppressive structures as divinely sanctioned activity. But Cone's insertion of God's approval in no way insinuates God's participation toward the removal of oppression. The theodical quandary of how black deprivation lingers in light of God's alleged endorsement of black people remains untouched by Cone's entire canon. In all his works, Cone quickly jumps from God to humans as the force behind any remedial activity to still the tide of black suffering.

While Cone (2011: 26–27) acknowledges that slaves and black preachers wrestled with God "about the deeply felt contradictions that slavery created for faith," nowhere does he similarly take issue with God for the lingering effects of past legacies of white supremacy and racial oppression. And thus, Cone's refusal to question God's passivity renders the theologian's attraction to another James's work quite curious. Cone informs us that James Baldwin's (1963) *The Fire Next Time* inspired him toward "a new way of doing theology that would empower the suffering black poor to fight for a more liberated existence" (Cone 1999: xxii). But in this passage Cone overlooks how Baldwin's (1963: 31) own treatment of theodicy posits an inquiry that preoccupied Baldwin's childhood as a suffering Christian: "And if His love was so great, and if He loved all His children, why were we, the blacks, cast down so far? Why?" A later work by Cone (2011: 28) does in fact cite this quote, acknowledging that Baldwin's frustration resonates with many black people wrestling with the contradictions of faith and systemic suffering. But Cone does not offer prescriptive analysis of Baldwin's indictment against God as it relates to Cone's own understanding of divine governance. So while the preponderance of black suffering and God's concurrent inaction do not seem to bother Cone, they are what crushed the other James's faith, as Baldwin scholar Clarence Hardy confirms: "Any promise [Baldwin] initially found in the faith of his youth was undermined by the betrayal of a God who was not only silent but also hostile to the life chances of black people and their own sense of worth" (2003: 41). In contrast to James Baldwin's theodical angst, James Cone's theological vexation only focuses on "how whites reconciled racism with their Christian identity" (Cone 1999: xiii). Nowhere in Cone's seminal texts and autobiographical statements do we ever see him questioning why black people seem especially targeted for a variety of health maladies, vulnerabilities, and other dysfunctions, and why it is taking so long to see measurable evidence of a divine reprieve.

Whereas the core tenet of Cone's theological innovation rests on the notion that God identifies closely with masses of subjugated African Americans (Cone 1969, 1970, 1984), the emancipatory tactics of Cone's black theology project are entirely dependent upon humans to balance the scales of justice. When Cone speaks vaguely of God's liberating presence among black people and claims that "God is always to be found in the sufferings of victims" (1984: 173–174), what tangible results God's presence generates for black people is a conundrum permeating Cone's entire canon. The pioneering theologian never calls down fire from heaven against white supremacists nor raises the possibility of God constraining evil against black bodies, and to the very end of his days Cone refused to voice public concern about why God seems to allow so much structurally injurious mayhem to pervade black communities and bodies without interceding.

If Cone deserves special distinction as its architect, J. Deotis Roberts is black theology's consummate deist. Even more blatantly than Cone, Roberts swiftly sidesteps addressing God's capabilities in the context of black suffering, preferring instead to consider anthropological channels to address it. Roberts (1987: 93) begins one essay by asking, "What accountability does God have, as creator, in the suffering that human beings inflict upon each other?" and conceding, "if God is a creator and provident God, the question is inescapable." But only moments later, Roberts stonewalls the very question he frames as unavoidable, choosing to focus solely on the role of humans to be co-workers with God to relieve suffering and promote goodness. Similarly, Roberts (1989: 265) contrasts the folly of supernatural hope against the more reliable modern mechanisms of black power:

> In a land of plenty, in the land of the free, the lot of the person in black skin must no longer be crumbs from the rich man's table. Over against an escapist and sentimental religious hope based upon a crude Jesusology, Black Power juxtaposes a this-worldly, secular and tough-minded understanding of what can be done to humanize structures of power to enable Blacks to hope.

Here Roberts assertively frames remedial measures for black suffering as a carnal endeavor rather than as the result of divine mediation. Like in his earlier statement on the black man's God (1971), Roberts offers a Christian response to evil and suffering that evades clarifying God's role behind alleviating black oppression:

> The questions arising from reflection on evil and suffering are often discussed so as to justify the justice of God. The goodness and power of God, as absolute attributes, are examined. While I am aware of these profound discussions and will refer to the aspects of the same, my approach will not involve God directly but will focus on human responsibility for evil and suffering. (2003: 169)

The last sentence best summarizes black theology's refusal to involve God directly and its exclusive focus on "human responsibility for evil and suffering." Roberts concludes the same essay, "Thus, an awesome responsibility rests on Christians and churches, through the power of the Spirit, to be transformers of the evil structures of the present world. With God as our Helper, we can do much to alleviate pain and suffering" (2003: 178). What exactly Roberts specifies by adding "through the power of the Spirit" and "with God as our Helper" at the end of his recommendation for constraining evil remains unexplained. Like Cone and successive generations of black liberationists, Roberts utilizes tangential God-talk to marshal troops, while placing all his faith in humans to offer black people a more equitable future.

Jaramogi Abebe Agyeman, formerly known as Albert Cleage, argues that blacks, like the Israelites of the Old Testament, are God's chosen people (Cleage 1989). But unlike the Israelites who benefit from supernatural intervention on numerous occasions, black people's "chosen" status appears more symbolic than actual. When encouraging young people not to become atheists, Agyeman alludes to the existential strength black people can tap into knowing God created them with dignity but makes no mention of divine mediations to relieve their struggles. Agyeman's focus is entirely on the capacity for humans to unite and secure their own power and liberty. His notion of redemptive theodicy appears at first glance to be theological in how it compares African Americans to Old Testament Israelites exiled to the wilderness for their faithlessness and frames African American faithlessness as the culprit behind their suffering. But contrary to the biblical idea of faithlessness as indicated by unholy or immoral activity, Agyeman reconceptualizes faithlessness as the absence of masculine courage. He writes:

> But the people who accept oppression, who permit themselves to be downtrodden, those people are faithless because God did not make men to be oppressed and to be downtrodden. And many times a man faces the choice between living as a slave and dying as a man. And when we choose to live as slaves, we are faithless and our children will be shepherds in the wilderness. (Cleage 1989: 267–268)

Agyeman's reformulation of theodicy makes black passivity and agentive action the respective cause of and remedy to black suffering. Thus, he offers only existential solutions to black suffering, and envisages a sidelined God rather than the active interventionist governor of history that the Bible depicts.

Joseph Washington (1970: xvii) begins with his own theodical question: "Why do blacks catch so much hell on the front lash, let alone the back lash?" Like J. Deotis Roberts, Washington offers no convincing answer to his own question, and is equally unable to present a direct role for God to end suffering. Washington concentrates on the durability, power, and strategic positioning of black religious institutions to meet the pressing needs of African Americans, not as conduits of God's power, but rather as administrators of social activities. Washington designates black religion as the base for justice and calls for black people to serve as God's humanizing agents. In Washington's theological project, it is not God who intervenes on behalf of black people, but black people who must function as God's "suffering servants" to utilize the institutional power of black religion to confront and remedy the inequities and injustices black people face.

Major Jones's (1971) message of theological hope is heavy on existential empowerment and light on specifics concerning how God can take concrete steps toward offering disproportionately poor black populations what they would need to achieve this state of hope. He alludes to the liberating intent of black theology as helping blacks connect with a deep core self that identifies with God's intention for black humanity, demonstrating how his work refers to God generally as an object of theological reflection while never treating God as a subject in history who executes actionable measures to relieve deprivation. Jones's theology is more like modern existentialism in offering a discursive apparatus for burdened black people to reclaim their dignity. Even in the chapter where Jones attempts to clarify the concept of God, alluding to divine love, wrath, and purpose, he never makes known how God exhibits those qualities in time and space to secure black liberation. In another work, Jones (1987) promises early on to develop a new frame of reference for understanding God's transcendence. But beyond establishing God's omnipotence alongside God's concern and love for black people, he never clarifies any tangible way divine power is activated for the task of removing black suffering. In other words, while Jones appeals to vague notions of divine love, he never indicates how God's love has real-world implications. Perhaps he does not consider how the very persistence and magnitude of black inequality and distress undermine his claims of divine love and omnipotence, making his framework vulnerable to another Jones's critique of divine racism (William R. Jones 1973). For if God is all-powerful and loves black people, as Major Jones claims, then God should have no qualms against intervening in a more decisive way to remove black oppression. Jones does allude to this quandary when he raises the issue of theodicy:

> If Black Theology is to be relevant to Black people, if it is to affirm God's power and love expressed in his creation, then it must also address the problems of evil and how they are related to God's character. The more Black Theology seeks to affirm God's goodness in the setting of Black human existence, the more difficult becomes the problem of evil. (1987: 61–62)

But here we see Jones write a theodical check that his project lacks the necessary funds to cash. He lists an array of historical approaches to the problem of theodicy and ends the discussion without ever reconciling how his conceptualization of God survives the very contradiction of triangulating God's omnipotence, God's love for black people, and God's enduring unwillingness to still the tide of oppression.

Fed up with its idle God, Cecil Cone (1975) calls out the black theology project of his brother James and colleagues, contending that the prayers, sermons, and testimonies of slaves, preachers, and other historical participants of black religion present an active God who is radically different from the passive portrayal of God in black theology. Cecil Cone argues: "Black Theology, if it is to remain faithful to the black religious experience, must look to God whom black slaves encountered as Almighty and Sovereign, thereby causing them to recognize him as the Mighty God Leader who brought them a mighty long way" (1975: 143). Here Cecil Cone anticipates Albert Raboteau's (1995) historical reflection on the ways that many Christian slaves and successive generations of African Americans facing segregation and discrimination believed in a God who intervenes in time and space to liberate sufferers and punish oppressors. But even as Cecil Cone is the first black liberation theologian to challenge his brother James and other proponents to recognize how their idle God contradicts the active God of black religious faith and experience, he ultimately falls short of providing any clarity on how such an interventionist God can stand up to the pressing questions of theodicy that a detractor like William R. Jones (1973) would propose. In other words, Cecil Cone overlooks the value of his brother's tactical deism in how it lowers the bar for divine efficacy so that the black theology project does not have to grapple with the contradiction of lingering inequities and struggles on God's watch. Thus, in an attempt to call out his colleagues for projecting a sidelined God, Cecil Cone falls victim to the problem of theodicy as it relates to the lack of supernatural firepower to still the tide of black oppression. By ascribing to God a more active place in history, Cecil Cone subjects God to more active criticism for failing to balance the scales of justice.

Dwight Hopkins, one of the most prominent second-generation black theology proponents, remains faithful to his predecessors' tactical deism, as none of his scholarly works offer any indication that God is anything more than a symbol of empowerment. Hopkins (2001) attempts to present continuities between black popular religion and academic constructions of black theology but overlooks Cecil Cone's aforementioned critique—how black theology's passive role for God is quite different from the active God of black popular religion. We see this disparity more clearly when Hopkins (2000) draws links between slave religion and black theology. He argues that the so-called "invisible institution" in which slaves gathered to worship in secret meetings away from their masters' watchful eyes nurtured early formations of black liberation theology. But Hopkins seems oblivious to (or deceptively reticent concerning) how the active interventionist God of slave religion controverts the sidelined God of black theology. Like James Cone, Hopkins claims that God offers a liberating presence and describes God as "an emancipating being for the oppressed of the earth" (2000: 162–163), without listing one tangible act performed by God in time and space to balance the scales of justice for the very same black people.

One of the few moments of levity in *Gangster Paradise: Jerusalema* presents a theological vantage point quite different from Dwight Hopkins's perspective on how God operates in time and space. The teenage protagonist Lucky and his buddy Zakes have just ventured upon a new life of crime and are in the middle of their first carjacking when Lucky and the victim find out that Zakes can't drive a stick shift. Now sensing that he is not only endangered by Lucky's gun but more so by Zakes's suspect driving skills, the petrified victim cries out, "Oh God, God of Israel, send your angel!" While meant to provide comic relief, the carjacking victim's desperate utterance inspires one to inquire if Dwight Hopkins or any proponent of black theology could instinctively cry out to God for immediate help should he come across gun-toting scoundrels like Lucky and Zakes. The answer is no because the God of black theology is more of an object of contemplation than an intervening subject in time and space.

Contemporary works in black theology continue to project a God who plays no active role in removing black suffering and oppression. For example, while Kelly Brown Douglas (2015: 193) positions God as "present in the harsh realities of black living," she never offers any indication of how God intervenes to prevent the kinds of racialized violence against black bodies she discusses throughout her work. Similarly, Keri Day's (2014) delineation of four camps of African American theology does not mention any group of black theologians who clarify how God intervenes to help oppressed black people. And Day's (2012) own book-length study on the black church depicts it as a social institution not a dynamic extension of God's spiritual kingdom, while branding herself more as a social ethicist than a theologian. Perhaps the future of black liberation theology requires a similar acknowledgment that black theology is more about social justice theory than clarifying the nature of God and religious faith.

While the above proponents largely focus their attention on Christianity, not all notable black theology projects do so. Sherman Jackson (2009) assesses how the Sunni Muslim theological tradition survives under William R. Jones's theodical critiques against liberation theology. Patrick Rael (2000) exposes the dynamic relationship between suffering and antebellum Black Nationalism. Torin Dru Alexander (2016) evaluates the usefulness and novelty of Jaramogi Abebe Agyeman's theodical teachings in light of his black liberationist presuppositions and commitments. None of these works endorse or even hint at God's active role in human history. Likewise, Will Coleman (2000) integrates Christian and non-Christian religious resources, including the idioms and perspectives indigenous to West African cosmologies and epistemologies, but shows no interest in explicating the role of God in alleviating black suffering, as his "tribal talk" never explains why ethnic suffering tends to fall upon black people more than most and how divine favor factors into that demographic reality.

Jawanza Eric Clark (2012) explains how Protestant doctrines of exclusivity and original sin perpetuate disdain and lead black Christians toward blithe dismissals of indigenous African religion as an ammunition depot of idolatry. Clark advocates for a black theology project that privileges indigenous African religious paradigms and concepts, more specifically, the important symbolic role of ancestors. While such a reclamation project may increase intra-racial solidarity, it does not offer any indication of how a West African cosmology expressed in indigenous perspectives and idioms addresses the core theodical problem of the transatlantic slave trade and its lingering effects. Like Coleman, Clark broadens black theology with greater hermeneutic alertness to a West African sacred cosmos without showing how such a renovated cache of theological resources helps to resolve theodical inquiries on the origin, perpetuation, and disproportionality of black deprivation.

In contrast to most liberation theologians and religion scholars who, unlike Cecil Cone, do not seem at all bothered by a God who does nothing to stop the surge of black suffering, William R. Jones (1973) proclaims that God's lack of direct intervention to controvert systems of oppression, injustice, and inequality against black bodies is a problem for and embarrassment to any theological position that presumes that God fights on the side of the oppressed. Jones goes so far as to call attention to the possibility that failure to resolve God's sovereignty with the disproportionality of black suffering leaves God susceptible to the charge of racism:

> To speak of divine racism is to raise questions about God's equal love and concern for all men. It is to suggest that He is for some but not for others, or at least not for all equally. It asks whether there is a demonic streak in the divine nature.

The charge of divine racism, in the final analysis, is a frontal challenge to the claim of God's benevolence for all. (Jones 1973: 6)

That black theology does not offer a cogent retort to Jones's challenges is something its architect James Cone (1989: 197) surprisingly confirms:

No one has provided a deeper challenge to Black Theology than has the philosophical critique of William Jones. His book, *Is God a White Racist?* (1973), shook Black theologians out of their "liberation complacency" and forced them to deal with the problem of theodicy at a deeper level. If God is liberating the Black poor from oppression, as Black theologians say, where is the liberation event that can serve as evidence of that fact? The question has not been answered to anyone's satisfaction, and thus continues to serve as a check against the tendency of substituting liberation rhetoric for actual events of freedom.

Hence, if Jesus is the champion of oppressed black people, as black theology proclaims, then Cone's quote tacitly concedes to William R. Jones's contention that the champ lacks punching power against the prevalence of evil and suffering. Jones endorses a humancentric form of theism that points to human agency as the cause of and solution to all problems black people endure. But by now it should be clear that Jones's "humanocentric" theism is merely a more deliberate way of sidelining God. And so Jones overlooked how proponents of black theology inadvertently endorsed his humanocentric perspective with their tactical deism.

Anthony Pinn (1995, 2004, 2010) also makes theodicy the focal point of (and greatest challenge against) black theology. And like Jones, Pinn renders the hypothesis that God fights on the side of the poor and the oppressed as disconfirmed by inequality and oppression which pervade black lives disproportionately. But Pinn (1995, 2012) goes a step further by extending an interpretive approach that replaces theism with nontheistic humanist theology; a project that draws strength from the rebellious spirit and positive expressions of complex subjectivity found in a diverse range of artistic expressions including the blues, hip-hop, and the creative artwork of Jean-Michel Basquiat. Pinn's method is best summed up in his belief that "humanity is far better off fighting with the tools it has—a desire for transformation, human creativity, physical strength, and untapped collective potential," than seeking for signs of God's presence or accepting trite theistic rationalizations of redemptive suffering (1995: 158).

Inspired by Jones's and Pinn's critiques against black theology, Andre Key (2011) attempts to articulate a Hebrew Israelite ethno-religious identity that rejects the notion that black suffering has redemptive value or comes as a result of failing to live up to God's demands. What makes Key's undertaking so provocative is how he situates his auto-ethnography and critique. For if William R. Jones's accusation of divine racism "is a heuristic concept designed to test what Jones believes are the liberation-defeating qualities of black theology" (Hart 2011: 100), and if Pinn summons the end of God-talk altogether, one might question how Andre Key can claim his study is rooted in black theology and the perspectives of black theology's two most notorious critics. Only when we consider black theology's tactical deism can we understand the priority of Key's intellectual partnership between black theology and its most persuasive detractors. For whether it's James Cone or Dwight Hopkins, William R. Jones or Anthony Pinn, each party understands rather vividly that God is a minor player in the cause and removal of black oppression. Andre Key appreciates this point more clearly than others: that black liberation theology, with all of its perfunctory allusions to divine presence among and preference for black people, promotes a theological outlook that in all practicality is not very different from Jones's humanocentric theism or Pinn's nontheistic humanist theology; and that the future of black theology resides in a more overt understanding of its sidelined God.

So what one can infer from Andre Key's consideration is that William R. Jones (1978) spoke too soon when contending that black theology has not taken seriously the inescapable occurrence of secularity. Key understands that Jones and Pinn explicitly express what black liberation theologians more tacitly (and tactically) imply: that God is a symbolic touchstone rather than an active subject in history. In the same way that Pinn (2004) presents the biblical character Nimrod as an archetype of humanist potentiality, black theology de-reifies God, making humans the focal points of justice and change. Retracing the path of modernity's first adept de-reifier, Feuerbach (1841), who reclaims humanity's ethical and creative usefulness, redirecting human contemplation away from the heavens and shifting it back toward Earth and human potentiality, black theology is quite "Feuerbachian" (or to pirate Pinn's biblical metaphor, "Nimrodian") in its erasure of divine efficacy and excellence, offering a compatibly anthropological outlook, while keeping God relevant as a sidelined coach and cheerleader. And if Ludwig Feuerbach got the ball rolling toward converting theology into anthropology, womanist theology is another late modern iteration of Feuerbach's project. For if we can accuse the aforementioned proponents of black theology of neglecting to "draw as fully as possible on the spiritual narratives and religious experience of African American women" (Evans 1992: 66), then we can subject womanists to a similar critique of overlooking the vast differences between the God of biblical Christianity to whom millions of black women adhere, and the sidelined God of womanist theology.

WOMANIST THEOLOGY

As a response to black theology's failing to address issues regarding gender and feminist theology's neglecting to confront issues regarding race, womanist theology is a thriving subset of black liberation theology that more specifically addresses issues regarding gender and race, while also tending to problems concerning class and sexuality (Williams 1993; White 2014). Womanist theology can be framed as a black liberationist intellectual discipline, existential outlook, and political dynamism (Kirk-Duggan 2014) that "critiques structures, systems, and sociopolitical realities that foster domination/oppression of African American women particularly, the African community, and humanity in general" (Crawford 2002: xiv). But what makes womanists less distinctive from their counterparts in black theology and more dissimilar to Bible-toting black female laypersons pervading churches across America is how womanists never provide any specifics concerning God's interventionist capabilities to alleviate black female oppression. What Delores Williams's (1993) pioneering book accomplishes explicitly, her peers and successors achieve more implicitly: to reduce God from active subject to symbolic resource for black women to employ on their own paths of survival.

Katie Cannon (1995) analyzes how theodicy is presented in particular texts, offering no indication of what a womanist approach to theodicy should entail. Even as Cannon addresses the patriarchal delimitations of black preaching, she offers no insight concerning how womanists can address the problem of evil and why God seems unable to provide black women with more equitable and flourishing futures. Cheryl Kirk-Duggan (2001) explores the interface of violence and religion, using refiner's fire as a metaphor of social change. But God is not the active subject behind any of her womanist solutions toward stopping violence, notwithstanding her unclear allusions to the power of God's grace, creative energy, and presence. What she offers primarily, like most womanist scholars, is a liberal feminist agenda rooted in Enlightenment ideals of freedom, equality, and individuality contextualized toward important issues she and other womanists frame as black women's struggles. God is not the subject behind black women's liberation; only human hands accomplish this task. M. Shawn Copeland (2010) is more explicitly anthropological in her interpretation of womanist aims, as she locates womanist theology within a focus on embodiment, and as even her analysis of Jesus's mission on Earth is reduced to its anthropological efficacy.

Stacey Floyd-Thomas (2006) depicts womanism as a revolutionary paradigm shift in which black women depend on themselves instead of others for their liberation, and nowhere in the twenty-two essays that fill her anthology do we get any indication of how God intervenes to balance the scales of justice for black women. Likewise, Floyd-Thomas's (2008) notions of "embodied theodicy" and "embodied theos" have nothing to do with God's interventionist capacities and everything to do with black women's struggles and agentive solutions in navigating white male-dominated academic environs. Emilie Townes (2006) treats evil and suffering from a cultural perspective without offering a trace of expectation of divine intervention to remedy black women's problems. JoAnne Marie Terrell (2005) distinguishes the spiritual, social, and political components of theodicy that are intrinsic to the relationship between gender and race without answering any of the pressing questions of black female suffering related to theodicy, and without clarifying God's contributions to recuperative efforts on behalf of black struggles. In this way Terrell, like Copeland (2010), assesses the meaning of Christ's crucifixion in light of the historical realities of black oppression while remaining reticent regarding its supernatural capabilities toward alleviating black suffering. Copeland and Terrell recapitulate Kelly Brown Douglas's (1999) concentration on Christ's symbolic potentiality to black communities without considering the prospect of Christ's interventionist power to eviscerate black struggles. If Christ for womanists has any power, it is only in providing representational inspiration and accountability.

Elaine Brown Crawford (2002: 14) concedes that the topic of theodicy compels inquiries concerning black women's reactions to malevolence and anguish: "Did their suffering negate their concept of an all-powerful God? Did the Christian religion and the Bible legitimize their suffering? How do black women understand the nature of a God who allows the suffering of black human beings?" But Crawford never provides a womanist response to her poignant theodical questions as they relate to the persistence of black female suffering. Crawford cites testimonies from ex-slaves who demonstrate belief in God's supernatural delivering capacities, but nowhere does she connect such theological claims to womanist theodicy. Similarly, Jacquelyn Grant (1989) acknowledges the prominent role the Bible has played in helping black women develop their "God-consciousness," without considering how the biblical endorsement of supernatural power goes untapped by womanists. And Diana Hayes (2011) claims that God takes sides and identifies with those most in need, but her Catholic womanist perspective offers no practical example of what divine favor translates into in terms of tangible support to those in need. As with her womanist colleagues, all of Hayes's prescriptions involve anthropological or humanist exhortations, never offering supernatural intervention as a remedial force in the world.

Stephanie Crumpton's (2014) study on womanist pastoral theology documents the stories of six black women who suffered violence and sexual abuse as children and some more recently as adults. Crumpton bears out the complicated relationship between black women as worshippers and spiritual citizens of their churches and black women as unprotected victims, while spelling out black churches' complicity in the abuse. Assessing testimonies that revisit traumatic assaults against these women's bodies and minds, the book neglects to offer a trace of intellectual energy toward explaining the womanist position on God's silence and nonintervention. God appears throughout Crumpton's tome as a sociocultural mechanism of identity and comfort, but never as an active subject exerting metaphysical power for the benefit of black women. Like most womanist reflections, Crumpton refuses to wrestle with God's absence or question why God does not play a more direct role to mitigate the threats and vulnerabilities that black women face or to punish the perpetrators of such crimes. Notwithstanding the great significance of Crumpton's undertaking, the author appears less like a theologian and more like an insightful social ethnographer.

Karen Baker-Fletcher's (1998) seminal work epitomizes the refusal of womanists to tackle the important theodical implications of their own theological positions. She embraces a panentheistic view of process metaphysics but never attempts to clarify why God is not culpable for the destructive outcomes of natural evils in light of the fact that panentheism as a theological outlook asserts that God interpenetrates all of nature. In an important passage she alludes to the theodical challenge of her panentheistic position without ever adequately resolving its implications for her womanist perspective:

> While Emerson's essay *Nature* emphasizes what I would call nature's awesome side, we humans are also confronted with nature's awful side. Nature affects us with these two experiences of awe; the first form of awe is often euphoric while the second form can be terrifying. Both forms of awe lead to questions about God and theodicy—the problem of evil and why God allows it. Is God in the hurricane, the tornado, the earthquake? Or is that just nature living its own life, doing what it must do to exist, to live, to express the fullness of its life-force? Is God in nature or not? Perhaps God is in nature, but nature is not God. Nature reveals God, because God is present in all that lives, in all that is. But God is larger than any part of Creation as the power of creativity itself, the life force of life in and beyond all others. (Baker-Fletcher 1998: 34–35)

Baker-Fletcher recognizes and then circumvents the theodical conundrum of her panentheism. If God is in all things, then, by implication, God is in the awe-inspiring beauty of nature (which Baker-Fletcher affirms with her pensive rebukes against environmental injustice), and God must also reside in the hurricanes, tsunamis, and viruses that kill many people, a fact that Baker-Fletcher sidesteps by attempting to suggest God transcends nature's destructive impositions. If her womanist project presumes that God is in all things, by suggestion God must permeate viruses too, which would include the AIDS virus that disproportionately kills black women worldwide. And

God must have been in the 2010 earthquake in Haiti that killed over 100,000 (mostly black) people as well as in COVID-19, a pandemic that disproportionately kills black people. Baker-Fletcher's refusal to resolve theodical challenges inherent in panentheism is a microcosm of womanist theology's overall reluctance to articulate God's direct role behind constraining natural or moral evil and removing oppression against black women.

Monica Coleman's (2008) study of leading proponents of womanist theology confirms their anthropological focus. Early in her work, Coleman explains her concept of "making a way out of no way," as an expression that explicates "black women's experiences of struggle and God's assistance in helping them to overcome oppression" (2008: 12). Thus, Coleman's folksy mantra initially leads readers to believe she will elucidate God's active participation in the womanist quest to alleviate subjugation—better yet, how God will make a way out of no way to help black women survive. But shortly after raising interventionist expectations, Coleman preps readers for the vertical boundary ascriptions that pervade all of her assessments of leading womanists: "Collectively, womanists understand salvation as a social activity of teaching and healing that leads toward survival, quality of life, and the holistic transformation of the world" (ibid.). In other words, Coleman reveals that salvation for womanists is entirely up to women and involves no salvific activity from God. And Coleman's perceptive evaluations of five womanist theologians confirm their tactical deism, as none of Coleman's assessments attribute to her womanist subjects any supernatural or interventionist component in God's redemptive capacities. Similarly bereft of supra-social content is Coleman's own essay and accompanying third-wave contributions to her anthology (2013), which leads us to believe that the second generation of womanists is similarly apathetic about God's interventionist capacities toward alleviating the suffering and oppression of black women.

Womanist and Black Feminist Responses to Tyler Perry's Productions (2014) is another anthology that includes important essays corroborating the sidelined God that has long characterized womanist theology as a movement and perspective. Andrea White's contribution asserts that filmmaker Tyler Perry's humanist project of self-cultivation falls far short of womanist aims toward collectivist activism. White argues that "Perry's films sidestep the more difficult questions of divine justice, and by emphasizing hope and faith as human dispositions rather than theological concepts, he places the onus on the human person and human agency, rendering God redundant" (2014: 82). But in light of their diminished role for God, one could claim womanists are guilty of the same oversight. For if faced with the task of assessing the notion of divine judgment in the context of the liberation of black women from oppressive systems and conditions, would not the entire womanist project crumble under William R. Jones's (1973) critique of divine racism? White's critique against Tyler Perry centers upon her own conflation of divine justice with womanist tactics of political resistance and structural analysis. But such a collapse of distinction can only be comprehensible in the context of God's demotion to cosmic coach. Whereas the biblical notion of divine justice always involves active intervention on God's part, Andrea White's understanding of divine justice is reduced to political theorizing and social activism on the part of humans fighting oppression. If we turn to Cheryl Kirk-Duggan's (2014) contribution in the same anthology, we can see a tacit concession to this sidelining of God in her attempt to rebrand their project as "womanist theological anthropology," a move reminiscent of M. Shawn Copeland's (2010) earlier call for womanists to consider how black female embodiment inspires new categories for theological anthropology. What Tyler Perry does in fact share with White, Kirk-Duggan, Copeland, and the best and brightest of womanists is the implicit acknowledgment that only human hands can solve problems that black women face, a poignant theodical message we also find in cinema.

In Lee Daniels's critically acclaimed drama *Precious* (2009), shortly after Precious discovers she is HIV positive, she writes in her notebook two words: "Why Me?" The troubled teenager is not asking for a logical explanation, for she is cognizant that her new condition is the effect of her father's repeated rapes. Her question seeks clarity concerning what she did to deserve such a fate. More importantly her question raises the issue of theodicy, challenging the justice of a universe run by a God that would allow a victim of incest and sexual assault to face a potential death sentence. The answer is implied: God is not in the business of preventing the predatory activity of a father nor in the business of protecting the victim of said predation from contracting HIV. And the sexual assaults are just part of the abuses in Precious's life. The film's most intriguing theodical moment unfolds when her unstable mother sparks a vicious brawl and Precious barely escapes with her newborn son. They roam the streets until she hears the melodic voices of a choir rehearsing in a nearby church. As she approaches the church's window to watch the choir practice, we see the church's title: "Thy Will Be Done Christian Ministries." This title is bewildering, not in the context of Christian theology, but when viewed through the prism of Precious's tragic life. The very notion of God's will provokes the question: What does a poor, despondent teen whose father raped and twice impregnated her, infected her with HIV, and whose mother condoned those rapes and physically and verbally abused her think about the possibility of divine providence when considering her own existence?

Rather than entering the church, Precious stays outside, drawing upon the resources of her imagination to sing in the choir and enjoy life with caring Christian peers. But when her fantasy ends, Precious walks away from the church, preferring to seek help from a supportive teacher rather than a pastor.

In a later scene, Precious is no longer fantasizing but now enjoying real love and existential nourishment, not in a church committed to doing God's will, but in the home of a lesbian couple. Precious never visits any more churches nor conjures up any spiritual answers to her earlier question, "Why me?" as she becomes too preoccupied preparing for the future to worry about dying. The film ends with Precious pursuing a G.E.D. and setting her next goal, which is college. In her very last scene, we see Precious exhibit a hopeful smile to match her newfound optimism, because in a world in which God does not intervene to protect Precious, she draws support from others and finally learns how to fight for her own future.

Lee Daniel's film *Precious* pushes one to ponder what kind of spiritual counsel or theological comfort a womanist theologian could offer the troubled teen to articulate God's response to her plight. Since Karen Baker-Fletcher's panentheistic God resides in the HIV virus infecting Precious's body, does that mean that God can be counted on to mitigate its effects? Could Monica Coleman address her financial problems by assuring Precious that God will make a way out of no way? Is JoAnne Marie Terrell's God willing to offer any direct change in the protagonist's situation, or is the womanist God entirely dependent upon human hands to improve Precious's life? These questions are rhetorical because we have already uncovered the answers in the form of black liberation theology's unwavering commitment to tactical deism. Similar to how Precious does not depend on God but on the intervention of helpful advocates until she learns how to help herself, black liberationists point to human hands as the source behind securing social justice and change as their God does nothing in time and space to liberate black women or men. Hence, liberationists are quite like filmmakers in ascribing rational boundaries to divine governance or, in some cases, in negating the notion of divine governance altogether. Perhaps the sole difference between black liberation theology and filmic treatments of black suffering is that the former is often fastened to a theory of redemptive suffering (Pinn 2002), whereas films (with few exceptions) code and narrate black suffering without teleological packaging.

CONCLUSION

Latin American liberation theology, black theology, and womanist theology—movements that make up what Mark Scott (2011) calls theodicy at the margins—are replete with representations of God as ultimately devoid of supernatural efficacy. While Scott situates theodical disputations of liberation theology within pragmatic and specific contexts of human suffering, what his notion of theodicy at the margins shares in common with cinematic theodicy is Christos Yannaras's (2005) supposition that the starting point for engaging the divine is acknowledging God's incomprehensibility; in other words, a retreat from trying to understand God's interventionist role within history, and movement toward a progressive focus on human responsibility. We see this realization manifest in *Gangster Paradise: Jerusalema* in how it closes with the criminal protagonist recently escaped from prison and safely relocated to the coast, expressing his agentive philosophy, "What's important in life is to set goals and go after them." Lucky has already proven quite savvy at achieving goals and hence we can predict his relocation will only provide new opportunities for entrepreneurial success.

Lucky's modern viewpoint echoes the takeaway message of the anticlimactic ending of Voltaire's philosophical tale *Candide* where Candide rejects previous attempts to understand God's intervention (or lack thereof) in world events and focuses instead on mundane horticultural pursuits. The lesson one can learn from the ending of *Candide*, from a provocative South African movie like *Gangster Paradise: Jerusalema*, and from a theologian like Christos Yannaras is to relinquish all attempts to understand the contours of God's governance over a world replete with tragedy and suffering, and instead preoccupy oneself with cultivating one's garden. In the case of liberation theology, cultivating one's garden translates to occupying oneself with the busy work of social theory and collective activism to fight oppression and inequality. Notwithstanding their noble efforts to steer Christian faith toward the struggle against social inequality and human suffering, and despite their firm appropriations of divine will in advocacy of the poor and oppressed, what makes liberation theology and filmic emissaries theoretically aligned with Voltaire's deistic perspective in *Candide* is how they place no expectations on and proffer no explanations of God's direct involvement toward protecting the innocent and eradicating injustice.

Black liberation theology, like scores of films assessed in this present work, focuses on the crimes and redemptive acts of human hands and leaves no place for transcendental breaks into human history to punish the wicked, save the oppressed, or reward the faithful. As sacred/secular anchoring systems for the negotiation of tragedy and trauma, black liberation theology and cinema exert anthropological and sociological astuteness toward constructing evil and rotating the affective gears of suffering. They carry out the cultural work of secularity by explicating complex causal factors driving suffering, crafting trauma narratives that recreate suffering on a human and emotional level, and coding and narrating evil in ways intended to persuade their readers or viewers to take sides. Put more crudely, liberation theologians and filmmakers present evil with a modern makeover by transforming its manifestation from the local domain of personal decisions, actions, and character flaws to structural levels residing within depersonalized complex systems, which in turn influence (or distort) the individual consciences and personal decisions and actions of oppressive antagonists.

Undergirding their perspectives and missions with the notion of divine support by claiming that God's preference lies on the side of the oppressed makes proponents of black liberation theology consummate artisans of sacred/secular mutuality. My distinction of the black liberation theologian as a tactical deist is another way of classifying her as a champion of theodical secularity. But while black liberation theology erupts and resonates within the walls of academia, we can only speculate how its reverberations would sound hundreds of years earlier in the slave quarters that housed the Wolof, Akan, Benguela, and other West Africans who suffered severe punishments and endured nightlong torture sessions in Mexico for holding steadfast in their renouncement of the Christian God of their enslavers (Palmer 1975). If black liberation theologians could go back in time, could they make a convincing case to these newly minted slaves fresh off the arduous Middle Passage journey that God is actually fighting for them? Along these lines, one should be perplexed by black liberation theologians' common practice of citing David Walker's (1829) incendiary appeal, while remaining reticent concerning how their own anthropological musings are incommensurate with Walker's supernatural notions of divine justice. For the passive God of black liberation theology could not be more alien to Walker's active avenger who rules armies in heaven, punishes oppressors, and liberates the oppressed. Unlike proponents of black liberation theology who conflate divine justice with human tactics toward fighting for social justice (White 2014), Walker's sense of divine justice relies on divine intervention to crush evildoers and right the wrongs of history.

One should also make certain the enormity of difference between black liberation theology's cosmic coach and the God of evangelical holdouts to theodical secularity, like the Pentecostal preacher who anoints sick people with oil as a prelude to offering the prayer of faith that she believes will make the sick well again. Unlike Pentecostal believers in the power of prayer, proponents of liberation theology are more akin to participants of Nancy Ammerman's (2014b) study and the praying soldiers in *Glory* in how they don't ask or expect God to do anything on behalf of sufferers. And those who read Andre Key's (2011) study will see a sharp contrast between the God of Hebrew Israelites who is alleged to have inflicted a natural tragedy like Hurricane Katrina as an instrument of correction to disobedient and pagan New Orleans residents, and the passive God of black liberation theology who stood by and watched the very same natural disaster (and human culpability in the form of unprepared levies) without lifting a preventative finger. Key describes his own personal shock upon hearing a rabbi offer such a providential interpretation of Hurricane Katrina during a reading of the Torah and at that very moment Key decided to reject this blame-the-victim theodicy of sin and accept the alternative: to "limit the power of God rather than make God the source for suffering" (2011: 205), a choice that resonates within three generations of black liberation theology.

One of the ironies of black liberation theology is that while it decodes prophetic black church traditions into expressions of black power in an attempt to preserve the relevance of black Christianity against the threat of secularizing forces (Glaude 2007), it is ultimately captivated by the restraints of rationality in the process. Hubert G. Locke (1999) recognizes another irony: the same 1960s that propelled the death-of-God movement into notoriety, incubated a liberationist theological outcry claiming that God is alive and well, that God is listening to and aligning with the cries of the oppressed. But an even greater irony concerns how black liberation theology (like its Latin American counterparts) puts divine approval in the forefront of the struggle against oppression without requiring that same God to lift a finger toward liberating the oppressed. If black theology prompts us to remember that this is God's world (Lloyd 2018: 13), then we must ponder why God does nothing to mitigate systems and conditions that keep disadvantaged groups from flourishing.

Hopefully this discussion will spark a more comprehensive analysis of God-talk in multiple generations of black theology and womanist theology. Such an undertaking will substantiate what the above sample of many leading proponents already demonstrates: that black theology and womanist theology confirm Harvey Cox's (1965) playful accusation that the gods have bolted and so world supremacy must now be left in the hands of humans. Cinema's and black liberation theology's consistent portrayal of God as sequestered to the sidelines of human history reminds us that the borders of vertical boundaries are entirely arbitrary in the analysis of theodicy when impressive levels of human suffering are front and center. Put another way, only a thin line separates varying strands of Protestant liberalism, Latin American liberation theology, black liberation theology, humanocentric theism, process theology, or radical theology when humans experience tragedy. For all these theological projects share in common how they offer much by way of modern liberal critiques but nothing by way of divine interventionism. Whether one believes that God fights on the side of the oppressed, abandons the oppressed, or doesn't exist at all is a minor quibble if the alleged divine intervention only manifests through human hands. In the context of black suffering and evil, most liberation theologians (like filmmakers) treat God like a metaphorical figurehead and moral fulcrum for collective activism, rather than as an active interventionist subject in history. Their God-talk opts against tapping into the spiritual efficacy deployed in Souleymane Cisse's film *Yeelen*, preferring instead to endorse the passive divinity of Mahamat-Saleh Haroun's film *A Screaming Man*.

It is worth pausing to note that William R. Jones's call for black liberationists to take theodicy more seriously would not have been a necessary exhortation for post-Holocaust Jewish philosophers and theologians who required no such inspiration to grapple with God's absence and who were quite vocal about their inability to reconcile the vast human waste that accrued in Nazi death camps against the promises of protection proclaimed by the God of the Jewish covenant. While there has always existed an impressive historical dialogue in Jewish philosophy on evil in the backdrop of divine governance (Leaman 1995), the genocidal campaign against Jews during World War II presents a historical rupture, propelling scholars to create new interpretative frameworks to ascertain the Holocaust's challenge to an all-powerful God who is in covenant with Abrahamic descendants. As Eliezer Berkovits (2001: 98) puts it, "The question after the Holocaust ought not be, how could God tolerate so much evil? The proper question is whether, after Auschwitz, the Jewish people may still be witnesses to God's elusive presence in history as we understand the concept?" Richard Rubenstein (1966: 176) argues, "No Jewish theology will possess even a remote degree of relevance to contemporary life if it ignores the question of God and the death camps." Rubenstein calls for an inversion of the Jewish understanding of providence, maintaining that God's inactivity toward preventing the genocide of six million people is a warning to all surviving Jews that the governing God of Jewish tradition is dead in the sense that such a God can no longer be trusted to protect and preserve a covenant.

While cautious against cosigning the full extent of Rubenstein's nullification of the covenant, Emil Fackenheim agrees with Rubenstein in positing that the commanding voice of Auschwitz appears to have annihilated any notion of providence (1970), arguing that Auschwitz offers no divine explanation, no redeeming voice, and no ultimate response from Jews other than the will and commitment to survive (2001). Arthur Cohen (1993) comes to a similar conclusion that such terror and human waste form a defining event for the Jewish faith that cancels all moral categories for assessing or pronouncing the parameters of evil, while Eliezer Schweid (2005) acknowledges that the notion of God's calling to redeem humanity became a throwaway affectation for most Jews after the Shoah, adding that he doesn't perceive any realistic chance the situation will be reversed. David Blumenthal (1993) proposes that theological protest and sustained suspicion against an abusing God are proper responses to the Holocaust. And when contemplating Auschwitz where his mother perished at the hands of her German aggressors, Hans Jonas (1996: 133) repeatedly asks, "What God could let it happen?" Jonas contends that what took place at Auschwitz calls for the Jewish notion of the God of history, the God of creation, justice, and redemption, to be questioned and eventually re-conceptualized toward the elimination of divine omnipotence and acceptance of divine self-limitation.

But in response to the despondency of post-Holocaust Jewish theology, Eliezer Berkovits (2001) warns Jews not to react too extremely in questioning the viability of God's covenant, because that would negate the pre-Holocaust past and post-Holocaust future that are Israel's responsibility to negotiate. In other words, Berkovits reminds his comrades that Auschwitz is not the be-all and end-all of Jewish identity and experience. Fackenheim (2001) similarly concedes that evil in Jewish history long precedes Auschwitz, while expressing angst against allowing Hitler to dictate the terms of Jewish religious life. Melissa Raphael (2003) contends that in contrast to a patriarchal Jewish framework of God dependent on a notion of masculine power, a feminist Jewish framework does not indict God's hiddenness in Auschwitz but rather recognizes God's presence to restore and purify the world of Auschwitz and lead Israel toward its future.

Inspired by Berkovits's, Fackenheim's, and Raphael's calls for Jewish temperance, one might be tempted to warn black liberation theologians against abandoning God in the way Jewish theologians, philosophers, and rabbis rejected the covenant or in the way that Anthony Pinn (2004) defected from his Christian faith as a youth when he could no longer make sense of the perplexities of divine supremacy against the backdrop of black historical sufferings. But three generations of black liberation theology reveal such an admonition as superfluous since, unlike post-Holocaust Jewish thinkers, so few black thought-leaders in theology wrestle publicly with God's hiddenness or silence. And thus, one is left to ponder why there is no pessimist camp in black liberation theology responding in anger and frustration to the durability of black suffering in the context of God's alleged justice and preference for black people. The answer resides in the tactical deism of black liberationist faith; that long ago proponents of black theology and womanist theology made peace with a modern God.

Chapter 3

Cinema and American Slavery

Will the shocks of American slavery resonate long into the future? A careful response considers the emotional cost of preventing past sins from succumbing to senescence. But what helps toward overcoming uncertainty is cinema's ability to saturate our mindsets with images of slavery's indignities. Just when Americans think they can put the matter to rest, a new slavery film emerges to stir up sympathy or reignite outrage. As an effective mechanism to elicit candid valuations of national identity (Gordon 2015), cinema stimulates appraisals of the distresses of slavery and the struggles to resist it (Davis 2000). Each theatrical release turns back time for contemporary Americans to confront the peculiar institution and all its terrors.

Long before the advent of film, anti-slavery campaigns, "largely inspired and led by evangelicals" (Taylor 1999: 26), used speeches, pamphlets, autobiographies, and vivid depictions of life on slave ships to convey the viciousness of subjugation in hope of winning new converts to their abolitionist cause (Rediker 2007). Had these mobilization efforts enjoyed access to cinema, they could have utilized scenes from Steven Spielberg's film *Amistad* (1997) to teach the American masses more about transatlantic traumas of the slave trade than any lecture or leaflet could convey. But in the process of weaponizing *Amistad*'s signifying potency, those same evangelical abolitionists would have to confront a disturbing caveat: God's contiguity to the cruelty of slavery. Such a proviso confirms that there are few better case studies on theodicy than cinematic representations of religion's complicated connections to the horrors of chattel servitude.

Amistad begins with Africans executing a successful mutiny of a slave ship as it sails off Cuba's coast. Their respite as free men and women ends when a U.S. Navy vessel seizes the ship near the coast of Connecticut. The Africans are detained on American soil and the plot zeroes in on the international trial that determines their fate. When Cinque takes the witness stand to testify about their abduction in Africa and experience on the slave ship, a flashback exposes disquieting occurrences. A crewman shoots an African in the head to the background cries of children, an African woman commits suicide by jumping off the ship with her newborn in arms, and fifty Africans are thrown overboard due to the captain's underestimation of provisions needed to feed everyone. *Amistad*'s producer Colin Wilson reveals in the Production Notes to the DVD that the reenactment of Cinque's testimony tore members of his production team apart emotionally. But the film's skill at signifying Middle Passage misery is matched by its aptitude for generating theodical tension.

Cinque's flashback also includes a brief but important moment when a European priest is holding up a small cross in one hand and a Bible in the other as he prays for each new slave embarking on the ship. Steven Spielberg supplements this sacramental intrusion with the cracking sounds of a whip lacerating African flesh. This clever concurrence should provoke viewers to question how God's earthly emissary could consecrate such moral chaos. But a more overt theodical conflict unfolds later on the mainland with the Africans in confinement. Aware that his friend can't read, Cinque confronts Yamba about his sudden interest in a book he confiscated from a Christian proselytizer. Yamba proves his attentiveness is genuine, as he articulates to Cinque a crude but surprisingly accurate summation of God's salvific activity among Jews and Christians which he ascertained simply from perusing visual illustrations accompanying Old and New Testament narratives. But Yamba's fascination with the God of Christianity suffers a setback when he later recognizes the cross he encountered throughout biblical images as the same symbol positioned on top of the slave ship that brought Yamba and his African comrades so much distress. So the film's most pressing theodical moment comes when Yamba struggles to reconcile how the cruelty of slavery fits together with the redemptive message he deduced from his new book.

Cinque's testimony and Yamba's cognitive dissonance disrupt the simplistic impression of God presiding over history to reward the faithful, heal the sufferers, and punish the evil doers. From the vantage point of millions of African victims, the notion of divine justice engenders the enigma of how it can coincide with the greatest system of human exploitation the world had ever known, and how the exploiters of that system were for the most part believers in God. This chapter contends that *Amistad* and many cinematic representations of slavery reveal how one way to crack the above conundrum is by ascribing boundaries to God. In this way, the God of cinema survives the ferocious strikes of theodical disputation via a demotion from omnipotent ruler to a cosmic coach who, stripped of supernatural efficacy, cannot be blamed nor shamed for slavery and its supplementary terrors. As such, in most slavery films, it is no less difficult to pinpoint divine intervention on behalf of the confused African standing unclothed and unprotected on the auction block than it is to perceive providential care for the cornered plantation slave standing frozen in fear as the soon-to-be victim of sexual assault.

That slaves' protective pleas to God go perpetually unanswered only substantiates that the essential master of their universe is not the mighty God above, but mortal "Massa" who owns them. And if indeed mortal hands have bound the slaves under God's inefficacious gaze, then, as theodical secularity suggests, only mortal hands can free them.

This chapter clarifies how slavery films sequester God to the sidelines of human history, leaving it up to humans to make all the decisive plays in a game of life that appears rigged from the start against abject underdogs who suffer staggering losses. Even as our coverage of the Underground Railroad exposes how films frame slavery as against God's will, their plots ultimately focus on human capacities to fight against, escape from, or remove the peculiar institution, while simultaneously proffering sociological (rather than spiritual) accounts for evil, depicting slavery as a corrupt structure of human relations with tentacles extending to multiple facets of American and European religious, commercial, and political institutions. Simply put, cinema can most often be counted on to project both modern explanations for slavery and a cosmic coach who stays above the fray. And those filmic scenes that situate God's active involvement within the black victim's struggle against slavery usually culminate in dashed hopes of a divine solution or, in a few rare cases, offer mediation that appears absurdly intermittent.

Before proceeding to our filmic analysis, we should pause to consider how the reconfiguration of slavery through cinematic representation is not a natural or objective process but involves artistic choices. And more importantly, those artistic choices entail the potential for axiological variability, meaning they do not come with value hierarchies or moral instructions handed down in stone. Whereas a film like *The Birth of a Nation* (1915) fashioned the American institution of slavery as familial and nourishing to the wellbeing of the poor, naïve, but happy slave, *Uncle Tom's Cabin* (1927) counters that narrative and documents the trauma of tearing families apart when one slave is sold to another slaver hundreds of miles away. And if early films like *The Confederate Spy* (1910) and *Mammy's Rose* (1916) exhibit a relationship of loyalty between slaves and their servitude (Eyerman 2001), most contemporary films present slaves as victims while depicting masters as rapists, exploiters, and killers, or at best showing disregard for the humanity of the slave. Despite some early sympathetic outliers, the history of slavery films is replete with representations of the peculiar institution as unambiguously cruel. The fact that most contemporary movies moralize and memorialize the tragedy of slavery is not a necessary progression but rather a contingent sociocultural accomplishment. Slavery films have evolved into their roles as moralizing mechanisms and empathy machines.

If Underground Railroad films signify slavery as an unconscionable structure of human relations, and God as a sympathetic cheerleader for those suffering in bondage, other slavery dramas flip the script, so to speak, by feinting divine endorsement of the peculiar institution, not as a nostalgic proposal to sanctify servitude, but more tendentiously as a ploy to expose the epistemic fatuity of slave societies. Such films satirize a world of upside-down morality where traders, masters, and prominent citizens situate slavery as divinely sanctioned while simultaneously branding abolitionists as scoundrels. This clever inversion portrays past slave societies as axiologically distorted, while also cautioning contemporary audiences that, with the right concoction of cultural work, legitimating mechanisms, and social practices, virtually anything can be justified, socially sanctioned, or condemned. But while many slavery films either place God on the side of the slave or mock the inverted morality of slave societies by placing God on the side of the slavers, by hook or by crook they excoriate the system, actions, and people perpetuating slavery.

HARRIET TUBMAN AND THE UNDERGROUND RAILROAD

The Underground Railroad was an informal network of whites and free blacks providing food, lodging, and logistical support to runaway slaves heading to free states up North. After Congress passed the Fugitive Slave Act in 1850, runaway slaves were no longer safe in free states, thus necessitating the Underground Railroad to extend its pathways to Canada. Three films inspired by the Underground Railroad offer vital contexts in which to explore the interface of slavery and God-talk.

Set in 1850, Don McBreaty's *Race to Freedom: The Underground Railroad* (1994) begins with slave catchers returning Sarah's brother Joe to the plantation after his failed attempt to escape. Despite Sarah's desperate pleas for leniency, Massa orders one of his men to break Joe's foot with a sledgehammer as a lesson on the consequence of running away. In a later scene Joe, now crippled, urges his sister to leave the plantation with her love interest Thomas. Joe reminds Sarah, "Mama always says we have two rights: the right to live before God and the right to die, and it's better to die trying than to die giving up." Joe then asks Sarah if she wants her fate to be one where Massa works her to death in his kitchens, marries her off to any slave he chooses, and sells her babies when they leave her breast. Here Joe alludes to Sarah's prospects on the plantation, suggesting that escaping to Canada is her only hope of having a free life. Note how Joe conveys his mother's claim that they have the right to live before God without offering his sister any insight on God's perspective on or interventionist capacities toward securing that right. God didn't prevent his own capture and concomitant crippling, so it is unsurprising that Joe urges his sister to escape without alleging divine protection.

A Canadian scientist named Dr. Ross secretly meets with Thomas to divulge his stealth mission in the South as an abolitionist helping runaway slaves reach freedom through the Underground Railroad. Dr. Ross is functioning as an abductor, perhaps the Underground Railroad's most courageous tactician because the abductor must devise creative ways to contact slaves on plantations to persuade and facilitate their escape. Dr. Ross will also play the more renowned role of conductor later in the film when he facilitates Thomas's travel to Canada. Initially skeptical of Dr. Ross's overtures, Thomas eventually trusts the Canadian and convinces Sarah and another slave couple that Dr. Ross can expedite their escape. When the four slaves are discovered missing, the authorities suspect Dr. Ross's involvement and the Canadian is arrested and faces the possibility of a long prison stint or lynching. The absence of sufficient evidence compels the authorities to release him, but the arrest underscores the danger abductors of the Underground Railroad put themselves in to help slaves escape. The fact that a man of science is more committed to respecting the humanity of black slaves than men of faith who continue to hold black women and men in bondage is part of the film's implicit critique of Christian virtue.

Eventually the plan of the runaways becomes compromised, requiring radical revision on the fly as Sarah and Thomas are separated and the two slaves who escaped with them are less fortunate. Slave catchers kill the male slave, and his partner Minnie succumbs to a snakebite. In her dying words she thanks the Lord Jesus for not letting her perish as a slave. Such a sentiment absurdly implies that Jesus intervened to get Minnie off the plantation but failed to interfere to prevent her from getting bitten by a snake. It demonstrates how rare theodical discourse in slavery films crediting divine intervention often generates implications that contradict the humanistic overtones of the plot resolutions or leave God's interventionist capacities appearing quite inscrutable. The film proceeds as Sarah and Thomas press forward on separate tracks of the Underground Railroad. Dr. Ross catches up with Thomas to pose as his owner so they can travel North without garnering suspicion.

In their first practice session, Dr. Ross's melodramatic performance prompts Thomas to teach his green sympathizer a more convincing way to exert Massa's authority by calmly issuing casual commands like, "Over here boy, and bring my bag." Thomas explains to Dr. Ross (and the viewing audience) the imputed inferiority of the slave:

> It ain't in the words that come out your mouth. It's what you believe. You ain't gots to be loud or angry. I'm your property bought and paid for and owned by you. And don't ever let your slave look you in the eye . . . cause that mean you

might see something that you don't like, something human, something angry and then you wouldn't be able to do what you're doing no more.

This tutorial on the slave master's deportment and the slave's existential debasement exhibits cinema's adept ability to encapsulate the logic of chattel slavery in a way that both teaches viewing audiences and instigates emotional unease at slavery's reduction of complex humans into property.

Thomas's journey on the Underground Railroad eventually brings him to Harriet Tubman, offering another juncture to assess notions of divine representation against the quagmires of slavery. A white abolitionist asks Tubman to slow down her activities for a month or two because they've had ten people arrested in New York alone, reminding Tubman, "You yourself have a $40,000 bounty on your head." Tubman responds, "As long as God is whispering in my ear, this here Railroad moves ahead." The white abolitionist could have replied that God did not protect ten of their comrades from getting arrested in New York, and hence she should be more careful. Instead, he answers, "I can see why they call you Moses, Miss Tubman." But perhaps both parties overlook how the same reasoning that motivates Tubman to place her safety in God's hands implies that the ten abolitionists who were arrested in New York were not divinely protected. Shortly after, the sequence exhibits even more theodical complexity when Thomas refuses to go with Tubman because he is worried about Sarah, and Tubman tells him:

> Thomas, you ain't gonna do your Sarah no good if you go running out to nowhere. You get caught you just gonna fatten some slave catcher's purse. For every slave that make it to freedom, it's a hammer-blow to the economy of the South. You come with me Thomas, God take care of your Sarah.

Tubman's caution to Thomas awkwardly conjoins a humanist imperative with theistic hope. She warns Thomas that uncalculated quests lead to tragic apprehension, while blithely assuring him that God will protect Sarah. Tubman's response unveils the sort of ambivalence that besets the problem of theodicy when interventionist capacities of the divine intersect with occasions fraught with peril. Tubman equivocates between strategic action and trust in divine capacities, balancing her awareness that God offers no guarantees of safety for abolitionist efforts alongside her trust in heeding God's voice to lead more slaves to the Promised Land.

We finally do catch up with Sarah when, shortly after sending a resident of his town to prison for harboring runaway slaves, a judge comes home to discover that his wife is guilty of the same crime in sheltering Sarah and a young boy in their kitchen, as unknown to the judge, his wife frequently hides runaway slaves. The judge is outraged and informs his wife she is breaking the law, but his wife replies, "The law of God says 'clothe the naked, feed the hungry, and comfort those in need.'" She reminds her husband what is at stake if they get caught, thus compelling him to comply with her defiance against what she perceives as an unjust law. This demonstrates how the theological implications of slavery not only divided the geographical boundaries of a nation but also family members on what a godly response should necessitate. A husband and wife cannot agree on the proper Christian response to slavery or the responsible action a citizen should take when confronting the prospect of helping runaway slaves. Thus, once again we see cinema broker the social construction of morality in how particular activities regarding slavery are coded and perceived.

Sarah and Thomas do make it safely to freedom and reunite, as *Race to Freedom: The Underground Railroad* offers insight into the theological quandaries involved with escaped slaves heading North toward freedom. God is alleged to offer guidance, but it is tactical planning and the intervention of courageous humans that lead to success. And the fact that only two out of four slaves make it to freedom represents how slaves have no guarantee of divine protection as passengers of the Underground Railroad.

Paul Windkos's film *A Woman Called Moses* (1978) covers the vicissitudes of the Underground Railroad by focusing on its greatest facilitator, Harriet Tubman. The drama begins on Broadas Plantation in Maryland when young Harriet's sister Tilly is sold to a slave trader. Both Tilly and Harriet scream and cry at their separation, believing they will never see each other again. The very next scene offers the film's first theodical moment when Harriet, looking up to the sky, cries out to God, "You told me the Holy Spirit stay with me all the time. But they took my sister. You let them take my sister!" Here Harriet wrestles with what she perceives as promises of divine intervention against the bare truths of slavery that can forever separate close siblings at a master's whim. Such a prayer expressing disappointment is one that might have been offered by many Christian slaves in Harriet and Tilly's predicament. Her accusation, "You let them take my sister!" recognizes God as capable but unwilling to intervene.

Later when an overseer throws a rock at Harriet's head as reprisal for helping a slave escape, Harriet loses consciousness for days and when she finally comes to, we see her praying:

> Just show me a way for Master Ed to be dead. For Master Ed to be smite down. The devil's got him, he don't know how to be right. He ought to be dead with his evil ways. I pray every morning, every day, every night that he'd be gone. I pray now. Did you hear me Lord? Did you? Did you hear me?

In the very next scene Master Edward suddenly drops to the floor. The doctor diagnoses that something is wrong with his heart and Master Edward dies shortly afterward. Harriet repents for killing her master, acknowledging that even though he deserved it, she had no right to wish death upon him. So Harriet perceives a causal connection between her prayer and her master's death, failing to consider how her routine to "pray every morning, every day, every night that he'd be gone" increases the odds that his eventual death will come shortly after she has prayed for it. Be that as it may, this scene offers a rare cinematic suggestion of God's supernatural intervention at work for the benefit of a desperate slave to punish an evil master. But what Harriet does not address here is that her belief in God's interventionist power presents a conundrum concerning her own plight in slavery and God's earlier inaction when her sister was sold. Harriet's theology appears conflicted in how God intermittently intervenes but is nowhere to be found when God is most needed. And killing Master Ed while doing nothing to extirpate the institution that produces and perpetuates more like him, and the pain and misery of many slaves, seems like an inefficient use of divine firepower.

Harriet gets along better under her new master's rule until he degrades her with one of his so-called Darkie Pageants. In this cruel spectacle, Master Stuart forces Harriet to pull a loaded cart like a mule, while dressed in her Sunday best, generating great laughter from Stuart's peers who pose as patrons watching a carnival featuring Harriet's humiliation. But in contrast to her two Christian masters, the film depicts a Quaker woman who treats Harriet quite charitably, even allowing the slave to enter her home through the front door as a gesture of equality. And the person Harriet visits when she finally escapes is this very same Quaker woman who then gives Harriet instructions on how to connect to the next station of the Underground Railroad. Now on her way toward freedom, Harriet takes refuge with a pastor whom she informs that God speaks to her and willed for her to escape, to which the pastor replies, "God uses many devices to lead us to the path of righteousness." So the Quaker woman, Harriet, and the Christian cleric not only condone escaping slavery but also perceive it as a divinely sanctioned act. Later Harriet connects with the church-based Antislavery Society, allowing the film to depict religion and Christianity as indispensable to the Underground Railroad and God as on the side of the runaway slave.

Now free in Philadelphia, Harriet perceives and answers a divine call to become a crucial conductor in the Underground Railroad, guiding runaway slaves on numerous trips. The film represents Harriet as God's servant and God as a foe of American chattel slavery. For example, later in the film when the head of the Antislavery Society informs Harriet that slave masters have hired a special detective to capture her, and that there is a reward of up to $40,000 on her head, Harriet responds, "Mr. Steele, I can't stop what I'm doing cause they lyin' on me. My life is with God! They's is with the devil. And with God on my side, I got to go where He calls me no matter what evil is trying to stop me." Here Harriet draws a clear line of distinction, characterizing slave masters who are trying to capture her as fighting on the side of evil, while depicting herself as God's agent of change even though her activities are in fact illegal. And later, after rescuing her parents from slavery, when those very same parents try to stop her from continuing her Railroad heroics, Harriet responds, "Mama and Daddy, the last thing I ever want to do is cause you to worry, but it ain't up to any of us. It's a calling, a calling." After her father scolds her for walking away, she tells him, "I'm sorry Daddy, but you must forgive me if I say there's no force anywhere but God that would keep me from going to make this journey." Thus, *A Woman Called Moses* situates Harriet Tubman's Christian faith and connection to God as contributive to her success leading slaves to freedom and portrays the peculiar institution as an affront against God. Consistent with this theological framing, Harriet gives a speech at an Antislavery Society protest in which she calls the recently passed Fugitive Slave Act "an unchristian law," adding, "It's against the will of God." But even as Harriet acknowledges that God takes sides, she instigates another inquiry for theodicy concerning how slavery can exist for so long against God's will without God stopping it. It is telling that nowhere in Harriet's speech does she question why God did not intervene to obstruct the Fugitive Slave Act's passage.

Our third Underground Railroad film, *Harriet* (2019), is more attentive to the mayhem that ensues when escaped slaves are put in greater jeopardy after Congress passes the Fugitive Slave Act. Like the latter two films, *Harriet* positions the abolitionist heroine and a coterie of fearless facilitators of the Underground Railroad as fighting on the side of the angels. But writer and director Kasi Lemmons more perspicuously casts a role for God as a partner of runaway slaves, partisan of the Underground Railroad and patron behind Harriet Tubman's remarkable achievements. The film offers numerous real-time incursions of divine communication to Harriet that ward off danger or guide toward success. For instance, early in *Harriet*, a premonition from God that she is about to be sold by Master Gideon inspires Araminta "Minty" Ross to leave the plantation in pursuit of her freedom. The film is clear to insinuate that had Minty not heard from God and acted so decisively she would have missed her opportunity to escape. When she reaches Philadelphia and takes on the new name Harriet Tubman to mark her newfound freedom, she credits God's voice for steering her through the perilous journey.

During her first trip back to Baltimore as an abductor collecting slaves from their plantation, and as a conductor guiding those nine passengers (including her brothers) to freedom in Philadelphia, God inspires Harriet to change course and lead her passengers across a creek to evade impending capture. Her older brother Robert, perhaps under the delusion that he was in charge, initially resists this improvisation because the creek's depth was unknown to them and most of the runaways could not swim. But Harriet draws her gun on her own brother to force conformity to her new plan and then confidently walks across the creek by herself to confirm the soundness of God's message. So the film explicitly portrays how divine guidance helps Harriet and her passengers disappear in the fog to avoid detection by Master Gideon's team of slave catchers.

Her successful first mission wins the confidence of William Still, a station master of the Underground Railroad, who runs a strategic network of "angels" that helps abduct slaves from plantations and conduct their safe passage to free states. The successful journey bookends her earlier conflict with Still, which pit Still's reliance on rationality and tactical planning against Harriet's dependance on divine guidance. Their standoff began with Harriet interrupting a planning session to make a request: "I need your angels to help me get my husband and family." Still perceived a return to Master Gideon's plantation in Baltimore as a risky endeavor and explained to Harriet how missions have gotten considerably more dangerous with slave owners, federal judges, marshals, and slave catchers working together to prevent slaves from escaping. The argument climaxes with Still's stern exhortation: "Rescuing slaves requires skill and careful planning. It requires reading Harriet! Can you read a sign or map? Can you read at all?" Harriet responds by informing Still that she puts her attention on trying to hear God's voice more clearly. Refusing to heed Still's warning, Harriet leaves intent on proving Still wrong, believing that hearing from God can help her bring family members to safety. And her safe return with nine passengers without the aid of Still's tactical support convinces Still that God's voice can mitigate the liabilities that come with Harriet's inexperience and illiteracy; and, more importantly, that Harriet can be trusted with future missions. We will later discuss how the success of Harriet's first trip did in fact depend as much on rational planning and guile as on heeding God's voice.

William Still confirms his newborn confidence in Harriet's competence as abductor and conductor by introducing her to his secret coterie of station masters who coordinate activities for the Railroad. After this meeting, the film proceeds with Harriet emerging as Still's most valuable angel. Real-time guidance from God continues to be crucial to the success of her missions. For example, shortly after Harriet leads a new cohort of passengers to the Canadian border, God communicates through a series of images that her father Ben Ross was in danger of being arrested by a posse of white men. The visions prompt Harriet to travel 600 miles back to Maryland where her trusty assistant Walter confirms that Ben Ross is only moments away from arrest and probable torture on the charge of hiding slaves. So Harriet's obedience to God's voice led her back to Baltimore with just enough time to save her father.

But if Kasi Lemmons's film casts God as an important character and credits divine communication for Harriet's successes, then it should also blame some of Harriet's failures on God's silence, most notably, the brutal death of Marie, her friend and supporter. In one of the film's most tragic moments, Harriet arrives to the boarding house and hides while witnessing Bigger Long's brutal interrogation of Marie, who steadfastly refuses to give up information on Harriet. The petite woman is beaten to death for her defiance. Since God's guiding voice had already played a crucial role in Harriet's perilous missions rescuing and transporting slaves to freedom, it is perplexing not to see God's guiding voice play a similar role toward leading Harriet to the boarding house a few hours earlier to prevent Marie from encountering the menacing slave catcher Bigger Long and Master Gideon. This discrepancy sets up viewers to ponder why God would prompt Harriet to travel 600 miles to save her father, but refrain from directing Harriet only a few miles away to the boarding house to save a crucial advocate of runaway slaves who was instrumental in helping Harriet get acclimated to life as a free woman in Philadelphia and make her first trip as a conductor. In this case, God's uncommunicativeness allows an asset of the Underground Railroad to suffer an easily preventable death.

Divine reticence should also be credited for Harriet's inability to save her sister Rachel. At a crucial point in the narrative, Harriet goes back to Baltimore for Rachel. The siblings embrace before Rachel informs Harriet that she can't leave the plantation because "Massa Gideon and Miss Eliza been full of the devil since you and the boys ran off. They took my babies, won't tell me where they be. They know I won't go nowhere without my children." Harriet reluctantly accepts Rachel's refusal to take off with her to Canada and her only solace is to pray, "Lord, I need you to watch over my sister and her children till I can bring 'em to freedom. Protect her Lord. Don't let 'em hurt her worse." Perhaps a more strategic prayer for a woman with a solid track record of hearing God's voice would have been, "Lord, show me where Master Gideon and Miss Eliza hid my niece and nephew and the best time to retrieve them so that I can lead Rachel and her babies to freedom." But God's silence sets the stage for Rachel to die as a slave. And later in the film, when Harriet once again returns to the Baltimore plantation, this time to abduct Rachel's surviving children, she learns from her niece that her nephew had already been sold to a trader. So not only did Rachel die a lonely and painful death as a slave, but her son endured the heartbreak of being separated from his sister and, thus, would not enjoy solace from servitude presumably until after the Civil War. If God can be credited for helping Harriet save her niece in the film's final trip, God can be blamed for failing to guide Harriet back to Baltimore in time to save her nephew from being sold. For this is the same God who led Harriet back to Baltimore in two separate trips with just enough time to save her brothers from being sold and her father from being arrested. God's communicative efficacy appears disturbingly intermittent in this film, at times guiding Harriet and others from danger, at times remaining taciturn when just a simple message could avert tragic circumstances. But what is even more germane to theodical analysis than God's idiosyncratic forewarnings is the film's representation of God's taken-for-granted refusal to act more intentionally on behalf of slaves and vulnerable black people.

Kasi Lemmons casts God as a cosmic coach who communicates forebodings and visions from the sidelines but never steps on the field to make plays on behalf of suffering black people to relieve their vulnerabilities. For example, Harriet tells William Still how God gave her a premonition about her sisters being sold when she was thirteen years old, "to prepare me, I guess," without questioning why God did not lift a finger to stop the tragedy from occurring. Similarly, a bathing scene reveals how Harriet's ability to hear God's voice did nothing to protect her torso from Massa's whip, as her back divulges the vicious scars of servitude. God did nothing to stop a slave named Tilly from being physically abused by her master/father, nothing to prevent John from losing an eye as punishment for his wife's escape, and nothing to avert Marie from enduring a fatal beating from a slave catcher. God could not stop Congress from passing the Fugitive Slave Act, which, as the film demonstrates with remarkable clarity, put Northern cities in turmoil and stretched the Railroad hundreds of miles north necessitating Canada rather than free states as a destination. Even Harriet's own prayers indicate her somewhat nuanced understanding of the necessity to fight for her own freedom, as she reveals to Gideon late in the film: "Ever since your daddy sold my sisters, I prayed for God to make me strong enough to fight. And that's what I prayed for ever since. I reasoned that there was one of two things I had a right to: Liberty or death. If I couldn't have one, I'd have the other." Perhaps seeing her sisters sold South without reprisal offered young Minty an early indication of God's renegotiated contract to the sidelines of human history. And long after Minty transforms into the Railroad's super heroine Harriet Tubman, she continues to expect little from God other than His guiding voice as she deploys grit, threats of violence, and her own wits to lead slaves to freedom.

And if we can revisit that critical scene where Harriet and William Still argue over the viability of her returning to Baltimore for her first mission, Harriet conveys to Still that all she needs is God to embark upon her first mission as a conductor, and yet the ensuing scene clarifies the human dimensions of her preparation. We quickly learn that Harriet does in fact need more than God's voice for a successful first mission and, quite ironically, she ends up implementing just the kind of tactical planning that William Still alluded to in their heated exchange. Marie teaches Harriet how to dissemble as a free black when confronted by white officials and connects her with a broker to secure documentation to travel as a free woman of color under the name Dessa Dixon. Marie also furnishes Harriet with a dress fit for a lady and a gun fit to handle trouble "should trouble arise," as Marie puts it. So shortly after conveying to William Still that she concentrates on hearing God's voice more clearly and that she will make her first return to Baltimore on her own, Harriet receives crucial tactical assistance from Marie on how to survive the dangerous mission by impersonating a free woman and averting danger with a lethal deterrent. And one should not overlook the theodical salience of Harriet's armament. She does not tell Marie, "I walk with God, so I don't need a gun." Instead, we see her making good use of Marie's gun on her first trip and successive Railroad excursions. When Harriet's older brother Robert refuses to cross the creek, Harriet doesn't pray, she draws her gun to ensure compliance. Later in the film when she's riding horseback with Walter, she is not praying, she is firing bullets at armed officials to ensure their escape. Whether it's seizing her former slave mistress's children at gunpoint or shooting Gideon in the hand and stealing his horse, Harriet's gun appears throughout the film as more reliable and efficacious than God's intervening hand. And in the film's last trip, when Walter and Harriet realize they need a larger wagon for their augmented passenger manifest, they don't pray for God's interventionist mercy, they commandeer a man's wagon at gunpoint. Whether it's using false papers, lying to officials, or resorting to theft, Harriet breaks laws and biblical commandments to ensure her success. God's voice may be necessary, but it is far from sufficient to get the job done, as Harriet must become a ruthless pragmatist to lead her passengers to freedom. Thus, one of the greatest theodical ironies of the film is that its intense effort to highlight the helpfulness of God's voice toward Harriet's success underscores God's sidelined status. And so Kasi Lemmons's decision to cast a central role for God only generates more profound theodical questions and conundrums, namely why God seems unobligated to take a more active role in undermining the institution of slavery.

As an analogue to Harriet's ruthless pragmatism, the film covers Reverend Green's complicated existence as both a cleric and secret agent of the Underground Railroad. By day, Reverend Green offers obsequious sermons, warning his vulnerable congregants that God has a special place in hell for runaways, while exhorting slaves to obey and honor their masters. But by night, the reverend runs the local station of the Underground Railroad and helps slaves escape. So by day the man of God must calibrate the Christian gospel to appease slave masters, while by night he can sneak off to accomplish the work of the Lord with Massa out of earshot. That God's intervention to help slaves escape depends on Harriet's gun and clerical duplicity points to

God's sidelined status in the backdrop of evil and black suffering. Theodical secularity is at play in how God needs Harriet's grit and theft and Reverend Green's fraudulence to help suffering black people escape slavery. Reverend Green's conservative sermons against his covert liberationist antics present a sacred/secular compromise concerning what it means to serve and represent God and Christian virtue when considering slavery as an evil institution.

These three Underground Railroad films reveal the tremendous dangers slaves, abductors, conductors, and other accomplices faced negotiating treacherous excursions that included evading harm from the authorities, from the elements, and from the snakes, as Minnie unfortunately discovered. But even as they represent God inspiring slaves to take great risks to secure their own freedom while inspiring free people to act courageously for the interest of slaves, all three films ascribe rational boundaries to God's intervention. And in brief moments when such boundaries are alleged to be removed, God's interaction seems inscrutable, if not absurd. Underground Railroad films do more to promote a humanist message of uplift than to encourage trust in divine activity on behalf of suffering slaves and thus, offer a new understanding of secularity. But whereas Underground Railroad films disclose how God and religion motivated slaves escaping bondage, Quaker sympathizers, other Christian abolitionists, and a heroine like Harriet Tubman to facilitate the escape of dozens of slaves, a more radical batch of slavery films presents God and Christianity as manipulative tools of oppression and indicts God and Christianity for slavery's crimes against black humanity, while satirizing the inverted morality of slave societies.

GOODBYE UNCLE TOM

Goodbye Uncle Tom (1971) is written and directed by Italian documentarians Gualtiero Jacopetti and Franco Prosperi. The premise is simple: two Italian journalists (the directors playing themselves) venture back in time to study antebellum slavery in the United States. The mockumentary intermixes religion with slavery, raising pressing issues concerning theodicy. The opening sequence is inside the mansion of the elderly matriarch Mrs. Carston, who introduces the journalists to her distinguished dinner guests. A younger woman questions the religion of the journalists, which Mrs. Carston reveals is Catholic, prompting a middle-aged man to interject that the journalists should not be too stunned by what they experience regarding American slavery, because "after all, their pope who's most generous with his excommunications has yet to excommunicate a trader in black flesh." Another dinner guest chimes in:

Excommunication? Catholic priests here in the South between one "Our Father" and another "Hail Mary" they raise goats and slaves. And I must confess, they know their business! The last males I bought were sold to me by the same Indigo Jesuits in Maryland. Finest bunch I ever bought.

Hence, barely has time passed before the film allocates opportunities for the trade of human bodies to gain approbation from Catholic clerics. Slaves are callously classified in tandem with goats to suggest the priests perceive no great distinction between breeding and selling them.

As the dinner conversation lingers, a noted professor of history remarks that slavery is the law of God and nature, encouraging his fellow diners, "Let us remember that God is white and as long as God is white, we shall prevail over all other races." But another guest, Harriet Beecher Stowe, interrupts to express her confusion and distress at her Southern kinsmen for perpetuating slavery. Stowe ends her rebuke by asserting God's calling on her life to write a book that will enlighten her compatriots. So, this opening sequence provides discourse that both affirms slavery as part of God's natural order of white supremacy and Stowe's divinely inspired objection to slavery. The noted history professor's extravagant claim that God is white is an early indication of the film's theodical strategy to satirize (rather than merely to sideline) God as a way of making sense of slavery. From the filmmakers' perspective, only the frivolously distorted God of a frivolous and distorted slave society could allow such a destructive institution to persist.

Goodbye Uncle Tom pivots from the dinner table to the journalists' encounter with a slave ship that reaches the United States after almost a hundred days of traveling from Africa's Ivory Coast. The Italians witness a conversation between the ship captain and a trader named Mr. Simms while the camera captures Africans as dirty, sweaty, covered with regurgitation, rats, and large cockroaches. A slave refuses to eat so the ship's crewmen chisel out the slave's teeth to force-feed him, a gory scene interrupted by casual haggling between Mr. Simms and the captain over prices. Mr. Simms takes his purchased slaves to Fort Bastille, Louisiana, and the journalists narrate each step the Africans undergo as they are disinfected and prepared for the auction block. The fact that each slave is sodomized with a water hose to clean inside his or her anus and handled by veterinarians highlights the dehumanization of the processing station.

As the film progresses, the Italian journalists witness absurdity at every turn, including the removal of a slave's testicles and the sadistic approval of an elderly female bystander. She exhorts the journalists not to worry about the emasculated slave because, "Niggers, they don't feel nothing." More disturbing is how the journalists observe white laborers visiting the female slave quarters to rape the women, while the children of these victims watch from the balcony as if they are patrons at a horror flick starring their mothers and the men who ravage them. The vividness of the above scenes should prompt us to consider how the film's European production status emboldened its directors to go far beyond what any American film could represent. It is difficult to imagine such scandalous depictions surviving U.S. censorship in 1971. Less heavy-handed is the way the film lampoons the piety of genteel whites. For example, the journalists listen to a group of female aristocrats take umbrage at the allegation that their husbands, white Southern gentlemen, would deign to sleep with slave women. Their objections continue while biracial slaves serve them tea. One slave, Jason, has blonde hair just like the woman's husband, but the wife remains clueless to the convincing proof of her husband's intercourse with the very people she refers to as animals.

The journalists visit a Jesuit monastery where we see a priest praying over slaves while another priest receives money from a trader after having just sold slaves. The Italians also visit a Protestant church service and hear Reverend Strongfellow impart his justification for slavery from the pulpit:

> God recognized Abraham as the owner of slaves he had bought, commanding him to circumcise them. And Jesus ordained it that whosoever dare to raise seditious doubts as to the benevolence of the institution of slavery shall be cast out and scorned not only as a danger to the state but destructive to the true nature of the gospel. God decreed by law that slavery be honored and obeyed.

With the preacher's unbiblical claim that Jesus supported the institution of slavery, the film once again conveys that it takes a distortion of religion to undergird such a distorted institutional arrangement of human relations as American slavery. But the preacher's embellishment is mildly satirical in comparison to a Protestant slave master's nighttime prayer ritual. After conveying gratitude for all the wisdom and blessings bestowed upon him, the master also thanks God "for closing your divine eye to a few little transgressions I got planned for tonight." He ends the prayer expressing appreciation for stamina, no doubt alluding to the horizontal festivities he is about to commence with two slaves. With his pre-coitus invocation complete, the slave master boasts to the journalists that he and God get along well because he was created in God's likeness. He adds that God immediately regretted creating blacks, and "damned the entire race, leaving them without a soul, fit only to be my slaves." Then the slave master joins two young slaves in bed not long before a thirteen-year-old slave jumps into an Italian journalist's bed and tries to seduce him. While the film doesn't show the coital act, we can infer from the close-up of her facial expressions and from her vocalized intonations of sexual pleasure that the young slave's plan of seduction worked. Whereas most slavery films depict a sidelined God in the context of the sexual exploitation of slaves, *Goodbye Uncle Tom* presents God as a playful and pliable condoner of slavery and concomitant indulgences, including sex with young slaves.

The film offers a scene where the journalists explain how slaves draw upon biblical history and symbols of Palestine to extrapolate Judeo-Christian residuals to their religious experience. What the journalists carelessly depict as the primitive second-rate rehashing of Christianity, is what religion scholars more perceptively construe as the vibrant syncretism of African traditional religion and Christianity to address and mitigate the vicissitudes of slavery (West 1982; Wilmore 1998; Hopkins 2000; Raboteau 2004; Brown 2008). In this manner, the journalists overlook the creative resilience of black slaves to utilize African and Christian cultural tools to construct a new theological awareness that helps them survive, exegete their own experiences under the cruel technologies of slavery, and reclaim their humanity (Paris 1995; Hicks 2012; Jelks 2019).

Goodbye Uncle Tom also offers perhaps the first filmic look at a slave-breeding farm, capturing all its farcicality. A slaveholder named Wilson pays the owner of the breeding farm to allow Wilson's thirteen-year-old virgin to sleep with one of the breeder's roughest slaves. Unlike the journalist's earlier romp with a young slave, this time we see the actual sex act. The older slave manhandles the virgin and the distressed look on her face reveals the cruel way the institution of slavery reduced young females to semen receptacles and procreating machines. One of the journalists asks the owner of the breeding farm why some of the progeny have blond hair, to which the owner replies, "Well you see some are mine and some are my brother's . . . and some are from passing guests like yourself, and the priest hasn't been losing any time either." The priest's connivance in utilizing the slaves for purposes beyond spiritual mentorship once again underscores how *Goodbye Uncle Tom* executes a satirical campaign against God and religion in the context of slavery. Throughout the film, God and Christianity appear as supportive of slavery and in lockstep with white supremacy. Slave masters, traders, prominent citizens, and a Protestant preacher relish coding slavery and its dehumanizing technologies as divinely sanctioned conventions within a racial hierarchy rooted in God's creation order. A Catholic priest goes a step further to partake in sexual indulgences with defenseless slaves. To the theodical question, how could God allow such a cruel system like slavery to persist? *Goodbye Uncle Tom* answers by treating religion and God as manipulatable pawns of the white American power structure. God is not only sidelined but distorted and humanized as slave masters' co-conspirator.

SANKOFA

Decidedly less satirical in its depiction of God and religion and considerably more measured in its representations of the atrocities of forced servitude, Haile Gerima's *Sankofa* (1993) still gives *Goodbye Uncle Tom* a run for its money in displaying Christian complicity in the crimes of American slavery. *Sankofa* begins in present-day Ghana with a black American fashion model named Mona posing in a photo shoot on the old slave fortress where merchants once stocked, branded, and transported Africans during the height of the transatlantic slave trade. During the shoot, an elderly African man in traditional garb startles the model when he yells, "Back to your past! Return to your source!" insisting that Mona and her photographer are intruding on "sacred ground covered with the blood of people who suffered." The African also commands a group of tourists to leave the slave castle after reminding them, "It is from here that our people were snatched and taken by the white man!"

Order is restored once policemen remove the old man so both the photo shoot and the tour can resume. The tour guide clarifies the old man's status as a self-appointed custodian of the castle who converses with the spirits of the dead. But this guardian of sacred ground proves prophetic as the film transports Mona to an earlier time where she is captured and processed for the Middle Passage. Slavers strip Mona and then brand her as the property of her new proprietor the same way ranchers brand their cattle. Mona eventually arrives at an American plantation and mysteriously transitions into a slave named Shola.

Shola may have the privilege of avoiding grueling work in the hot sun, but her proximity to her master in the house increases her vulnerability to rape. And when she finally goes to the plantation's priest, Father Raphael, to inform him of her plight, he offers neither a rebuke to the rapist nor a healing message for Shola, which teaches Shola that Christianity is out of touch with a slave's painful struggle. All Father Raphael can do is to urge her to pray, and Shola narrates, "It seemed like the more I prayed the meaner the master got. Prayin' wasn't working, so I just stopped it altogether." Her recollection not only proposes Christianity's inability to confront sin and brutality, but also reveals the ineffectiveness of prayer to ward off evil. Shola eventually abandons her faith and joins the forces of rebellious slaves.

Sankofa makes its case for Christianity's insignificance to slaves, a disappointment Gerima contrasts against the film's more positive portrayal of African traditional religion, as embraced by a strong slave named Nunu. Shola recognizes Nunu's potency and in her earlier praying days requests, "Lord let me be like Nunu. Just give me a little of the power she's got right there in the center of my eyes." Nunu's subversive African spirit is contrasted against her biracial son's Christian collusion with the white power structure on the plantation. Joe, the offspring of rape during Nunu's Middle Passage journey, serves as a headman handling the master's dirty work in keeping slaves in check. He also spends much time with Father Raphael. Joe's fascination with Catholic iconography, the blessed mother Mary, and his Bible makes him malleable to the priest's will. Through Joe's relationship with Father Raphael, *Sankofa* not only insinuates Christianity's inconsequentiality to slaves, but also downgrades God and Christian dictates to psychosocial mechanisms of domination; forms of false consciousness distracting a slave like Joe from recognizing and rebelling against his subjugated state.

Under the directive of their master, Joe and another headman named Noble Ali build the whipping posts that Noble later uses to flog a pregnant slave named Kuta, while Joe counts the lashes. After the fatal punishment, Joe's mother Nunu rushes over with a machete and cuts open Kuta's corpse to deliver her baby. Noble is devastated by his obligatory contribution to Kuta's death, while Joe appears unfazed. The implication is that Christianity makes Joe callous to the pain and tragedy of slavery. Later that evening, Joe meets with Father Raphael at the church and the priest does not even ask his protégé how he feels about participating in the brutal death of a fellow slave. Instead, Father Raphael uses the time to extol the beauty of Christian paintings and doctrinal truths about Christ's resurrection. To reiterate, through Joe's relationship with his mentor, Gerima portrays Christianity not only as unable to speak to the revulsions of chattel slavery or provide an existential awakening, but also as a meaningless distraction to the slave.

Joe basks in religious sanctimony and perceives himself as better than the other slaves. When he does give in to carnality, lusting after Lucy, the erotic episode is followed by a pious rebuke against Lucy and renewed commitment to his faith. Unsurprisingly, Joe does not get along with his defiant mother Nunu, who finds her son's role as headman incomprehensible. Father Raphael's pious indoctrination eventually persuades Joe to perceive his own mother as a heathen stumbling block to his faith, a perception that, in due course, impels Joe to kill her. But the murderous act incites Joe to reevaluate his faith. In anger he strangles Father Raphael in the very same church where he spent so much time functioning as the priest's obsequious mentee, a redemptive act that signals Joe's long overdue rejection of Christianity and slavery.

Haile Gerima's film questions how a slave can find nourishment and solace in a religious system that the slave master manipulates to keep the very same slave under his power. *Sankofa*'s answer is that the slave can't, and hence must reject the master's God and reach back to Africa for a more relevant religious perspective. But Gerima unwittingly exposes the inefficacy of African traditional religion as well. Despite her spiritual power, Nunu endures rape during the Middle Passage and later dies at the hands of her confused Christian son. In other words, no matter how strong Nunu appears, her traditional African religious power can't protect her from defilement on the Atlantic waters and death on an American plantation. And so the film turns Nunu's religious worldview into an existential resource rather than an intervening force. But even as *Sankofa* both directly and indirectly advances poignant interrogations against any notion of divine intervention, its severest critique is aimed at Christianity and its God. The Christian slave master repeatedly rapes Shola with no fear of reprisal or challenge from the religious cleric to which he adheres. And it is the victim Shola, not the rapist, on whom Father Raphael performs an exorcism to rid her of heathen influences.

ADVENTURES OF HUCKLEBERRY FINN

Mark Twain's *Adventures of Huckleberry Finn* (1885) is as incisive in satirizing slavery as it is prolific in using the word nigger. While Twain's masterwork continues to generate both admiration and discord, one facet that remains underexplored is its theological implications in the context of its implicit critique of slavery. Alongside Harriet Beecher Stowe's *Uncle Tom's Cabin* (1852), Twain's novel is among the earliest American classics to offer an important and pervasive intersection of divine representation and black suffering in a way that lampoons the collective conscience of a slave society. Select filmic adaptations of Twain's novel are similarly skillful at exposing the upended moral logic driving slavery, presenting cinema as a formidable foe of the peculiar institution while posing intriguing implications for religion and theodicy.

J. Lee Thompson's 1974 film *Huckleberry Finn* is the only adaptation to begin from the perspective of Jim the slave. Thompson's film opens with images of Jim visiting his wife and baby flanked by scores of slaves heading for the fields with pitchforks in hand. And while the credits roll, we hear Roberta Flack sing the powerful lyrics of "Freedom," with the last verse conveying a sentiment in harmony with cinematic theodicy's vertical boundary work:

> God made the sun to rise
> And God made the Earth and skies
> God made the seas and plains
> God made the winds and rains
> And freedom, freedom, freedom,
> Man's got to make his own.

Flack's song ends proposing that slaves cannot depend on God to escape bondage but must rely on themselves to secure freedom, suggesting that God's interventionist capacities end with the creation of the world. The film's dialogue begins with Jim explaining to his wife that Miss Watson plans on selling him to a trader, so he must escape to avoid being shipped off to an auction in New Orleans. And thus, we quickly see how the lyrics to "Freedom" foreshadow Jim's proactive response to his desperate situation; he cannot passively wait on God but must secure his own liberation, with the help of his young comrade Huck.

An important way that Thompson strays from Twain's novel is by leaving out Huck's inner conflict over the moral implications of abetting a runaway slave. While he recognizes abolitionist activity as an infraction of the societal moral code, Huck never struggles with helping his friend escape. At the film's end when Jim is pursued by slave traders, Huck watches Jim run toward freedom and declares, "If there is a God up there—I ain't sure if there is or there ain't—He'll hear me praying for you Jim," revealing that Huck, despite his rejection of societal values to help a runaway slave, does not perceive himself as emphatically banished by God and destined for hell like he initially perceives his predicament in Twain's novel. But other filmic adaptations stay true to Twain's magnum opus by depicting a morally confused Huck grappling with the racist dictates of a slave society against his budding love for a friend and contempt of slavery. In the context of theodicy, these filmic adaptations capture Huck's cognitive dissonance concerning where he stands before God as the result of his illegal actions in aiding and abetting Jim's escape from slavery.

Peter Hunt's *Adventures of Huckleberry Finn* (1986) includes important moments that juxtapose God and religion against the rigors and rites of slavery. Early on Miss Watson presses Huck to pray and go to church, while perceiving no contradiction between owning Jim and living out her Christian faith. When a slave trader offers her $800 for Jim, Miss Watson tells her sister, "Isn't that grand? Well isn't it? That's a lot of money and we really haven't any more use for Jim." The Widow Douglas responds, "I don't take to it Sister. We've always told our slaves they'd never be sold downriver; you know that." But all Miss Watson can say in response is, "The man offered me $800!" So not only does Miss Watson's Christian virtue do nothing to prevent her from defaulting on a promise not to sell her slaves downriver, but her faith also fails to pique her moral sensibilities against reducing a human being to a commodity.

After Huck helps Jim escape and the two are separated, Huck meets another boy who mentions in passing that a runaway slave named Jim was just apprehended for reward money. Oblivious to Huck's partnership with Jim, the boy also informs Huck that the abolitionist who helped Jim escape is going to hell. This piercing reminder of what many people in his slave society believe prompts Huck to pray:

> Lord, I know that I shouldn't have done what I done. And I know I should sit down right now and write a letter to Miss Watson and tell her where her nigger is. But I was brung up wicked. So I am much to blame. Except of course there was that Sunday school I could have gone to and they'd have learnt me that people that act as I've been acting about that nigger goes to everlasting fire. So what I wants to say is . . . well, I found out one thing, you can't pray a lie.

Here we see Huck apologizing to God for helping Jim escape, assuming it was a sinful act that he would have been less inclined to commit had he not skipped Sunday school. The suggestion is that the place where Huck should have ideally learned to be more Christlike and compassionate essentially would have better conditioned him to be a compliant witness to the debasement of humans. Filled with guilt, he then writes a letter to Miss Watson informing her where Jim is and how to get him back. Upon finishing, he holds the letter to his chest, looks up to the heavens, and then rips it apart, crying, "Alright, I'll go to hell!"

Huck's angst demonstrates how thoroughly socialized he was on the evils of abolitionist activity. In the beginning of the prayer, he attempts to rationalize why he allowed himself to sink so low as to help Jim escape by reminding God of his lack of fine upbringing. As the prayer continues, we see a boy show remorse for doing what many people today (and slaves and abolitionists of his day) would readily conceive as the morally correct thing to do. But Huck's young psyche is an artifact of a slave society, and he therefore appears shamefaced at his culpability in Jim's escape, an act he believes destines him to hell. However, his love for Jim eventually leads him to the conclusion that saving Jim is worth suffering eternal damnation. This sequence (that is left out of Thompson's adaptation) codes chattel slavery as a corrupting force against the American conscience such that it cannot correctly decipher right from wrong. It reminds viewers that a conscience is no objective magistrate of virtue; it is an acculturated mechanism of society. And if societal logic on slavery is epistemically contorted, then the same may hold for each individual conscience. But the film, like Twain's novel, also shows that love for a fellow human being can trump the defective conditioning of a slave society. The film's ironic message is that law-breaking Huck is morally superior to Miss Watson and her sanctimonious slave society, and that his devotion to Jim is more Christ-like than the acts of any of his more finely cultured peers.

An earlier filmic version of Huck and Jim's excursion also assembles moments germane to any discussion of theodicy. In MGM's *The Adventures of Huckleberry Finn* (1960), directed by Michael Curtiz, after two scoundrels referred to as the king and duke expose Jim as a runaway slave, Huck sneaks into the place where Jim is detained and listens to Jim account for getting caught by pointing to God's punishment against him for being a sinner. Huck responds, "Ah, you're always chattering about sin. You ain't never sin. Except for running away from the widow and I ain't even sure that's a sin." Earlier in Curtiz's version, Huck was sure Jim's escape from slavery was sinful and wrong but at this point in the plot he seems uncertain. Jim tells Huck he also sinned by not revealing that the dead man they saw on the houseboat was Huck's father Pap and that God is now chastening him. Here Jim is offering a theodicy of sin, not unlike the Old Testament narratives that explain Israel's captivity to enemies as penalty for violating the covenant. According to such a calculation, God's benevolence refrains from intervening to help suffering people because said suffering is the divinely sanctioned penalty for their sin.

But Huck isn't buying Jim's theodicy of sin. His response reflects a humanist shift, "You know who the Lord helps Jim? Them that helps their selves." Huck then smiles and runs off as if a new idea compels him toward immediate action. He goes to the sheriff dressed up like a girl, pretending to be Mrs. Douglas to redeem her runaway slave. While the sheriff falls for Huck's ruse and goes off to get the king and duke, Huck is left alone with the sheriff's wife who easily deciphers he is a boy. Huck changes his story and tells her that abolitionists are forcing him to help them free slaves, which she believes and becomes quite sympathetic. When she leaves to get him lemonade, Huck steals the sheriff's keys and runs off to set Jim free. Huck takes Jim's vest to trick the sheriff's dogs with its scent, and Jim swims across the creek to free land on the other side. The sheriff (accompanied by the king and duke) eventually catches up to Huck, and Huck offers his best lies of the film, first in telling the sheriff that Jim drowned trying to cross the creek, and second in posing as the king's abolitionist apprentice to bring suspicion upon the king, declaring, "I ain't blaming you for getting mad mister. The job you gave me was to get him free and not to get him drowned. So it wouldn't be right keeping this," and then hands the king the gold piece he secured earlier in the film for an entirely different reason. Incensed by Huck's revelation, the sheriff snatches the gold piece to use as evidence that they are in fact dreadful abolitionists. Huck chimes in, "I reckon, I'm as bad as they are Sheriff. What chance does a poor little boy like me have with grown-up slickers?"—correctly calculating that the sheriff would have mercy on him because of his age.

So Huck's earlier clarification to Jim that God helps those who help themselves inspired a plan that involved deceit and theft to achieve its objectives. Huck uses guile and societal hatred of abolitionists to facilitate his plan. Instead of adopting societal norms, Huck cleverly subverts them. We should point out that Huck's conclusion that God helps those who help themselves is simply a folksy way of sidelining God and pointing to human creativity and diligence as the way to win the day or ward off evil. But Huck also grows in assurance that helping a runaway slave is the godly thing to do when earlier in the film he considered it a sin.

It is worth noting that another adaptation, Herbert Swope's *Adventures of Huckleberry Finn* (1955), excludes any mention of slavery, replacing Jim with Huck's friend Tom Sawyer. Jim's absence in this film is a testament to the perplexing dilemma of slavery's presence in American history, which has important implications for any discussion of religion, God, and black suffering. Like Swope's revisionist erasure of Jim, perhaps many people wish they could wipe away slavery's place in history and all the suffering and death it incurred upon black bodies. Fortunately, most filmic versions of Twain's novel take the issue of slavery head on and provide some of cinema's most profound treatments of theodicy. They code and narrate slavery as an institution that corrupts the moral conscience of its society. And through Huck's ingenuity, these films present solutions that sideline God.

THE AMAZING GRACE

Jeta Amata's *The Amazing Grace* (2006) covers the transnational slave trade from Nigerian, British, and American perspectives. The story is inspired by a slave ship captain named John Newton who wrote the Christian hymn "Amazing Grace." Amata's film offers a window to Newton's spiritual awakening. Early in the film we find black Africans in a region now known as Nigeria, speaking of a supreme being that resembles the God of Christianity, which offers intriguing implications for theodicy when some of these same West Africans are captured, killed, and brutalized under God's watchful eye. The foreshadowing event occurs when a warrior named Etim awakens from a dream of his village being raided. His wife reassures him, "Nothing will happen, after all, you're here to protect us," to which Etim responds, "God will protect us." Etim's prediction is disconfirmed when John Newton's ruthless partner Oliver and his crew attack the village, killing Etim's wife and child in the process and abducting the surviving villagers as new slaves to meet their quota. Viewers might question why God would reveal an impending disaster and do nothing to prevent it. Similarly prophetic is how, moments before the raid, the village griot warns his people there will be a time of justice for turning their backs on God. And while the raid is taking place, the same griot cries out to God, "Forgive us Father. Do not forsake us at our time of need. We have sinned and lost glory in your sight oh Creator of the universe. Turn not from your children. Forgive them Father, for they know not what they do." The griot's assertions create more uncertainty regarding God's failure to protect Etim's village by suggesting the Africans had it coming for past sins, a move reminiscent of the Old Testament practice of coding brutality and genocide as retributive acts of God. Such theodical reasoning is simple: God punishes people for sinful behavior by removing protection and allowing tragic events to take place. Thus, from the vantage point of the believer, God is ultimately exonerated for non-intervention when evil events occur. It is an exegetical strategy that posits all the causal power for evil and suffering to sinful people. It turns tragedies into tools of justice while keeping intact God's sovereignty. A theodicy of sin has the downside of making God look monstrous.

Maria Davis was a young girl when Oliver's crew raided her (and Etim's) village and is now an older slave in America serving as the film's narrator retelling her story to her daughter. Maria describes the long walk after the raid, how they went without food or water for two days and nights, how children clung to their mothers for support and mothers looked up to God, asking "Why?" During this long and painful trek to the coast we learn from Maria that "Some fell and could make it no more. They were abandoned and left to rot." Maria also mentions how "people hoped for a miracle, a savior to come release us from our bondage." Nowhere in Maria's narration of the pain and suffering of her captured people does she confirm her griot's earlier assertion that their unfaithfulness led God to abandon them. Later, while we hear the moans of slaves chained up in agony, Etim inquires "Why has our Creator allowed this to happen?" Notwithstanding the griot's early attempts at blaming their suffering on their sin, the film never adequately answers Etim's question.

As the story shifts back to its aim, a confrontation between Christianity and the ruthlessness of the slave trade, Captain Newton rebukes his crew chief Oliver for the sin Newton euphemistically classifies as fornicating with savages, a strategic recoding of Oliver's actual practice of raping African women. But Oliver bites back, referencing Newton's own hypocrisy in participating in the trade of humans while cognizant of the cruelty awaiting them in American plantations. Newton's only retort is to insist that black Africans are not made in God's image, like himself as a human and an Englishman, to which Oliver responds, "Do not try to protect your morality by thinking these poor fools as less than human." Their debate about the humanity of black Africans ends with Newton asking the key question of theodicy that haunts any intersection of divine governance and slavery: "For why would God permit such cruelty were it not that our actions take these unblessed closer to salvation?" Oliver, a slave-raider, rapist, and murderer, takes the moral high ground as he indirectly answers Newton's question: "When you return to England you shall go to church and thank God for your safe return from your pillage and plunder. And for your sake, Captain, I hope that God is an Englishman." Oliver impels the sanctimonious ship captain to confront his own hypocrisy and thus Newton for the first time is conflicted. The rest of the film unfolds his progression toward a new respect for the humanity of his captured Africans.

The Amazing Grace continues to project ambivalent (if not incongruous) theodical implications about the slave trade. On the ship, after Etim and other Africans save John Newton's life during a storm, Maria's narration tells us, "He was destined by God to be saved by his prisoners. It was to fight their cause some day. He was destined to receive the Amazing Grace." So Maria's chronicle places God's providence in service of saving an English captain of a slave ship so that one day he can write a great song about grace, while the same God, by implication, did not lift a finger to stop Etim's wife and child from being ruthlessly murdered, did not intervene to prevent the death of countless other black Africans during the long trek to the coast, and now, at this point in the film, allows Africans to suffer on the Middle Passage voyage. By introducing God's purposeful orchestration of events, the film makes God appear even more inscrutable when the times in which God does nothing to save men, women, and children from viciousness and death are brought into focus. Oddly enough, the subsequent line from our narrator, after mentioning God's hand behind Newton's rescue, is: "The next day, while John Newton was unconscious, Oliver and his crew executed some of the slaves for rebellious acts. Your grandmother was one of them. The rest of us were rounded up and sent back to our dungeon." Maria's own mother was killed on the slave ship at the whimsical dictate of Oliver and yet, just a few moments earlier, Maria's voiceover frames Newton's rescue from the gusts of a storm as divinely orchestrated.

We later learn from a white crewman who speaks the Africans' language that the repeated song the slaves sing on the ship asks why God has forsaken them and how they can find grace without God's help. The melody of the slave song eventually influences John Newton to write his hymn "Amazing Grace," but if all Newton's efforts were divinely orchestrated just to produce an amazing song, it seems like there were more cost-effective ways for God to generate a hymn. What is more surprising is that the film ends with a caption informing viewers that John Newton continued slave trading for several years after this life-changing experience. So this impactful trip in which he experiences a spiritual awakening and affirms the humanity of black Africans is enough to inspire a great song but not enough to instigate a clean break from the very slave trade that impels Newton himself to draw upon God's grace. That Newton continued trading Africans even after he found grace is a testament to the film's perplexing treatment of black suffering, while simultaneously confirming how rare cinematic attempts to introduce God's plan and intervention in the confines of the unfolding misery of the transatlantic slave trade end up producing impenetrable problems for theodicy. This no doubt explains why so many filmic treatments of the horrors of slavery opt for a sidelined God who remains estranged from the unfolding events of slavery and its technologies of oppression and dehumanization, save when films satirize God as the architect behind racial hierarchy and dehumanizing cruelty.

In a strange coincidence, Jeta Amata's *The Amazing Grace* was released in the same year as Michael Apted's film *Amazing Grace* (2006). In Apted's film the setting is not the West African coast but the British Parliament's contestation over the issue of slavery through the political efforts of William Wilberforce. But certain commonalities exist beyond the two films' eerily comparable titles and release dates. They both delineate the degeneracy of the transatlantic slave trade and showcase John Newton while doing so. Whereas Amata's film features the Englishman as a young slave-ship captain, in Apted's film Newton is long retired and plays a supportive role in motivating Wilberforce's political affront against slavery. Now old and blind, Newton still has enough faculties to offer Wilberforce a firsthand account of the cruel methods by which slaves were flogged on the wharfs, as well as names, ship records, ports, and other meticulous details of the trade that still haunt him. More importantly, Apted's film features other eyewitness accounts of the horrors of slave ships and how a Christian nation is shamed by its participation in slavery.

UNCLE TOM'S CABIN

Harry Pollard's filmic adaption *Uncle Tom's Cabin* (1927) bears the same name as Harriet Beecher Stowe's (1852) classic novel and is an early cinematic effort to portray the inhumaneness of American slavery. The film begins with Tom eating dinner with his family in their humble slave quarters. Tom declares to his wife, "We's got a lot to be thankful for. De Lord's been mighty good to us," shortly before Eliza comes knocking at his window with news that Master Shelby has sold Tom and her son Harry to a rival landowner. Eliza plans to escape with Harry and asks Tom to join them, but Tom stoically accepts his fate. A later scene shows Tom's family and other slaves on their knees praying in desperation while Tom rides off on the wagon, never to be seen by any of them again. Whatever those prayers from the slaves entailed, they lacked the spiritual force to reverse a man's heartrending dislocation from his family and friends. If Tom's earlier sentiment expresses how God has been good to his family, then one should ponder what his permanent estrangement from his family does to alter that perception.

Tracking Eliza and Harry's escape, the film offers a cinematographically innovative ice floe scene in which they evade slave catchers by traversing across the winter river. Hanging over the falls on a tree limb, a Quaker sympathizer named Phineas Fletcher risks his life to save them. He brings Eliza and Harry to his home where he and his wife nurture them back to health. Whereas in Stowe's novel Eliza makes it to Canada and doesn't appear in later chapters, Pollard's adaptation extends her presence in the plot by adding an upsetting twist. Slave traders abduct Eliza and Harry, leading to the gloomiest moment of the film when young Harry is sold to a family and Eliza desperately chases the wagon that carries her son away. We should pause to consider how the film's diversion from Stowe's novel demonstrates cinema's commitment and signifying capacity to capture the devastation of slavery. As a ritualistic performance, it moralizes and memorializes the tragedy of slavery, allowing parents in the viewing audience to connect with a mother's grief upon seeing her child fade away from her life forever. Eliza's agony might prompt even the most conservative defender of slavery to imagine watching his or her own child ride away with no chance of ever reconnecting. The fear of being sold downriver was a frightening reality for many slaves and the film offers its viewers two salient opportunities to see what the breakup of families looks like in real time with real human anguish.

In a farfetched coincidence, Tom and Eliza reunite when Simon Legree purchases them. In an even more fantastic twist of fate, her purchase reunites Eliza with her mother, one of Legree's slaves. The fluke of a mother and young daughter being separated and later reconnecting through those same market forces points to the precarious nature of slave families under the peculiar institution's caprices. Tom never sees his family again and Eliza loses Harry just as her mother lost Eliza decades earlier via the vagaries of buying and selling human flesh. Cinema as an empathy machine compels viewers to confront this rational yet most regrettable component of a slave economy.

Things quickly go badly for Tom when henchmen bring him to their master claiming, "Dis Nigger's been makin' trubble 'mong de hands—preachin' an' a-prayin'!" Legree grabs Tom and tells him, "I'll do all the prayin' around here!" The Special Features section of the DVD of *Uncle Tom's Cabin* reveals that the censors rejected Legree's original response to Tom, a line that ultimately captures the logic of American slavery in the context of theodicy better than the redacted version. In the original screenplay, upon hearing from his henchmen that Tom is carrying out spiritual activities among fellow slaves, Simon Legree informs Tom, "I am your church; do your praying to me." The censors deemed such a declaration as offensive, but we can't overlook how the original line does offer an adequate summary of the theological conundrum of Tom's existence as a Christian owned by another human. No matter how much praying and hoping a God-fearing slave like Tom could put forth, at the end of the day, the slave was a mere pawn in the earthly master's kingdom. Essentially, the slave master was in fact an authoritative institution like the church (or better yet, God) to the vulnerable slave. But even as the unredacted line captures the sovereign presence Legree looms over Tom and other slaves, Tom refuses to concede such a point when Legree is standing over him and asks, "Didn't I pay twelve hundred dollars for you—ain't you mine, body and soul?" A debilitated Tom responds, "No Massa! My body may belong to you, but my soul belongs to God." Tom gets up and Legree knocks him down again and then orders Sambo and Quimbo to give Tom the worst flogging he's ever had.

In contrast to the "Uncle Tom" archetype deployed in contemporary culture to symbolize weakness and servility, Tom in this film is heroic and defiant. When Legree orders Tom to whip one of the female slaves, Tom refuses, which angers Legree enough to send Tom crashing to the ground with a blow to the head. And later when Legree demands to know the location of Eliza and her mother, who are hiding, Tom refuses to tell him and receives a fatal flogging for failing to comply. When Tom dies, we hear the Negro spiritual "Swing Low, Sweet Chariot," which once again juxtaposes Tom's suffering against the backdrop of his Christian faith. But Tom's story and death reminds viewers that slaves were bought, sold, and separated from family members and died without ever experiencing life as free human beings, despite their belief in an all-powerful God. Like many films assessed in this chapter, Harry Pollard's *Uncle Tom's Cabin* presents God and religion as ineffectual toward preserving the physical wellbeing of the slave.

OTHER FILMS

Richard Fleischer's film *Mandingo* (1975) offers a shocking portrayal of plantation life in the Deep South. A line from the lyrics performed by Muddy Waters during the opening credits best summarizes the desperate slave's emotional state: "Dear Lord in heaven can you hear my lonesome cry?" Another line captures the slave's bleak prospects: "I was born in this time to never be free." Over dinner, the doctor asks the plantation owner if he has any religion for his slaves. Maxwell responds, "Hell no! The more religion they gets, the onerier they gets. Harder to drive." The doctor curiously inquires, "Don't worry nothing about they immortal souls?" to which Maxwell retorts, "They ain't got no immortal souls. They gets to thinking they got souls, they gets to thinking they as good as white folk." A visiting slave trader jumps into the conversation to point out that some people believe slaves have souls and go to heaven too, and the doctor adds, "Them abolitionists up North telling us they as good as whites." Master Maxwell responds by sharing his divine defense of slavery, his dehumanization of slaves, and his contempt for abolitionists: "Them sons of bitches! Slavery was ordained by God His self. Niggers are right happy eating, working, fornicating. Abolitionists—cracks and loonies!" Not long after, two older slaves prepare a young virgin for sex with Maxwell's son by bathing her and providing her with instructions on how to conduct herself. One of the consulting female slaves is the virgin's mother who informs her daughter, "You supposed to reckon it a prideful honor for white Master taking you first." Throughout the film, female slaves are mostly referred to as wenches and have no choice in matters regarding their bodies, sexuality, and whether their babies get sold or stay with them. Slave babies are called "suckers" as if to put an exclamation mark on their dehumanization. Maxwell's early statements about denying slaves the dignity of religion is corroborated, as slaves are continuously mistreated throughout the film as disposable tools, sex objects, or fighting animals.

Quentin Tarantino's stylized spaghetti Western *Django Unchained* (2012) offers many scenes that signify debasing aspects of slavery. We see a slave named D'Artagnan ripped apart by dogs as punishment for his attempt to escape, and others treated as property rather than people—chained, muzzled, and whipped for the smallest of offenses. Through a flashback we see an overseer of slaves named John Brittle preparing to whip Django's wife Hildi. Django pleads with John not to whip her, first reminding the overseer that Hildi works in the house and so Old Man Carrucan "ain't gonna appreciate it if you messes her skin up." Django continues to plead for mercy, offering a last attempt to stop the whipping by referencing John's Bible, but to no avail, as Hildi does receive a brutal beating to the sadistic pleasure of John and his brothers. As we hear the cracking of the whip causing great pain to Hildi's back, the camera offers a close-up of John's left hand in which we do in fact see a Bible. After Django's flashback ends, the film jumps to the present time where John and his brothers are wanted murderers and Django and Dr. Schultz are bounty hunters ready to enact retributive justice. John, assuming a new name as an overseer on a new plantation, is up to his old tricks, getting ready to whip a slave for accidentally breaking a few eggs. As John preps with a couple of practice cracks of his whip, we see what looks to be the same Bible in the same hand, and John recites the scripture, "The fear of ye and the dread of ye shall be on every beast of the earth" (Genesis 9:2). But before he can administer his biblically inspired punishment, Django enacts his revenge by putting a bullet in John's chest. Like Haile Gerima's *Sankofa* and other slavery films, Tarantino strategically incorporates a spiritual component in the persona of slavery's technician of cruelty to underscore how the ferocity of chattel servitude intersects with the sanctimony of Christianity.

Tomas Gutierrez Alea's *The Last Supper* (1976) has one of the most eccentric premises of any filmic treatment of slavery. Set in the eighteenth century during the Holy Week, it unfolds how the owner of a sugar mill attempts to recreate the Last Supper with twelve of his slaves. After washing their feet like Jesus did for some of the disciples, the count prepares a feast on a long table reminiscent of the one depicted in many Renaissance paintings of the Last Supper, with the slaves joining him to indulge in food and conversation. What makes this dinner (and film) so unusual is the amount of time devoted to the count conversing with his slaves like they are his equals, an event perhaps never repeated in successive filmic representations of slavery. While happy to enjoy great food and drink with their master, the slaves convey the failure of Christianity to speak to their plight, as one of them tells the count, "The slave is cursed by God, born to suffer."

Intending to teach his slaves through his example of humility and his dinner-table ruminations on Christian doctrine, the count tells them a long story about St. Francis and then finally sums it up: "The moral of the story is, of all good things Christ gives, the best is to suffer pain and injury for His divine love. The other things aren't ours, they belong to God. Sorrow is the only thing that is truly ours, the only thing we can give to God with joy." The absurdity of an owner of a sugar mill operated by the backbreaking work of slaves teaching some of those very slaves about honorific suffering and Christian humility is not lost upon the count's dinner guests, as they all start laughing, prompting the count to ask, "You understood the moral?" One slave responds, "Let me see if I understood. When the overseer beats me, I should be happy?" His question generates more laughter from his peers, to which the clueless Christian count responds, "Yes, that's it. If you understood this, you will be happy, happier than the whites." Later when the count brings up Paradise, one slave asks if Paradise has overseers, explaining that the priest once told them that Jesus Christ is an overseer, thus making this slave think Jesus must be cruel like their overseer Don Manuel. This long dinner sequence attempts to contextualize Christianity toward the daily struggles of slaves and in the process reveals Christianity as quite absurd, at least from the suffering and exploited slave's perspective.

CONCLUSION

Steven Spielberg's historical drama *Lincoln* (2012) ends with the sixteenth president delivering one of his most stirring orations, the Second Inaugural Address. The scene infuses theodical tinges to the film, as Spielberg's coverage captures the historical speech verbatim and commences at the point when the president triangulates human suffering, divine retribution, and national healing:

> Fondly do we hope, fervently do we pray, that this mighty scourge of war may speedily pass away. Yet, if God wills that it continue until all the wealth piled

by the bondsman's two hundred and fifty years of unrequited toil shall be sunk, and until every drop of blood drawn with the lash shall be paid by another drawn with the sword, as was said three thousand years ago, so still it must be said, the judgments of the Lord are true and righteous altogether. With malice toward none, with charity for all, with firmness in the right as God gives us to see the right, let us strive on to finish the work we are in, to bind up the nation's wounds, to care for him whom shall have borne the battle and for his widow and his orphan, to do all which may achieve and cherish a just and lasting peace among ourselves and with all nations.

Here Lincoln indicates the notion of God using the Civil War and its associated traumas as both retribution for and redemption of the scourge of slavery. The scene fashions Spielberg's most daring cinematic statement on theodicy since *Schindler's List* (1993). Bold and prophetic in its claims and rebuke, this part of Lincoln's Second Inaugural Address presumes a providential understanding of history, one in which God not only acts and intervenes, but also administers justice. Since President Lincoln raises the possibility that the Civil War is God's scourge against the national sin of slavery, it is only fitting that we offer a few challenges to his theological understanding of slavery and social justice.

Raoul Walsh's romantic drama *Band of Angels* (1957) climaxes with Hamish Bond revealing to his lover Manty the dirty details of his earlier involvement in the transatlantic slave trade, including how he allied with a vicious African king who invaded villages to secure slaves. Plagued by guilt and regret, Hamish tells her, "I can still hear them. The puking and the screaming and the praying. Packed into slave shelves with hardly any turning room." Hamish's only justification for his complicity in this system challenges President Lincoln's allusion to providence, "But I didn't make this world. I didn't even make myself. And if the Creator didn't like it, He should have done the world a favor and sunk those hellish ships under the sea along with the whole black coast." Hamish raises a striking point concerning theodicy: that an all-powerful God could have obliterated the slave system if God had a problem with it. Another challenge to Lincoln's teleological appropriation of divine justice comes in Charles Burnett's film *Nightjohn* (1996), when Clel is about to beat a slave as punishment for visiting a woman on the plantation of Clel's brother. Jeff tries to stop this, reminding his father that the slave is his hunting buddy. Perplexed by his son's declaration of friendship with a slave, Clel responds, "Friends? Jeff, son. God made this boy to pick your cotton!" Similarly combative to Lincoln's assertion is how slave masters and traders in films like *The Amazing Grace*, *Goodbye Uncle Tom*, and *Mandingo* justify the slave's oppression or presumed ontological inferiority as established in God's decisive designation of race within the creation order.

And as this chapter demonstrates with impressive prolificacy, other slavery films demonstrate that God is not the kind of deity that gets hands dirty intervening in human affairs.

So Lincoln's presumption of divine providence generates a pressing question for theodicy, namely, if America's long participation in the slave trade incites divine fury, and if the Civil War is restitution for the sins of slavery, and if God wills for slaves to be free, then why did God take so long to put a final end to slavery? Lincoln's position provokes an even more pressing theodical inquiry, namely, if God is the ultimate administrator of justice and nothing happens outside of God's will, as many proponents of ethical monotheism claim, then is God culpable for something as egregious as the transatlantic slave trade? Molefi Kete Asante's answer to the latter inquiry comes after he first poses similar questions from the vantage point of the newly minted African slave during the height of the transatlantic trade. Asante's poignant questions and decisive answer unfold with the scholar positioned near a West African slave castle for dramatic effect in the most compelling theodical moment of Owen Alik Shahadah's documentary *500 Years Later* (2005):

> The thing that disturbs me most is that right here behind me was a church situated over the dungeons and all around this church were dungeons where hundreds of Africans were held in bondage. And on Sunday morning, you could hear the wail and the moans of the African people combining with the sacred or so-called sacred hymns of the Christian people to produce the most terrible dirges of death you would ever hear. And the African people would always say, as I say even till this day: Where was God then? Where was God when all of the horrors that happened happened here, the brutality that happened to the Africans?

After questioning divine whereabouts during the zenith of the greatest system of human exploitation the world had ever known, Asante pivots by insisting that humans alone were responsible for the slave trade and its associated misery. But Asante's generosity in letting God off the hook does not come without cost in the form of an implicit but conclusive assault against Lincoln's understanding of divine providence and sovereignty. Asante minimizes God and elevates the agentive capacities of humans for unchecked evil. Hence, Asante's answer concerning God's culpability in slavery brings attention to cinema's most tactical instrument when confronting the perplexities of black suffering: a modern God.

Chapter 4

Ousmane Sembène
Toward a New and Modern Africa

Within the span of a month the world lost two legendary filmmakers. The broadcast of Ingmar Bergman's death in 2007 reverberated around the world, while Ousmane Sembène's passing received less intercontinental attention. Such is the discrepancy of admiration that characterizes any comparison between the two, as scores of tomes tackle Bergman's existential classics, while scholars devote considerably less attention to the African pioneer's masterworks. This is not to suggest that Sembène's career lacked global reach, as his works enjoyed multiple screenings at important film festivals and stimulated more scholarly coverage of African auteurs (Tsika 2015). But while Sembène's standing as the continent's most noteworthy filmmaker remains unobstructed, he, like many African filmmakers, was at a great disadvantage in comparison to Europeans like Bergman who possessed greater levels of support. As Roy Armes confirms:

> The situation of the African filmmaker is a difficult one. There is no standard procedure for organizing production and no conventional source of film finance, and inevitably African films are personal creations in a way that films can never be in the context of an industrialized film industry. (Armes 2011: 134)

Bergman never had to shoot in locations where there was no electricity, as Sembène often did, and Bergman's base in Europe gave the Swede more visibility, wider distribution, and better resources than Sembène ever enjoyed as a product of Senegal's film industry. Thus, Bergman was able to make more films and generate greater acclaim owing to conditions largely outside of Sembène's control.

Experiencing vastly different careers and levels of global recognition, there is one trait that Bergman and the father of African cinema do share in common, and that is their penchant for tackling theodicy. And even in this place where they stand on common ground, such terrain is unevenly balanced in favor of the Swede. Bergman is valued for his piercing encapsulations of God's silence in *The Seventh Seal* (1957) and *Winter Light* (1962), provocative valuation of God as a spider in *Through a Glass Darkly* (1961), and plentiful handlings of human suffering and the problem of evil, while Sembène has never been credited for his theodical ingenuity.

But asymmetric appreciation is not their only difference on the subject. For Bergman, cinematic theodicy offers artistic space to mourn the loss of humanity's teleological horizon, while for Sembène it represents the opposite, a chance to signify pragmatic veracities for continental survival. If theodicy is a meaning-mocking enterprise for Bergman's nihilism, then for Sembène, theodicy is a meaning-making naval vessel retrofitted to help Africans sail the torrential tides of modern momentum. And if there are any meaning-mocking armaments in Sembène's theodical arsenal, they are deployed as truth-seeking missiles to obliterate the religious, social, and political machinations that drive oppression and impede human flourishing.

This chapter assesses Sembène's treatments of God and religion within the architecture of African tragedy and a mushrooming modern landscape. While his films pay homage to religions as aesthetic touchstones and indigenous incubators of African cultural forms, they ultimately portray religion and God as ineffectual toward resolving the many challenges Africans face. Both traditional African religions and major world religions take hits when Sembène places them alongside African vulnerability and suffering. In his early short film *Borom Sarret* (1963), we see great poverty as well as the social disorientation and unpreparedness of a peasant Muslim trying to make it in a modernizing country. A bourgeois black man manipulates and abandons this peasant and a policeman humiliates him and strips him of his livelihood. Only seconds before this sad encounter, the peasant prays both to Allah and the gods of African traditional religion for protection on his excursion to downtown Dakar. Sembène here presents Islam and African traditional religion as unable to help disadvantaged people negotiate the politics and economics shaping their suffering.

In *Ceddo* (1977), Sembène presents the dictates and practices of the imam as provocations against Senegalese villagers. The message we extract from the film is that Islam did not come to liberate but rather to oppress, take over, and destroy African tradition, while imposing its perspective and practice onto unwilling participants. *Ceddo* presents Islam not only as a major source of black suffering, but also as a manipulative tool to conceal specious motives within one's struggle for power and ascendance, as the imam justifies killing and enslaving under the guise of religious sanctimony. Sembène offers a more benign treatment of this theme in his earlier film *Mandabi* (1968) when both a beggar and a businessman use Islam in their attempts to deceive the protagonist out of money. With both films, Sembène obliges compatriots of an overwhelmingly Muslim nation to confront the prospect that Islam contains cultural tools that can be used to manipulate and exploit its own believers.

In *Emitai* (1971), Sembène subtly suggests that, when facing an unrelenting challenge from a powerful conqueror, it is better to die fighting (like the village chief) than to consult the gods. The film's pressing communiqué is that the gods of African traditional religion can only distract people from fashioning their own fates. In *Guelwaar* (1992), Sembène offers his most inflammatory theodical implication via a confab between a prostitute and a priest: that sex workers are more dependable sources of sustenance toward African survival than God. Sembène goes so far as to designate two prostitutes as sole patrons of their fathers' religious pilgrimages. Sembène's last film *Moolaade* (2004) reveals the ways in which traditional authority intersects with religion to perpetuate evil and suffering with a resolution that calls for a rejection of aspects of tradition and religion that oppress. In this film, Sembène codes the traditional practice of female circumcision as irrational, dehumanizing, and evil. Hence, *Moolaade* suggests a modern makeover that affords girls and women free choices about their bodies and their lives. Sembène exhorts Africans not to submit blindly to tradition but to have the courage to think and live for themselves. Throughout his oeuvre, Sembène's treatment of theodicy offers signifying transparency and precision concerning the costs of a changing African landscape, and secularizing intelligibility regarding what he perceives to be ameliorative solutions to African suffering. In other words, if Sembène's films spell out questions, challenges, and contradictions regarding what it means to be African and modern in the postcolonial era, the elucidations they endorse require religion, tradition, and God to play diminished roles.

BOROM SARRET

N. Frank Ukadike (1994: 71) describes the significance of Sembène's short film *Borom Sarret*: "When it was exhibited at the 1963 Tours International Festival in France, it not only made history as the first black African film seen internationally by a paying audience but it also made an impression on the international scene by winning a prize. . . ." Similarly, Manthia Diawara reveals how Sembène's first filmic effort inaugurated a new post-independence era of black African films:

> Sembène's discovery was that film could be used to give Africa back its dignity, just as it had been used by colonialists and racist films to destroy the image of black people. The quest for dignity in *Borom Sarret* reflects the culture and

politics of the independence movements of the 1960s, with Ghana and Guinea as the most illustrious examples. (2011: 83)

Ukadike and Diawara recognized *Borom Sarret*'s role in orchestrating a postcolonial black African cinematic aesthetic. We consider here the short film's underappreciated theodical significance.

Set in Senegal, like most of Sembène's later features, the short's opening moment displays the busyness of city life to foreshadow a confrontation between the challenges of modern Africa and the vulnerability of peasant life. The protagonist's profession in this new milieu is hailing riders in a horse-driven cart. Shots of a mosque are followed by the first images of the cart driver in his prayer circle at his humble home. After beseeching Allah's blessing and fortification, the cart driver puts on amulets, Sembène's clever allusion to the protagonist's fusion of Islam and traditional African spirituality. Years later, his fellow Senegalese director Amadou Salaam Seck makes a similar move in *Saaraba* (1988) when a Muslim villager obeys the counsel of a witch doctor to sacrifice his own daughter, an act fortunately prevented when another villager intervenes to stop him. Both examples offer contexts in which to see cultural adulteration at play, revealing that postcolonial Africa's adherence to the dictates and practices of a major world religion does not inevitably expunge the cultural memories of its religious past. Sembène revisits such a synthesis in a later scene of *Borom Sarret* and other future films. Beyond its subtle displays of religious syncretism, what makes *Borom Sarret* relevant to theodicy is the way in which its allusions to God coincide with evidence of God's non-intervention in the lives of the cart driver and suffering people he encounters. The greater message Sembène conveys is that Allah is unable to mediate the vicissitudes of peasant life in an increasingly modern Africa.

The first words we hear from the cart driver come in prayer, "Merciful Allah, protect me and mine from the Law and the Infidels." Shortly after his entreaty, his wife blesses him before he goes off to work, "May God be with you!" But what follows her benediction is a sad reminder, "We've no food for lunch." Sembène here cleverly contrasts the notion of God's blessing with deprivation, as the protagonist must head off to work leaving his wife and child with nothing to eat. Another reference to God comes after his first passengers fail to pay him, leaving the cart driver frustrated as he ponders, "How will I feed my horse and family?" But he quells his own inquiry by adding, "Let's wait for God's mercy." And not long after he assesses his predicament of nonpayment, the protagonist comes across a crippled beggar beseeching assistance, "For the grace of God, have pity on me." Instead of responding, the cart driver rather callously compares the preponderance of beggars to flies. In a later scene, the protagonist transports a foreigner and a small corpse to the cemetery where the foreigner is told he lacks the proper certificate to entomb his child, whereupon the driver heads off in his cart, abandoning his passenger at the cemetery. The deserted and dejected foreigner then contemplates, "God knows I'm a believer! What's to become of my child?"

So with these four allusions to God—the wife's appeal to God's blessing, the cart driver's own reference to God's mercy, the beggar's petition for God's grace, and the foreigner's reminder to himself that God knows he is a believer—we see situations offering no indication of divine mediation concerning their troubling plights. In the most heartbreaking case, the foreigner is twice abandoned by God, in the loss of his child and not being able to bury him because of bureaucratic requisites. The protagonist's acknowledgment that beggars are everywhere also challenges the notion of God's grace on their behalf. The wife's divine blessing on her husband is mocked only seconds later with recognition of her deprivation. People appeal to God but do not seem to receive any help from above. But a later occurrence in *Borom Sarret* more explicitly brings to light the film's import for theodicy by exposing the protagonist's disorientation and lack of preparedness for modern Africa.

This crucial scene comes when the cart driver agrees to take a black man clad in a business suit to the downtown area of the city, which restricts horse-drawn carts. Initially reluctant, the cart driver disregards his better judgment after the passenger promises him both remuneration and protection through his powerful contacts in downtown Dakar. As they approach the restricted area, the protagonist petitions both the saints of his traditional gods and the God of his Muslim faith for safety. But none of those spiritual sources safeguard him, as a policeman almost immediately stops the cart. The protagonist suffers the humiliation of the policeman's reprimand, a fine, and desecration of his medal when the policeman steps on it after it accidentally drops to the ground. More demoralizing is how the protagonist has to sell his cart to pay the fine. Instead of employing his powerful connections as promised, the bourgeois passenger sneaks off without even paying the fare. So as a result of his venture into the most modern part of the city at the behest of a bourgeois passenger who offered him false promises of protection and money, a destitute peasant sinks to a more desperate socioeconomic plight, a devolution no doubt replete with symbolism for poor and uneducated people in postcolonial Africa. The cart driver's demise, like the foreigner's inability to bury his child because he didn't have the correct certificate, signifies the difficulties peasants face as they navigate an increasingly bureaucratic and intricate modern Africa. And the man in the suit represents how Senegalese elites can exacerbate peasant vulnerability, a characterization confirmed by the dejected protagonist's reflection on his passenger's grift, "They all know how to read and lie!"

But in addition to indicating a contrast between traditional and modern black African life, this seminal scene offers a salient statement on theodicy: God (and the gods) won't help vulnerable peasants escape the iron cage of bureaucracy. The cart driver prayed both to his gods of traditional African religion and to his God of Islamic faith and none were able to protect him in downtown Dakar. And as the cart-less protagonist heads home, his despondence reaches suicidal proportions as he deliberates, "I might as well die." When he gets home and updates his wife about their bleak situation, she responds by promising they will eat that night upon her return. And so the last vista of Sembène's first film shows the driver standing in his prayer circle watching his wife leave the compound. It is no accident that *Borom Sarret* ends with the protagonist standing in the very same place Sembène introduces him in the film's opening moments, his prayer circle. But this time he doesn't offer any prayers because they have already proven futile. His dejected demeanor reiterates the film's message about the protagonist's appeals to God—they do nothing to feed his family nor help similarly vulnerable peasants overcome the harsh realities of modern life.

MANDABI

If his first feature film *Black Girl* (1966)—which doesn't mention God or religion—offers an even gloomier treatment of black African vulnerability than his inaugural short film *Borom Sarret*, Sembène's second feature *Mandabi* (1968) presents a lighter but equally pessimistic view of the mires that marginalized Senegalese citizens must circumnavigate in modern Africa. *Mandabi*'s protagonist is a poor and illiterate peasant named Ibrahima Dieng who receives a money order from a nephew working in France. The entire plot revolves around the challenges Ibrahima encounters attempting to cash it. Immediately after his two wives learn about the money order they purchase food and clothes on credit. Word of Ibrahima's good fortune quickly spreads throughout his surroundings, as people make petitions before he is even able to turn the money order into cash. Ibrahima procures funds on credit to cash it, thus adding to the money order's liability. The protagonist discovers it is more difficult than he had imagined satisfying the administrative requirements.

When Ibrahima tries to retrieve the money order from the post office, the attendant tells him he needs an official identification card, something he is unaware exists. When he goes to his local precinct to get an identification card, the clerk tells him he needs a birth certificate and photos, neither of which Ibrahima has so he has to go to city hall to pick up his birth certificate and on the way gets ripped off trying to secure a photo. In an interview with Francoise Pfaff (1984: 128), Sembène discusses his protagonist's quagmire:

> He is caught in a situation that goes beyond him because he has always thought he was, as Ibrahima Dieng, a personality in his neighborhood where everybody knows him. But as he goes out of his own traditional culture, he goes to a modern culture where the identity card has nothing to do with internal autonomy within a group where he was not an anonymous person. Out of his culture, he becomes an anonymous person. In this context, identity papers are needed.

The money order is the film's mechanism to expose how ill-prepared a poor illiterate peasant is to meet the mounting necessities of a modernizing Africa. The film's ending proves tragic when a family friend named Mbaye swindles Ibrahima out of the money order.

Like in *Borom Sarret*, Islam is part of the backdrop in *Mandabi*, as Ibrahima conducts himself as a righteous Muslim. Early in the film he scolds his wives for failing to wake him up for Friday prayers. Intermittently, we see Ibrahima greeting his neighbors with references to Islam and giving praise to Allah as often as he can. But Allah does nothing to help this illiterate believer negotiate the rigors of modern Africa. Instead we see tricksters manipulating religion to take advantage of him. The first example involves a street beggar who pleads with Ibrahima in the name of Allah to have mercy on her because she desperately needs bus fare to take care of urgent matters. Ibrahima obliges and gives her money from the stash he borrowed. But later that day when Ibrahima comes across her again, she does not recognize him from their earlier encounter and approaches him with the same pitch, which incites outrage from Ibrahima. What must have been most shocking to Ibrahima (and Sembène's Senegalese viewers) is that this female beggar appeals to the holy name of Allah for deceptive purposes.

But a more consequential manipulation of Allah comes later when Ibrahima, still unable to solve the bureaucratic puzzle, signs over power of attorney to his bourgeois friend Mbaye to cash the money order. The protagonist naïvely assumes Allah has finally provided a solution to his problem. A few days later, Ibrahima returns to his friend's home only to hear Mbaye rather cavalierly proclaim that after he cashed the money order he was the victim of a pickpocket and that all the money is gone. In an attempt to bolster the credibility of his story, Mbaye asserts that Allah is his witness that he was the victim of such a crime. Ibrahima is devastated and pleads with Mbaye for mercy, reminding his friend he has to feed his family and that the money order wasn't even all his to spend. Then Mbaye callously asks Ibrahima, "Don't you believe in Allah?" as if to suggest that Ibrahima must accept Mbaye's story because of his claim that Allah is his witness. Earlier scenes clue viewers in to Mbaye's sinister motive for bankrupting his friend Ibrahima.

Francoise Pfaff (1984: 138) sizes up the protagonist's fate quite succinctly: "The victim of a world he does not understand, Ibrahima becomes an existential and isolated anti-hero, ill-equipped to function in modern society." Like the peasant protagonist of *Borom Sarret*, Ibrahima is bamboozled by a slick bourgeois predator, and left in a situation that inspires contemplation on how poor vulnerable people will survive the postcolonial African landscape. Going a step further than the slick businessman in *Borom Sarret* who only rips off the cart driver of his fare, the bourgeois grifter in *Mandabi* makes an appeal to Allah to sanction his exploitative deed. With *Mandabi*'s tragic ending, Sembène not only reveals religion and Allah as inept forces in the context of African survival, but also demonstrates how they function to undergird peasant vulnerability. Hence, *Mandabi* points viewers to an uncertain postcolonial African future where peasants fall prey to manipulative representations of Allah.

EMITAI

If *Mandabi* displays how shifty educated people can utilize God for selfish gain, then *Emitai* (1971) offers a supplementary critique of divine representation as false consciousness. Inspired by a historical incident during World War II, the film delineates how a Senegalese village, having already experienced the loss of its youngest and strongest men through forced enlistment in French regiments, decides to resist additional demands from French military officers to provide them with their rice harvest. The French officials, accompanied by African soldiers at their command, resort to extreme measures to acquire the rice harvest from the villagers. The focal point of the film is how the gods of African traditional religion distract male elders of the village from offering a courageous response, and hence the gods become part of the problem.

Sembène discloses in a 1971 interview, "The meaning of [*Emitai*] is that it belongs to the people to decide about their destiny, not the gods" (Hennebelle 2008: 22). The standoff with the French raises the question of what to do when faced with an oppressive situation, and from Sembène's appraisal, the women of the village perform far better than the male elders in answering such an inquiry. Instead of surrendering, the women hide the rice harvest and are forced by the French officials to languish in the hot sun as recompense for their cat and mouse game. Sembène discusses this in a 1972 interview with *Cineaste*: "I just wanted to show, by gestures, that the women are tired, their legs are tired, their arms are burdened—one woman has the sun shining in her eyes, another two are sleeping. All this is shown in silence, but it is a silence that speaks" (Weaver 2008: 30). But while the women suffer under the beaming rays of the sun, the male elders consult the gods, thus wasting precious time and appearing quite cowardly in contrast to the women's calculated defiance.

However, some of the elders do question the utility of their gods in responding to the pressing threat by French colonial power. For example, alluding to the forced enlistment of the village's young men, one of the elders ponders, "I wonder if our gods see the situation we are in. I am worried about their silence." And later, their frustrated chief asks his comrades:

> But where were the gods when the whites razed the village? When the whites took our sons for their war? Remember, Kabebe? You remained all day long tied in the sun. Where were our gods? We all suffered the same humiliation. Where were our gods? Where are they now?

The chief's growing skepticism eventually leads him to form his own makeshift band of warriors to fight against the soldiers operating under French command. Their small resistance is quickly crushed and the chief is fatally wounded in the struggle. The chief's dying conviction is the film's theme: that it is better to die fighting in dignity than to appear weak and ineffectual in offering sacrifices to gods.

One should evaluate the indecisiveness of most of the male elders of *Emitai* against the valor exemplified by villagers in *The North Star* (1943), a popular Samuel Goldwyn film. The fact that Sembène studied filmmaking in Moscow only heightens the likelihood that a popular pro-Soviet movie like *The North Star* is on his radar when he writes and directs *Emitai*. As with Sembène's film, the plot of *The North Star* centers on a village's response to European aggression during World War II. But the Soviet village responds quite actively and heroically compared to the dithering elders of *Emitai*. When Nazi troops invade the North Star village, the residents don't spend time praying for direction but instead offer an immediate call for resistance, as illustrated by the village leader's speech after the first round of German airstrikes:

> Comrades, we have good reason to know that our country is at war. In our small village alone thirty people have been injured, eleven people killed. But this is not a time for mourning. It is time for revenge. We will divide into two groups, each to do his duty from this day until death.

The first group is composed of guerilla fighters who hide in the village and take the Nazis by surprise, and the second consists of people who burn all the homes and destroy everything before the Nazis arrive. So when faced with a formidable foreign challenger, the North Star villagers quickly mobilize a resistance force, burning all of their assets to spite the approaching Nazi ground troops, while simultaneously committing themselves to die fighting with dignity. And as the film unfolds, fearless villagers transport crucial supplies to guerilla soldiers and continue to resist the Nazi occupation. Even the Nazi colonel calls attention to the valor of North Star villagers. The effort of the resistance fighters proves successful in withstanding the Nazi takeover and thus provides, at least presumably from Sembène's perspective, a useful counterexample on how to meet a challenge with strategic action, and how to die with dignity.

Sembène's film *Emitai* has a far more tragic ending than *The North Star*, as the French destroy the village without facing much opposition from the gods of the elders. Thus, the only heroes in *Emitai* are the chief and a few accompanying men who die fighting, and the women of the village who are never seen contemplating the gods. With *Emitai*, Sembène exhorts his contemporaries against making appeals to divine intervention to solve the most pressing problems of their country and continent. This message exemplifies the filmmaker's overall assignation to human hands the solutions for problems plaguing Africans. Sembène reiterates this message in an interview discussing the movie: "The gods never prevented colonialism from establishing itself; they strengthened us for inner resistance but not for an armed resistance. When the enemy is right there, he has to be fought with weapons" (Ghali 2008: 80).

The film rekindles a historical memory within the national consciousness of victims of European aggression in a way that converts a siege on a small village into a crime against Senegalese and black African humanity. From Sembène's vantage point, the village's suffering has symbolic tentacles reaching Ghanaians, Nigerians, Cameroonians, and other compatriots in the African nations that agonized under colonization. If *Emitai* reimagines a mid-twentieth-century episode of collective African trauma, then his later film *Ceddo* continues the cultural work of trauma signification by extrapolating theodical talking points from a more distant past.

CEDDO

Ceddo (1977) may be Sembène's most critically acclaimed and controversial film. Set in the eighteenth century, the conflict driving the film is an African king's conversion to Islam and how his imam's edicts defy the traditional way of life in the village. The villagers who wish to retain traditional religion and culture clash with the imam and so they kidnap the king's daughter in protest.

Slavery is an important undercurrent, as a European trader intermittently barters rifles and gunpowder for villagers. The fact that the imam's disciples are armed with rifles not only divulges the cleric's growing strength in the village but also implicates the imam's past dealings with the white local trader. With the imam's dirty hands, Sembène intimates that both black Africans and Islam colluded with Europeans in the transatlantic slave trade.

The brave outsiders (or ceddo) who challenge the king's authority disclose how the imam's oppressive practices and bartering of villagers to secure weapons are the catalysts for their rebellion. Fighting against the imam and Islam means fighting for the African people, as they see it. But toward the end of the film when the ceddo are under siege by the imam's jihad and face a clear and present choice: convert to Islam and accept the imam's oppressive practices or arm themselves to resist, the ceddo choose the latter option—which means doing the same thing for which they excoriated the imam, trading their own people to the local European retailer. This catch-22 that the ceddo encounter skillfully uncovers how Africans selling Africans can exist within an intra-village (or inter-village) arms race for power and existential survival.

After the imam crushes the ceddo, kills the king, and secures total control over the village, he issues dictates demanding absolute compliance to Islam. And it is during his mass conversion ceremony that the king's daughter returns from captivity and kills the imam to avenge her father's death. But the film ends with no indication that the imam's death will diminish Islam's grip over the village. When one considers that the overwhelming majority of people in Sembène's country embrace Islam, one can imagine that the death of the imam in *Ceddo* was like a drop in the bucket concerning the historical trajectory of Islam's presence in Senegal.

As an aesthetic footnote to Sembène's treatment of theodicy, each sequence portraying the selling and processing of villagers into slavery features black gospel music. Similarly, when the imam's disciples burn down the village, we hear the same gospel tune. Perhaps Sembène's use of gospel music is a subtle jab at Christianity, which historically played a far more critical role in the transnational slave trade than Islam. Or maybe a better answer in the context of theodicy is to envision this anachronistic musical infusion as Sembène's attempt at irony. The object of worship in the hopeful song does nothing to remedy the hopeless situation that the newly christened slave encounters as she is primed for an arduous trek to the coast followed by a much more grueling sail across the Atlantic. But more relevant to our conversation is the way Sembène introduces African and Islamic culpability into the collective trauma of the transatlantic slave trade.

In the PBS documentary *The African Americans: Many Rivers to Cross* (2013), Henry Louis Gates confirms the important role Africans played in the transatlantic slave trade: "Though some find it difficult to face, the crucial role of Africans in the slave trade is now well documented. Historians estimate that the overwhelming majority of the slaves shipped to the New World were captured and sold by African Kingdoms." Gates's comment points toward the opportunistic African kings, merchants, and powerbrokers who participated in various stages of the slave trade by seizing, transporting, and selling other Africans to European dealers at handsome profits (Davis 2003; Rediker 2007). Films like *Band of Angels* (1957), *The Legend of Nigger Charlie* (1972), *Amistad* (1997), and *The Amazing Grace* (2006), along with the television mini-series *Roots* (1977) offer poignant optics or verbal accounts indicating the transatlantic trade's dependency on Africans abducting Africans and trading them to Europeans. Those gripping sequences may be shocking to viewers who presumed only Europeans were to blame for the tragedy of slavery. Ousmane Sembène is the first black African filmmaker to represent the intra-racial mechanics of bartering African bodies.

If Sembène had stopped at the accomplishment of offering an early filmic recapitulation of African involvement in the slave trade, it would still be a noteworthy feat, especially when considering his status as one of Africa's cherished artists. But the most direct and commanding statement about evil and black suffering that we can extract from *Ceddo* makes a more provocative contribution by situating Islamic power within the exploitation of black bodies to secure weapons to take over villages—an even more audacious move for an African filmmaker who reps a Muslim country. If his earlier film *Emitai* converts local suffering into a collective trauma of continental colonization, then *Ceddo* utilizes equally powerful imagery to connote collective black African trauma as homegrown and fertilized by Islamic aggression.

One might speculate that many Senegalese citizens were not pleased with their most noteworthy artist portraying their principal religious representative (imam) as an ambitious, power-hungry, slave trader and manipulator in *Ceddo*. Perhaps a tense response by Senegalese nationalists was the real culprit behind the country's ban of the film upon its initial release rather than an alleged dispute over how to spell *Ceddo*. Perhaps this also explains why Sembène, in the midst of depicting great religious dysfunction and mayhem on the part of both Muslims and Christians in *Guelwaar* (1992), redeems the role of an imam by having him act bravely toward achieving the conflict's resolution. So while Muslims appear in *Guelwaar* as erratic and violent, at one point so out of control that they pose a serious threat to the Senegalese police, their imam appears as a calming presence and man of peace, unlike his callous clerical counterpart in *Ceddo*.

MOOLAADE

In an interview with Samba Gadjigo in 2004, Sembène commented on how his goal in *Moolaade* was to present a clash of values:

> In *Moolaade*, there are two values in conflict with each other: one the traditional, which is the female genital excision. This goes a long way back before Jesus, before Mohammed, to the times of Herodotus. It's a tradition. It was instituted as a value in order to, in my opinion, continue the subjugation of women. The other value, as old as human existence: the right to give protection to those who are weaker. When these two values meet, cross, multiply, clash, you see the symbolism of our society: modern elements and elements that form part of our cultural foundation. On top of these add the elements that belong to the superstructure, notably religion. These are the waters in which this group, this film, sails. (Gadjigo 2008: 191)

The "female genital excision" that Sembène references as a tool of female subjugation ignites the fundamental conflict of the film. A new cohort of young girls is scheduled to undergo this practice rooted in tradition and religious sanctimony, but six girls break away from the group before the procedure is accomplished. As Sembène points out, the film's other value involves the moolaade, which allows a weaker party to seek the promise of protection from a more powerful party. Two of the six young girls disappear early on while the four remaining dissenters petition for the moolaade with a middle-aged woman named Collé, who honors their request. But the film unfolds in a manner that makes it less of a balancing act of African values and more of an indictment against a regrettable African tradition. For even as its invocation is crucial to the plot's formation, the moolaade as a traditional mechanism offers no practical strategy, discursive repudiation, or systematic reevaluation of female genital mutilation. Sembène's unfolding plot instead issues a powerful challenge against excision through modern values.

As Sembène indicates with his above reference to superstructure, Islam plays an important role in providing religious legitimization to female genital excision throughout the film. Village elders play up the religious connotations of the ritual, even though the Koran and Islamic teachings lend no official authority to the purported necessity of mutilating clitorises. And while proponents infuse the ritual with spiritual efficacy, the film's heroine Collé rejects all discursive attempts to sanctify what she perceives as gratuitous incisions. For instance, when an elder woman reminds Collé that she "purified" Collé long ago, Collé responds by acknowledging that the elder woman is the one who cut her up. From Collé's perspective, cutting a young girl's clitoris doesn't result in the girl's purity; it only brings her pain. Collé is similarly subversive when she challenges the villagers' attribution of the practice to Islam, arguing that millions of uncircumcised Muslim women travel to Mecca for their yearly pilgrimage, thus rejecting the notion of its universality to Muslim communities.

In addition to using her words, Sembène deploys Collé's body in the service of recoding female circumcision as evil, dangerous, and bound to produce great harm to its victims. Complications from the resulting wounds of her excision later made childbearing so difficult that she lost two babies and her only surviving child had to be delivered through Cesarean section. The film's most heavy-handed recoding of the ritual comes aesthetically through juxtapositions of present-day discomfort Collé experiences during intercourse against the flashback of Collé as a child going through the ritual. Within this penetrating sequence, we see the pain and trauma expressed on the face of young Collé, followed by close-ups of her present day passionless gaze during sex with her husband, thus confirming that Collé's cut clitoris consigns her to a lifetime of callous coitus. When her husband finishes depositing semen into her, Collé is sore and bloody and must soak herself, adding more clarity on how female genital mutilation is not only dehumanizing but also physically harmful, erotically unpleasant, and existentially malicious: the product of an old way of thinking that needs to be jettisoned in a new modern Africa. For the pain and loss she endured (and continues to suffer) due to the ritual, Collé refused to allow her own daughter, now a teenager, to be circumcised as a young girl.

Eventually the villagers learn that the two missing girls committed suicide by jumping into a well. And when the men discover their corpses, instead of assigning culpability to their ritual, they blame Collé for discharging a subversive spirit in the village that inspired these girls to reject the ritual. Similar tragedy ensues when the mother of one of the four girls residing under Collé's protection lures her daughter away from Collé's home to have her circumcised. During the procedure a complication occurs that ends the girl's life, making her the film's third young casualty of the ritual. The dead girl's mother, once a staunch advocate of excision, now basks in guilt and grief.

Angered by Collé's defiance, the men confiscate all radios in the village as an attempt to protect their traditional way of life, which they claim has been adulterated by outside ideas. The village chief's son, who just returned from living in Paris, can only laugh at the desperate efforts of the men, remarking that disconnecting Africans from world communities is not possible in the times in which they live. Perhaps this silly radio ban is Sembène's subtle jab at the Senegalese officials who issued a similarly implausible injunction against *Ceddo* more than a decade earlier as possibly the desperate attempt of traditionalists to obstruct his modern deliberations. Beyond its usefulness toward settling old scores, Sembène's satirical radio ban offers an unexpectedly positive depiction of media as mechanisms connecting African villagers to larger and freer communities dispersing practices and perspectives beyond the confines of tradition. The socialist filmmaker of earlier years might not have offered such a positive role for media, but in the twilight of his career, a more pragmatic Sembène, like the chief's son, recognizes that dialogue with outsiders is important for the transformation of identities toward a more liberal consciousness.

The chief's son plays an important role in the film's negotiation of modernity against the village's recalcitrant grip of African tradition. Sembène's camera work catches a close-up of the crisp bills the son uses to pay his father's debts, money that appears in contrast to the crinkled bills we see other villagers use to purchase items from the local shop. His time in Paris provides him with both new ideas and new money in contrast to the traditional ideas and fiscal deprivation that persists in the men of the village. For even the most powerful man in the village has to wait for his son's return from Paris to pay his bills, heightening the contrast between modern Europe and the traditional village. A conflict later develops when the chief objects to his son's choice to take Collé's daughter as his bride, simply because she is shunned by the elders for remaining uncircumcised. The son's directive for the chief to mind his own business provokes the chief to physically assault and disown him. In this tense exchange, Sembène shows how a modern ideal of individuality inspires the son to rebuff his father's attempt to manipulate him through religion and tradition. Sembène's message is clear: the next generation of African leadership must be willing to come into conflict with the status quo and discard hegemonic aspects of past tradition to forge a path toward a new liberal society.

Moolaade presents the female circumcision ritual and its legitimating religious and traditional discourses as practices rooted in male hegemony, exposing how both social customs and religious perspectives undergird such domination. The heroine of the film is publicly flogged by her husband in a last-ditch effort for men of the village to uphold patriarchy. But Collé receives the beating without relenting to their demands and hence renders male power as desperate and ineffective. With this film Sembène mocks a kind of paternalistic African male privilege rooted in African tradition, revealing its frantic strivings for supremacy and relevance along with its imminent expiration date, while situating it as part of the collective trauma of black African suffering. And like other Sembène films, the men also lack moral authority as they represent the futility of attempts to preserve their power in a new era connecting Africans to world populations and new ideas. The local shop owner Mercenary, the only other moderately heroic man in the film, is like the chief's son, also well-traveled and more modern than most of the villagers. The men later kill Mercenary as retaliation for putting a stop to Collé's beating.

Moolaade represents the last page of a new pragmatic chapter in Sembène's political vision, calling less for a socialist revolution and more for symbiotic engagement between Africa and world communities: an interaction where ideas are freely exchanged, democratic values are extolled, modernity is tempered with the best of African cultural values, and people are able to thrive and maximize their potential as autonomous citizens. Whereas Sembène's early films use dark colors to paint the canvas of modern Africa's bureaucratic, political, and fiscal relationship to its poor masses, in an astonishing reversal Sembène's last films offer more hopeful visions of the modern African person, nation, and continent. The film's theodical takeaway point insists that radical critique of African tradition (and religion) is a means by which to confront evil and assuage suffering in Africa.

GUELWAAR

Guelwaar has a premise that could easily mark the film as absurdist. A Catholic activist known as Guelwaar dies and his corpse gets mixed up with the cadaver of a recently deceased Muslim. Gora, the chief of police, investigates and eventually uncovers that Guelwaar was erroneously buried in a Muslim cemetery where the newly departed Muslim is thought to be located. The rest of the movie stages the conflict between the family and friends of the dead Muslim who trust their loved one is resting in his designated grave, and Guelwaar's family, friends, and supporters who believe Guelwaar is there and want to recover his body to administer a proper Christian burial. While one might predict that mixed-up corpses make for rollicking amusement, *Guelwaar* is by no means a slapstick film. Tensions are high, as Muslims vow jihad against anyone who digs up the grave. Finally, it is the imam who takes Gora to the precise location where the Muslims insist their comrade is buried so the police chief can confirm that the Catholic agitator is mistakenly resting in the Muslim's place. The imam brings calm and resolution to the standoff after his followers have stirred up threats and a few acts of violence.

The misplaced burial and concomitant religious conflict serve as Sembène's device for developing a film that speaks to political, social, and economic issues of postcolonial African life. Guelwaar's missing corpse is not nearly as important to the film's overall message as Guelwaar's life as a political agitator. While Guelwaar is no idealized character, as a flashback shows a disgruntled husband chasing a younger and naked Guelwaar out of his mistress's house, what Guelwaar stands for is the theme of the film revealed in perhaps one of Sembène's strongest messages to his continental compatriots: Africans must reject foreign aid. Accompanying this message of African self-reliance is the film's powerful denunciation against African leaders.

Guelwaar's son Barthelemy, a sophisticated man who abandoned Senegal at a young age to live in Paris, has returned to his homeland to bury his father. Early in the film, his interactions with Gora leave him lampooned as an ex-compatriot and lover of all things European. But as the film progresses, Barthelemy becomes the film's insightful guide to an educated man's frustrations with postcolonial Africa. *Guelwaar* ends with Barthelemy and the police chief no longer verbal combatants but unified in their analysis of African depravity and united in their belief that African youth hold the power to a positive future. The two men share common contempt for the misappropriation of foreign aid by African officials and are equally disdainful of the greed of African leaders who hide their assets overseas and enjoy jetsetter lifestyles at the expense of the people.

Along with its discourses on foreign aid and its trenchant denunciations against African corruption, *Guelwaar* has important implications for theodicy. Through a penetrating dialogue between Helene, a prostitute in Dakar, and a priest named Father Leon, we see the inability of religion and God to offer solutions to African economic hardship.

The scene begins when Helene, a friend of Guelwaar's daughter Sophie, appears to pay her respects to Sophie's family during their time of mourning. Helene enters the compound clad in an elegant evening gown that is a bit too chic for the ceremonial gathering. So upon her entry, she draws immediate attention and Father Leon sizes her up. Helene informs the priest that she works with Sophie in Dakar; significant information as Father Leon knows how Sophie makes a living. In response, Father Leon asks Helene if her parents are still alive, as if to suggest she is shaming them—a furtive jab at her chosen profession. Sensing where the priest is going with his inquiry, Helene reveals that her parents are alive and then jumps right into her story: "After getting my diploma, I went to Dakar in the hope of finding a job. I searched for six months but there were none to be had. So I became a registered prostitute." Before the priest is able to offer one word of condemnation Helene discloses:

> No one in my family has to beg. My young brother has enrolled for his first year of medical studies. I must help him. I paid for my father to go to Yamoussoukro for the consecration of Notre Dame de la Paix. Father, you see this? [She grabs hold of the small silver cross she keeps on her necklace.] He brought this back for me. I'm told the Pope blessed it. Sophie too paid for her father's pilgrimage. You know where he went? Jerusalem.

Helene here summarizes how her chosen vocation derives out of heroic necessity to support her family, revealing that she will sponsor her sibling in medical school, and more surprisingly, that she already financed her father's visit to the capital city of the Ivory Coast. The basilica in Yamoussoukro is a notable hajj for African Catholics, and so Father Leon is speechless at the proposition that this young prostitute is the patron behind her father's pilgrimage there, allowing him to even meet the pope. Father Leon listens to Helene while slowly pacing and finally replies, "It's good to talk. Did you go and greet the pope when he came to Dakar?" Helene responds, "Yes, I was one of the first at the airport. Judge not, so that ye be not judged," an exhortation the priest acknowledges is in fact biblical before adding that all he asks of her is to dress more decently because "this house is in mourning." The scene ends with Father Leon taking Helene away to find clothing better suited to the somberness of the occasion.

What is most telling about this exchange is that Father Leon's reproach is limited to Helene's attire and offers no commentary on her profession. Sembène constructs Helene's career choice as one emanating out of deprivation, revealing the young woman's unsuccessful attempt to find other work. But Sembène goes a step further by rendering Helene as the sole supporter of her family. With this inclusion of Helene's patronage of her father's religious pilgrimage, Sembène makes a subversive jab at none other than God. Consider the irony of a man depending on his daughter's sex work to make the most important religious pilgrimage an African Catholic can undertake on his continent. Similarly, Helene informs Father Leon that Sophie funded Guelwaar's pilgrimage to Jerusalem, a revelation that leaves the priest equally thunderstruck. Nowhere does the priest interject that God could have stepped in to provide the money for Helene's and Sophie's fathers to make their religious hajjes so that their daughters would not have to use immoral activity (from the priest's perspective) to fund them. Nor does he challenge Helene's claim that no one in her family has to beg because of her support. The priest simply has no retort to Helene's testimony.

Helene's conversation with the priest is the most dramatic of several allusions to sex work. Earlier in the film, Sophie reminds her younger brother Aloys that her work in Dakar keeps everyone fed. And later, we see a flashback of Guelwaar with his wife Marie discussing Sophie's profession, seemingly for the first time. When Marie tells him, "Sophie works as a whore to feed us," Guelwaar responds, "Don't you know that I prefer to see her as a whore than to see her panhandling? Rather dead than begging." Marie then insists their daughter's profession desecrates her dignity as a mother, adding, "I would prefer to feed myself from charity than to know about the life my daughter leads in Dakar." But Guelwaar rejoins that he would rather die than to live off foreign aid and thus he affirms his daughter's profession. And later when Father Leon accuses Sophie's older brother Barthelemy of condoning Sophie's career choice, Barthelemy responds by acknowledging that while no one wants to see his family member resort to such a profession, Sophie's lifestyle is undeserving of condemnation because "there can be no virtue in destitution and poverty." Once again, Father Leon is left with no reply concerning the pragmatic prospect of prostitution as a means of survival in face of scarcity.

Sembène presents Helene and Sophie as gallant providers, an affront against both African masculinity and trust in divine provision. Sembène's message is clear: Sophie's and Helene's families must depend on their sex work rather than Senegal's economic infrastructure or God's manifold blessings to survive in postcolonial modern Africa. Perhaps this is the most provocative statement on the problem of evil and black suffering in Sembène's oeuvre. As the film validates the can-do spirit of two prostitutes who support their families, it indicts Senegal for not having an adequate source of jobs for its people, and lampoons God for not being able to provide remedial intervention within African destitution. Put more bluntly, prostitutes appear more able to feed their families than the God of their Christian fathers.

So if Sembène's earlier film *Emitai* contends that when facing conflict people should fight with dignity rather than waste time seeking divine intervention, then *Guelwaar* adds a new filament to that tapestry: that God is maladroit at absolving Africa's economic despair and so individuals must resort to their own wits to feed their families. Sembène uses the oldest and most denigrated profession he can muster up to articulate that even such a vilified occupation is more adept at meeting African needs in the face of economic despair than going to church, praying, and depending on God. Sembène's deployment of Sophie and Helene's entrepreneurial ingenuity foreshadows the filmmaker's optimistic embrace of corporate success in *Faat Kiné* (2001) and demonstrates his newfound pragmatism while unleashing caustic rebukes against African leadership and tradition.

FAAT KINÉ

Faat Kiné is about a woman in her late thirties named Kiné who is a successful executive running a gas station and the single parent of a daughter and son who recently completed high school. Kiné overcame difficult early years to raise her children with no male support and ascend from the lowly rank of gas station attendant to the privileged position she now enjoys at the controls of the entire enterprise. The film opens with the protagonist presented as a loving parent and successful single woman, but flashbacks reveal how her accomplishments would have been less predictable two decades earlier when she became pregnant with her first child Aby as the result of an affair with her teacher. The teen was kicked out of high school before she was to complete her final exams and receive her diploma, and the fact that her father disowned and tried to kill her was an even more severe blow to endure. A year later, Kiné became pregnant again by another man who deceived her and robbed her of her savings before landing himself in prison. Abandoned by both children's fathers and her own father, Kiné faced grim prospects.

Though Sembène's early films deftly depict how the whirlwind of modern change makes traditional African peasants quite vulnerable, *Faat Kiné* (like *Guelwaar* and *Moolaade*) presents tradition as problematic, while it celebrates modern ideals as requisite assets to reset Africa toward a more prosperous future, and features Kiné as the film's modern heroine. *Faat Kiné*'s first reproach against tradition occurs early during the flashback in which Kiné's father violently rejects her under the premise that her pregnancy brings shame to the family. Her father attempts to throw scalding hot water on her, but her mother, "Mammy," jumps in the way, subjecting her own back to severe burns. Sembène clarifies how traditional thinking about familial indignity sparked the father's rage, a stark contrast to how a modern parent might exhibit a more tempered response if his daughter were to become pregnant out of wedlock, exactly the kind of parent Kiné becomes as an affront against her own parents' traditionalism. Sembène's close-up of Mammy's charred torso offers a poignant visual indictment against traditional notions of shame. But surprisingly, the very same African tradition led Mammy herself to confer dishonor upon her daughter's pregnancies. As mother and daughter reflect on this difficult chapter in their past, Mammy reveals, "Every day I begged God to kill me so I could escape public shame. I also prayed for you to die." Kiné cries when Mammy relives this dark episode.

After Sembène confronts the excesses of tradition that inspire parents to wish death upon their child, he seamlessly transitions the mother–daughter confab from earlier shame to present-day pride in Kiné's accomplishments; a reversal in which Mammy's traditionalism is retroactively rebuked by her acknowledgment that her modern daughter has become the better parent. Mammy tells her daughter, "Kiné, thanks for everything. You gave your children what you did not have as a child." Mammy also declares, "Now I am your daughter. I praise you," a striking declaration from a once traditional African parent. Sembène also juxtaposes Mammy's past sins of parental shame against her present affirmation of her daughter's children. For it is obvious through their interactions that Aby and Djib, the grandchildren who initially brought Mammy near-suicidal disgrace under a traditional framework, now bring her great joy. Hence, it is equally apparent through her pronouncement of her daughter's resilience and success that Mammy now regrets her earlier dispensing of shame. Sembène uses the flashback to critique deductive formulations that lead to tragic consequences like violence and familial abandonment, while conveying the new modern African values that Kiné exemplifies that Mammy would celebrate (not condemn) in the birth of new grandchildren.

Sembène puts Kiné's current parental mechanics on display, as she negotiates with her children and supports their individuality. Even when they disagree, we never see Kiné employ African tradition as an apparatus of control but instead we see her utilize rational arguments in attempts to persuade them to accept her perspective. Aby and Djib possess great latitude in self-expression, even if at times they can emit hurtful sentiments to their mother. By contrasting Kiné's parental tactics of negotiation and free communication against her own parents' traditional understandings of familial shame, Sembène accentuates modern liberal values toward a flourishing African future. Sembène's message is clear: when shame becomes an obtrusive tool of tradition and religious sanctimony, then there is something profoundly wrong with your tradition and religious worldview. Kiné is a modern Muslim parent who does not offer shame or rejection, but only unconditional acceptance and love.

Faat Kiné also challenges tradition by celebrating its protagonist as the purveyor of a brazenly sexual brand of Senegalese feminism (Tsika 2015). Throughout the film, while her family assumes she would be more complete with a husband, Kiné appears as a well-adjusted single woman enjoying life and economic privilege. David Murphy and Patrick Williams (2007: 53–54) affirm the feminist power of Kiné and her friends: "Far from the virtuous virgins and wise old mothers of tradition, they are complex human beings with their own sexual and emotional needs, who are well capable of surviving without men." Kiné mischievously satisfies her sexual appetite by paying a suitor named Mass to service her, and when Mass's wife finds out about their arrangement and confronts Kiné in a parking lot with a violent threat, Kiné responds by spraying mace into her eyes and then scolds her, "When I need a man I pay your husband for his services. He is the king of gigolos and you are the queen of whores." So similar to how Kiné enjoys corporate power in the workplace to hire or fire male employees, she flaunts fiscal power in the bedroom to hire and fire a manservant to achieve her sexual desires. And one should also note how Kiné's Muslim identity does nothing to constrain her sexual indulgences.

But Sembène's most explicit contrast between tradition and modernity occurs during a heated exchange at Aby and Djib's graduation bash when Aby's father Gaye joins Djib's father B.O.P. in an attempt to pressure Djib to submit to African tradition by humbly soliciting his father's forgiveness. B.O.P. thinks he can appear in Djib's life for the first time and still demand respect. And Gaye, who himself remained distant from Aby's life, similarly believes he has the moral authority to compel his daughter's brother to honor his elders. When Djib resists, Gaye accuses him of being "a youth without moral values," a comment that generates sounds of dismay from Djib and Aby's friends who are now intently listening to this intergenerational altercation. Djib responds to Gaye's outburst:

> Monsieur Gaye, retired philosophy professor, excuse us. We, the loose youth! And you on the moral high grounds. Should I talk about your exploits at the all-girls high school? Twenty years ago, this pregnant student [pointing to his mother] was expelled from high school. Her father wanted to burn her. It was Mammy's back that shielded her from death.

Djib reveals how Gaye abandoned Kiné and Aby and fled to Gabon and then insists that "it is not I who should kneel down in front of this man [pointing to his father]. It is B.O.P. and Gaye who should kneel and ask this woman's [pointing to his mother] forgiveness." Gaye is so revved up by Djib's insolence that he attempts to strike him, but Djib intercepts his arm and then holds it in a vulnerable position. Kiné pleads with her son to let go, which he does only after declaring that Gaye and B.O.P. are the shame of Africa. In this shocking scene, Sembène not only allows a seventeen-year-old to disrespect his father and another elder but also to have the last word and moral high ground over the older men before Kiné kicks the two deadbeat dads out of the party. Sembène exposes African patriarchy for its hypocrisy, positioning young Djib as the marker where the filmmaker aims his hope for modern Africa.

A less contentious but equally relevant sequence exemplifying Sembène's assault against tradition involves a character named Alpha who has trouble making ends meet with his four wives. When Alpha comes to Kiné asking for money, she reminds him that he already owes her 30,000 francs and then refuses to help him. Alpha later asks Thiam for help, "Do something for me, Monsieur Thiam. God damn! That's the last time. You know what it's like to have a big family. It bleeds you dry!" But Thiam is unsympathetic, responding, "No, I don't know about big families. That was my grandfather's time. What I do know, however, is that you are inefficient and backward." Polygamy to Thiam is a practice lost in the past and not suited for the new modern African trajectory that he and Kiné navigate quite impressively. He scoffs at such an old-world way of living and Alpha responds to Thiam's mockery with the accusation, "You are the embryo of free market neocolonialism," the kind of jab that Sembène himself probably made many times against bourgeois people in his more radical days as a socialist. Thiam is unmoved by his friend's charge and responds, "You are an African from colonial times."

This exchange exposes how patriarchal African customs of the past like polygamy do not position people advantageously in the context of a competitive capitalist landscape. Alpha is broke, always borrowing from friends because he has not made the transition to a new modern Africa. Their attire intensifies the contrast of old and new Africa, as Alpha is dressed in traditional African apparel while Thiam sports an expensive business suit. And Thiam calls Alpha "inefficient and backward," terms that connote traditional ways that don't position Africans strategically toward a global capitalist future. Both Kiné and Thiam remain quite alert to their own freedom and power as independent and successful modern capitalists and unresponsive to the cultural constraints of a traditional past. This represents a striking turn in Sembène's oeuvre. In earlier films like *Borom Sarret*, *Mandabi*, and *Xala*, the African men clad in business suits were deceptive selfish elites who preyed on the vulnerable and uneducated poor masses. But in this film, the man in the business suit, Thiam, is the face of a more hopeful modern Africa. And what is Sembène's role for religion and God in this new Africa? He answers this question quite cleverly with the film-ending romance between Kiné, a Muslim, and Jean, a Christian.

Aby and Djib decide it is about time to find their mother a suitable mate. After a brief discussion, the siblings conclude that Jean, who is like an uncle to them, is the best candidate. Jean is a widower who runs his own successful business. Aby and Djib visit Jean to persuade him to marry their mother, at which Jean is surprised, not only because of their forwardness but also because, "I am a practicing Christian. Kiné is Muslim." Undaunted by Jean's religious affiliation, Djib cunningly rejoins, "Uncle, do you think Jesus Christ or Muhammad would be against your union?" and then utters a persuasive rationale for Jean to consider their proposition: "Uncle, you're a good person; an exemplary father. You are admirable, morally. And you raised your three children without a wife. Wonderful. You know Kiné. She is a fine woman. I would like to bring the two of you together." While Jean at this point has had enough of Djib and Aby's meddling and playfully kicks them out of his office, he never contradicts the cogency of Djib's ecumenical reasoning. It is important for viewers (particularly those outside of Senegal) to understand how radical a notion Djib conjures up with his insistence that Kiné's Muslim faith and Jean's Christian faith do not hamper matrimonial suitability. At the time of this film, a Senegalese Christian had to convert to Islam before marrying a Muslim. Djib proffers a progressive proposition for postcolonial Senegal (and Africa): that connubial compatibility need not be threatened by religious differentiation. And the fact that a seventeen-year-old makes this argument only underscores Sembène's hope in the youth for a new kind of modern Africa.

Djib and Aby don't relinquish attempts to harvest a new relationship between their Muslim mother and their Christian play-uncle. They concoct a plan with the help of Jean's son to get the two parents together at a restaurant. The plan works without a hitch, as Djib and Jean's son are delighted to watch their parents slow-dancing. But unknown to these plotting teens, the two parents had already consummated their relationship. We learn this when Kiné's girlfriends Mada and Amy tease Kiné by speculating that Jean will need Viagra for their inaugural encounter and Kiné informs them that she already had sexual congress with Jean at the hotel. When Djib and Jean's son optimistically begin to make plans for their parents' marital union, Jean's son says, "So let's legalize their partnership. But not at the mosque." Djib responds, "Not at the church either." And then both friends laugh and simultaneously blurt out their secular compromise: "At city hall!"

Kiné sneaks off with Jean to her bedroom and shortly afterwards we see the successful businesswoman sitting in her chair with her legs spread open inviting the successful businessman to come to her. The film ends with a close-up of Kiné's toes curling up perhaps to symbolize the toe-curling coitus the Muslim and Christian dyad will commence. But more important than the sex is the fact that the ending offers an ecumenical romance with implications for theodicy in the context of a new modern Africa. Such interfaith cooperation suggests modern Africa need not be hampered by religious divisions but instead occupy a new era where differences are minimized and commonalities toward human flourishing are prioritized. And the fact that both religions prohibit premarital sex and yet Kiné and Jean are still game for horizontal tango emphasizes how less obtrusive edges to Christianity and Islam enhance a new modern Africa. With the film culminating in sex, *Faat Kiné* offers the first hopeful ending of Sembène's oeuvre. From Sembène's perspective, if God and religion are to remain fruitful elements of African identity, secular boundaries must encase them.

CONCLUSION

This chapter begins by discussing how Swedish filmmaker Ingmar Bergman enjoyed several advantages over the father of African cinema that led to differences in their ability to generate intercontinental acclaim. One overlooked advantage is how Bergman did not feel as much pressure to tackle tendentious geopolitical problems as Sembène. Even though Bergman's career commenced shortly after Auschwitz, there were a bevy of filmmakers treating the social consequences of World War II and its impact on European life, ostensibly easing expectations of the Swede to do the same. Bergman's films, as complex as they can be, are situated within universal themes on the human condition. Conversely, postcolonial Senegal and Africa confronted challenges that Sembène felt compelled to address, first as an award-winning novelist and later as his country's and continent's first and most prominent black filmmaker. Accordingly, some of Sembène's brilliant moments may go entirely unnoticed by outsiders because his work is so firmly entrenched within the context of Senegalese and African survival.

A great example is how Sembène's film *Xala* (1975) contains social satire that demands more attentive interpretive work than most European films. When Rama, the outspoken daughter of the protagonist El Hadji, refuses to have a drink of Evian water with her father, there is more to this exchange than the insolence of youth and its disputations on liquid refreshment. Her refusal offers a subtle but powerful moment where a black nationalist woman confronts her father's obsession with all things European and separates herself from that colonial mindset by affirming all things indigenous to Senegal and Africa. The uninformed viewer could easily miss Sembène's subtle use of imported water as a site for the contestation of postcolonial identity and the assertion of African pride, while simultaneously ridiculing African elites as infatuated with Western artifacts. But you can rest assured knowing Senegalese elites felt the sting of Sembène's satire. Moments later when El Hadji questions why whenever he addresses his daughter in French she responds in Wolof, a Senegalese indigenous language, Sembène once again contrasts Rama's Pan-Africanist pride against her father's valorization of all things European. For Rama, African water and language are just fine by her even if they raise the ire of her father. Later in *Xala*, Sembène offers a quick shot of El Hadji's driver pouring a bottle of Evian into the car radiator shortly after he had similarly emptied imported water into a bucket for a street worker to wash the car. The inattentive viewer could once again miss this clever caricature of elitist improvidence.

These scenes from *Xala* offer just a glimpse of how the Senegalese filmmaker engages in incisive satire against African leadership and tradition. Conversely, Ingmar Bergman's films connect more easily with foreign audiences, and even his most mysterious musings are taken on the faith generated by his reputation for existential cleverness. Simply put, the African takes more swings against the status quo than does the Swede, as Sembène's satire uncovers the governmental, political, economic, social, and religious absurdities of his homeland. Sembène's approach is both diagnostic and prescriptive, using art to instruct, critique, and inspire a more promising future for a modernizing Africa. But a lack of awareness of those problems and struggles can cause one to miss Sembène's filmic ingenuity and resourcefulness.

Beyond asserting that Sembène's artistry stands on equal footing with the best of European filmmakers, this chapter shows that what has been most overlooked among Sembène's numerous accomplishments is his pensive treatment of theodicy. Serving as signposts for a culturally and religiously pluralistic modern Africa, Sembène's films express doubts concerning the ability and agility of God and religion to mitigate the suffering and oppression of black Africans. Whether it is diagnosing anguish generated by colonial oppression or reevaluating indigenous practices and perspectives, Sembène's films convert individual sufferings to collective identities of social trauma, while often extending troublesome roles to God and religion in the backdrop of black African survival. There is a sense in which his later films, *Guelwaar* and *Moolaade*, confirm Sembène's realization that progress comes through confrontations with tradition and young people standing up to their elders to insist upon new ways of living out African identities.

If *Moolaade* is a repudiation of destructive parts of African tradition and religion, then *Guelwaar* makes a firmer advocacy of carnal resources being more effective than spiritual assets to solve African problems. In contrast to the film's critical attacks against the first generation of postcolonial African leaders, *Guelwaar* presents Helene and Sophie as heroic prostitutes of the second generation who are able to provide education and sustenance to their families and fund expensive religious pilgrimages for their fathers. Sembène pivots prostitution from debased profession to pragmatic means of survival to mitigate the downturn of the Senegalese economy. In *Guelwaar* we learn that, in the midst of African struggles and poverty, prostitution can help religious families meet their basic needs; in other words, sex work can feed religious families better than God can. And when confronted with this reality in the form of a prostitute's powerful testimony, the priest has no riposte. For that reason, Helene's dialogue with Father Leon is one of the most provocative theodical moments in Sembène's oeuvre.

If we are keen to acknowledge Sembène's secularizing potency, we should also recognize the signifying capacities of his films toward mediating the social meanings of black suffering. Whether it is young girls experiencing excision in *Moolaade* or a poor peasant stripped of his livelihood in *Borom Sarret*, the filmmaker explicates how individual sufferers are part of vulnerable populations of black Africans that face collective threats. Sembène creates narratives of collective trauma and in doing so plays a crucial role in the establishment and potential mobilization of social identities by distinguishing those religious, political, and social culprits who caused or continue to perpetuate that suffering. In this way the six suffering girls of *Moolaade* who refused to be circumcised stand in proxy for thousands (perhaps millions) of girls around the world who suffer the pain and trauma of excision. More striking and subversive is the way Sembène identifies the co-conspirators behind such suffering as African tradition and religion. Sembène makes a bold move in converting a circumcision ritual with traditional and religious legitimation into a heinous practice, while recoding and narrating such a practice as inextricably linked to a collective experience of trauma, thus fashioning this religiously supported tradition as a crime against humanity. Similarly, if we return to his earlier work *Emitai* we see how the siege of an individual village represents collective trauma experienced on a continental level in which millions of black Africans can identify, as victims or descendants of victims of colonization (see Sembène's 1988 film *Camp de Thiaroye* for a more intense development of this theme). In *Emitai*, the French crime against the small village is a microcosm of Europe's crimes against African regions. Sembène's cinematic narratives clearly depict sufferers against oppressors, and by linking the individual sufferings to collective social identities, he makes the narration of social suffering and oppressive forces part of collective calls to action against oppressors, while issuing equally compelling collective calls to empathize with the humanity of the sufferers. Thus Sembène's artistry has immense political import in how he fashions and facilitates suffering communities and social identities and demonstrates the inherent sociological components of trauma signification.

Whereas his earlier films present modernization as a source of social disorientation—exposing the ways in which black African peasants are vulnerable prey to the machinations of bourgeois men, the strictures of rational-legal authorities, and the rigors of bureaucratic systems—his later films frame modern liberal ways of thinking as more prescriptively (and in the case of *Moolaade*, more proscriptively) useful toward a freer and better Africa. But even as we acknowledge such a dramatic transition in Sembène's oeuvre as the recoding of the modern imagination for a new, pluralistic, and more efficient African world community, one that is less reliant on tradition and God, we should also consider how Sembène's deployment of modern progression against what he posits as the regressive and at times destructive forces of tradition and religion does not imply the filmmaker has solely European adjurations of modernity in mind, a notification best exemplified in *Guelwaar*. All the madness that goes on with missing corpses in *Guelwaar* should not distract us from Sembène's primary interest in the protagonist's repudiation of Africa's dependence on other nations for the continent's survival. A comprehensive analysis of his other films and writings will inform the viewer that Sembène's modern recalibration considers how black inhabitants of his continent can act as subjective forces in the midst of their own dialectical confrontations between the past and the future. In other words, embracing modernity is no outright imitation of Europeans but rather implies that Africans surf their own continental waves of modern momentum.

If Sembène admits in a 1973 interview in *Jeune Afrique* that "It goes without saying that I am impatient for a socialist revolution," (Diallo 2008: 52), his later films suggest a newborn conviction that pragmatic progression rather than radical socialist revolution is the solution to Africa's pressing problems.

In this way, *Faat Kiné* is quite the adequate follow-up film to *Guelwaar*, even though almost a decade separates their release dates. The heroines in both films are women facing paltry prospects but who find ways to support their families. During Kiné's passionate debate with her children, she reveals how she was ready to do exactly what Helene and Sophia accomplished in Dakar to support their families rather than depend on others: "Twice a young mother, without husband, work, or connections. If I didn't have this job selling gasoline, I would have become a prostitute to raise you and send you to school." While in both films the modern is affirmed and tradition is rebuked or ultimately rejected, *Faat Kiné* offers a more explicit contrast between tradition and modernity and celebrates the notion of a new modern Africa in all its potentialities. With *Faat Kiné*'s positive and hopeful ending, we see an aging filmmaker's refurbished expectations of his nation and continent. The friendship of Djib and Jean's son, like the newly sparked romance between Kiné and Jean, represents Sembène's vision for postcolonial Senegal and Africa where religious differences are not stumbling blocks to African fellowship, sustenance, and survival. Sembène's new Africa is one in which Islam and Christianity, or any religion for that matter, can provide Africans with cultural continuity to traditional elements of their continental past, but must not become intruding forces that delimit Africa's future. Hence, it is within his filmic colloquies on the ways in which religion and tradition produce cultural value and yet harmful consequences that we see Sembène's treatment of theodicy flex its mighty muscles. Sembène sets forth a hopeful trajectory for African survival and advancement as long as religion remains unobtrusive, inclusive, and inoffensive (or what Jürgen Habermas calls post-metaphysical). Sembène's crucial theodical message for his developing continent is quite simple: what Africa needs most is a modern God.

Chapter 5

Contemporary African American Films

In an early scene in Tyler Perry's movie *Daddy's Little Girls* (2007), the protagonist Monty visits Katherine, the grandmother and guardian of his three daughters. Katherine, or Miss Kate as Monty sometimes calls her, is the mother of Jennifer, Monty's ex-partner and co-parent. Jennifer's romantic partnership with a drug kingpin strains her relationship with her mother. When Monty enters the apartment, his girls are beaming with joy, but Miss Kate isn't looking well and her cough confirms her frail state. When the girls are out of earshot, Miss Kate reveals to Monty that she has lung cancer and then urges him to file for custody of her grandchildren in fear that her daughter will gain custody of the girls after her death. After Monty reassures Miss Kate that everything is going to be okay, the frail woman responds with desperation, "Everything is not going to be alright!" Her warning proves prophetic, for in the very next scene we see Monty and others leaving Miss Kate's funeral. Her death results in the girls suffering psychological and physical trauma after Miss Kate's worst fear comes to fruition and Jennifer gains custody. If God had healed Miss Kate, Monty's daughters would not have suffered abuse. But that is not how God works in cinema, even when the writer and director is a devout Christian.

This chapter explores how *Daddy's Little Girls* and many other contemporary films with African American protagonists cast important roles for God and religion while setting reasonable boundaries on what God can do in a world replete with evil and suffering. The analysis starts with a crucial scene in Tyler Perry's fifth film *Meet the Browns* (2008). The protagonist Brenda Brown, a struggling mother of three, has a tête-à-tête with an elderly sage that sets up a filmic showdown of competing perspectives on black suffering: one that sees hardships and tragedies as theological problems requiring theological solutions, and the other that interprets the vagaries of life through a worldly lens. Next, the chapter returns to *Daddy's Little Girls* to discover how

Tyler Perry's ending offers an ungodly solution to quite the quagmire, even after the protagonist's pastor proposes divine intervention as the operative means to make all things right. The chapter then examines Spike Lee's provocative film *Red Hook Summer*, which questions how a struggling church and hopeful preacher can negotiate challenging urban environs through the eyes of faith, and how a loving God can allow a child to suffer sexual predation from his cleric. It then turns to Neema Barnette's film *Civil Brand* to see how black women suffer abuses in the prison industrial complex until they stop praying and start fighting back with armed resistance. The chapter continues with analysis of more contemporary works that juxtapose God-talk and various contexts of African American suffering. Before commencing with contemporary films, we must pause to consider a celluloid classic featuring a different kind of God from the sidelined deity we generally find in cinema.

On the surface, *The Green Pastures* (1936) resembles contemporary movies in how it contextualizes God toward human perspectives and cultural tastes, as the film's foreword suggests:

> God appears in many forms to those who believe in Him. Thousands of Negroes in the Deep South visualize God and Heaven in terms of people and things they know in their everyday life. *The Green Pastures* is an attempt to portray that humble, reverent conception.

The film displays quite the humanized deity, not only with God's embodied presence and Southern dialect, but also with God's lack of omniscience. We see God turn to Gabriel and other angels for information and schedule a visit to Earth to review how humans are progressing—redundant undertakings for an all-knowing deity. God also enjoys cigars and reacts in cantankerous ways, while heaven functions as a happening place with fish fries, friendly banter, and choir performances.

But despite its anthropomorphic indulgences, *The Green Pastures* presents a God who must not be mistaken for the sidelined deity we encounter in most movies. For even as the film's signifying capacity reshapes God, heaven, and Earth toward the social, cultural, and racial perspectives of a particular community, it does not deprive God of supernatural efficacy. The film brandishes a God who rules over heaven and Earth with obtrusive displays of supernatural power to punish sinners or rescue people from oppression. In other words, it depicts God as an active mediating force in time and space. Less than a decade after *The Green Pastures* hit theaters, *Cabin in the Sky* (1943) appears to follow its trajectory by showcasing a transcendent world where God responds to prayer and spiritual beings compete to influence the fate of black people. But the end of the film flips its supernatural script by unveiling how earlier sequences containing angels, demons, and an interventionist God were figments of the protagonist's dream. With the protagonist now awake in the real world, God is handicapped by the limits of rationality. This chapter explores contemporary films featuring black suffering and God-talk that emulate the ending of *Cabin in the Sky* by keeping God sidelined.

MEET THE BROWNS

In *Meet the Browns* (2008), Brenda and her three children withstand the vicissitudes of poverty. An emotional dialogue between Brenda and Miss Mildred, the elderly woman who watches over Brenda's youngest daughter Lena, is the film's most salient theological exchange. Miss Mildred attempts to console Brenda by insisting that God has been helping her family make it thus far and that her current setback only confirms that her breakthrough is imminent. She admonishes Brenda to keep praying. With tears streaming down her face, Brenda responds, "I pray! I try to pray. I try to live right. But where is it getting me? Look at me. If you would have seen the look on my babies' faces when that man turned my lights off." Brenda is referring to an earlier sequence when her electricity was cut off for failure to pay the bill. If Brenda's misfortune pushes one to ponder why bad things happen to good people in a universe governed by a loving and just God, then Miss Mildred's answer posits trust in God's purposive plan to make everything right in the end.

This dialogue between a destitute mother and a wise elderly woman is crucial to our discussion of theodicy in terms of how it represents historically divergent responses to African American struggles with slavery, segregation, lynching, racial degradation, and economic hardship. On one side of the spectrum is the response that frames African American suffering as divinely steered toward redemptive results, while on the other side of the spectrum reside interpretations of black suffering that either identify the socio-historical mechanisms of oppression and inequality at play to generate practical solutions or languish within a defeatist outlook. At this juncture, we can only speculate whether the film endorses Miss Mildred's theological understanding of Brenda's poverty or merely includes it for the purpose of providing a nuanced dialogue on black suffering. Put differently, we must contemplate whether Perry is teaching his audience a lesson on spiritual resilience through Miss Mildred's hope, or if he is subjecting such hope to deliberative interrogation.

While weighing the evidence we should consider that Brenda's struggle is commensurate with the plight of many single parents who endure the vulnerabilities of poverty: low wages, frequent loss of employment, difficulty ascertaining affordable childcare, lack of food, and loss of utilities. And we must not overlook the fact that Brenda's record as a hard worker and devoted parent remains unimpeachable throughout the film. So Brenda's issue is not laziness, unwillingness to work, struggle with addiction, bad habits, etc., but rather a perfect case study for theodicy in which a conscientious parent is overwhelmed by economic hardships seemingly beyond her control. Miss Mildred's claim is that amid Brenda's family struggles (loss of electricity, perpetual lack of food, recent loss of employment), God's interventionist power is preserving the family and preparing its eventual breakthrough from poverty.

A critic might counter that to take Miss Mildred's contention seriously is to admit that God either is not a very good provider or does not like Brenda's family very much, as its constant state of deprivation ostensibly defies teleological tinkering. Consider this, only moments before their conversation takes this theological turn, Miss Mildred offers food to appease Brenda's hunger and reminds Brenda that she often drops off Lena in a famished state. In a later scene, Brenda's older daughter Tosha scarfs down food like she hasn't eaten in a long time and then admits to Sarah, Vera, and Cora that her family often goes without. Brenda tells Harry in the hospital, "There are nights when I go to bed hungry 'cause I know they didn't get enough to eat all day." And there's that unforgettable morning when Brenda cooks the last scraps of oatmeal and goes without breakfast so her kids can eat. We also see how Brenda's son Michael does not have a decent pair of tennis shoes for his basketball games until a drug dealer surprises him with a new pair. So Miss Mildred's claim that God has been responsible for their survival could be met with the immediate riposte that God is not doing a very good job of sustaining them. Similarly, we can easily do the math to assess the durability of the Brown family's long hard slog with poverty. Brenda's oldest child Michael is seventeen and she's been struggling the whole time as a single parent, and so, for almost eighteen years, various formations of the Brown family have endured poverty, thus making it more difficult to believe that divine intervention has sustained them thus far—or is about to make things any better.

Whereas Miss Mildred spiritualizes Brenda's poverty, Brenda subscribes to a more natural explanation. Early in the movie, while reprimanding Michael to focus on school instead of even thinking about getting a job, Brenda identifies her lack of education as what's been hindering her from getting gainful employment. Brenda's assessment demonstrates a sociological understanding of her battle with poverty that makes her low education a causal factor behind her failure to get ahead. But Miss Mildred doesn't see it this way. Rather than encouraging Brenda to get her G.E.D. or train in new technologies to avoid low-wage jobs that leave her susceptible to the whims of corporate relocation which eliminated her most recent job, Miss Mildred exhorts Brenda to keep praying. The elderly woman isn't the only character to make Brenda's scarcity a theological issue. When Cora and Sarah find out about her financial struggles, they also urge Brenda to stay encouraged in her faith. And even Brenda shows ambivalence in how she perceives her plight and how to ameliorate it, sometimes offering naturalistic explanations and other times leaning toward God, as Michael's passionate retort to his mother reveals: "You work like a dog and what has it gotten you? You talk about God making a way. Mama, I'm not trying to die to get to heaven, I want mine here on Earth!"

In contrast to Brenda's vacillation, Michael displays no theological inquisitiveness concerning their plight. For example, whereas the spiritually minded Miss Mildred might have prayed with a demoralized Brenda moments after she lost her job, Michael reminds her they always find a way to make it, and rather than offering prayer, he persuades her to dance, which cheers Brenda up, at least until their electricity is abruptly cut off from lack of payment. Later in the movie, the shock of watching his mother beg his deadbeat dad for money prompts Michael to sell drugs with his buddy Calvin. And when Brenda confronts her son after his first night working with Calvin, Michael apologizes and adds, "Mama, I'm just tired of seeing you hurt and struggling." The fact that a promising teenager momentarily falls into criminal activity illuminates his worldly perspective—he deems dealing drugs to be a more dependable solution to reverse his poverty than divine intervention.

So *Meet the Browns* contrasts worldly and spiritual ways to frame a family's deprivation and how to alleviate it, juxtaposing the theological sanguinity of Miss Mildred and Cora against the modern perspective of Brenda (for the most part) and Michael. If Brenda prays, as she tells Miss Mildred, the audience never gets to see her supplication in real time. If Brenda trusts in God, as Michael conveys in his above comment, we never see such confidence manifest when she is facing daunting circumstances due to her lack of resources. While balancing the weight of each perspective to decipher the film's takeaway lesson, it is easy to assume that Tyler Perry, a Christian filmmaker who relishes deep and robust ties to black churches, ultimately sides with Miss Mildred's trust in an interventionist God who is waiting in the wings to make things right for Brenda's family. Lending credence to the latter interpretation, a prominent theologian analyzes Perry's films and concludes:

> Perry conveys the message that only happiness and success signify liberation and divine favor. His doctrine of grace is reliant on divine favoritism and works of righteousness. There is a causal relation between stronger faith, more fervent prayer, morally pure behavior, and a better life. (White 2014: 82)

One could infer from Andrea White's above summation of Perry's theological standpoint that Miss Mildred's exhortation for Brenda to keep praying and trusting in God for her situation to improve epitomizes Perry's normative message for *Meet the Browns* and other films. But a careful evaluation of *Meet the Browns'* unfolding plot reveals just the opposite, that the critical lesson we can glean from its resolution is not renewed faith in divine providence but rather a tacit endorsement of luck, good genes, and talent. God remains on the sidelines while carnal capacities set in motion Brenda Brown's escape from poverty in two stages.

The first phase of her breakthrough begins when Brenda and the family attend her father's funeral in Georgia and learn through the reading of his will that he left her his dilapidated house. Not having the money to make it livable, Brenda rejects the dusty broken-down house and the Brown family returns to Chicago. But unknown to Brenda, while she's back up North, her budding love interest Harry spearheads an expensive effort to renovate the house. In a later scene Brenda and her family return to Georgia to see the renovated home and are astounded by its beauty and charm. While other family members chipped in small amounts, Harry took on the bulk of the cost. So in a stirring scene, Brenda's family moves into a beautifully refurnished home. If one is tempted to interpret Brenda's first step away from poverty as the providential hand of God, such a construal overlooks the more obvious human motives behind the renovation of the house.

A well-to-do man helping out a poor but beautiful woman is no rare occurrence in contemporary life and cinema. Such an arrangement does not necessitate a divine act, simply an interested party who has the resources to make things happen. In this way, Harry's motivation for taking charge of the renovation is not even remotely philanthropic; he lives in Georgia and wants the woman he loves closer to him. Harry sacrifices money and time to make her life better because, simply put, Harry is a wooing party acting in his own self-interest. The fact that he eventually marries his relocated inamorata ultimately affirms the renovation as a sound investment rather than a spiritual act of altruism. Does such "woo-ability" require divine intervention for a suitor to act on behalf of a woman as dashingly beautiful and charming as Brenda Brown (played by the dashingly beautiful and charming film star Angela Bassett)? Would one be out of place to postulate that if Brenda were far less physically appealing, it would have been far less probable for the poor mother of three to sweep a former basketball star like Harry off his feet, inspiring him to bankroll an expensive renovation of her inherited broken-down home? As superficial as it may sound, one must be quite naïve to deny that Brenda's relationship with Harry is at least partially achievable due to her privileged status as a beautiful woman.

But moreover, at no point does Brenda give God credit for the renovated house. Even Cora offers Brenda quite the carnal lens through which to see Harry's benevolence when she confirms Sarah's claim that Harry put up most of the money for the house and then tells Brenda, "I think he likes you." Cora, a Christian woman who had already demonstrated a penchant toward perceiving life through a theological lens, simply refers to Harry's fondness for Brenda as the source of his generosity, rather than suggesting it was God pressing upon Harry's heart to bless her. Vera comes up with a different theory, framing Harry's act as a ploy to secure a bigger payoff, presuming Brenda's son Michael will soon become a professional athlete. While Vera's theory is ill-advised, it is nonetheless driven by an attempt to crack the puzzle of Harry's generosity, a conundrum Vera qualifies in her cutting query to Cora and Sarah, "Why else would a man be this nice to a woman with three, count 'em, three kids?" Certainly, Vera's snobbery causes her to overlook Cora's simpler explanation, that Harry did this because he likes Brenda. All the same, no one in the film even hints that God inspired Harry's investment of time and money to renovate the house. Thus, it is more exegetically sound to perceive the initial phase of Brenda's break from poverty as the natural outcome of her budding relationship with Harry rather than a blessing from God.

The second and more decisive part of Brenda's breakthrough occurs at the end of the film when Michael secures a professional basketball contract. If it were Tyler Perry's point to position Brenda's ascent as part of a normative message about divine intervention, it would seem necessary for the Brown family to credit God after Michael receives the contract. But this never happens; neither God nor divine provisional power is mentioned when Michael goes from struggling teen to a millionaire. Even during the press conference after Michael signs the big contract, he mentions how his mother broke her back to make sure he and his sisters had food on the table, but omits God from the equation. There is nothing in the plot that primes us to consider Michael's basketball talent needed a touch of divine intervention to seal the deal. Perry could have easily included a scene with Brenda on her knees thanking God or a quick sequence with Brenda revisiting Miss Mildred to tell her that God did work things out for her. Instead the film keeps God sidelined and credits the Brown family's breakthrough to human achievement. So Perry's resolutions to his protagonist's problem remain inattentive to Miss Mildred's theological hope.

Lisa Allen-McLaurin (2014) asserts that Tyler Perry infuses his films with a strategic use of gospel music toward asserting teleological design that comes through a heavenly focus. But as with Andrea White's earlier assessment, Allen-McLaurin misses the earthly undertones of Perry's spirituality in how the filmmaker offers a post-soul Christian-cool aesthetic that accentuates pragmatic solutions and self-actualization (Lee 2015). Despite the director's recurrent arrangements of black religious tropes and theological themes throughout his oeuvre, a sidelined God is a common feature in his films which ultimately place the burden on human will and self-discovery to rectify life's most pressing problems. In other words, Perry's plots feint spiritual jabs and then unleash humanist haymakers. And if *Meet the Browns* offers a surprisingly secular sucker punch with its resolution of Brenda's suffering, then the film that opens this chapter more resolutely knocks God out of contention as a viable solution to a pressing problem. For the theodical takeaway lesson of *Daddy's Little Girls* is indisputable: Don't wait on God for deliverance, create your own resolution!

DADDY'S LITTLE GIRLS

Fewer developments could be more distressing to a parent than discovering an unfit parent will gain custody of his kids. Faced with this situation, Monty plops on the couch and informs his boss and mentor Willie that Jennifer and her criminal boyfriend Joe now have custody over his three daughters and that his only recourse is to win back his children in the court system. Willie responds, "You know Jennifer and that crack dealer; they got long money. You're gonna need some help from God and two more white people to fight them!" Willie's suggestion that God needs two more white people to win the legal case against Jennifer and Joe's impressive resources is as amusing as it is indicative of vertical boundaries. And the very next scene offers a decisive rebuttal to Willie's calculation with Monty and his mentor seated in church listening to their pastor's exhortation:

> "Let us not grow weary in well doing," He said, "for in due season you shall reap if you faint not." I'm trying to tell you God is faithful. In His faithfulness He reminds us that in doing good you shall get weary. There is no sin in getting weary; the sin is giving up. I'm here to announce to you, you're so close to your due season, you're about to taste it, there is about to be a manifestation of God in your life and it's not time to throw in the towel. It's time to lift up your head because something is about to happen in your life and God is going to ensure it. The evidence that you're so close to your breakthrough, the evidence that you're so close to your payday and your reward for walking righteous is that you will feel like—you better hear this I'm telling you something—you will feel like you're about to faint and when you feel like you're about to faint don't faint because that says I'm right there next to my miracle, I'm right there, right at the door of my due season. I'm talking to those that walked into this church today with their head kind of hung down and just about to give up and about to lose your faith. I'm encouraging you to keep the faith, stay right there, don't faint, hold on, God is about to bring your due season.

Monty and the rest of the congregants seem quite encouraged by their pastor's appeal to God's interventionist capacities. It is as if the preacher's proclamation is prophetically attuned to Monty's situation because in the previous scene the mechanic was despondent. Now he can rest assured knowing, as the preacher prophesied, God is about to bring his "due season" which suggests that God will help Monty regain custody of his kids.

To revisit Willie's wisecrack, it suggests Monty needs God and two more white people to win his children back in a lengthy trial against Jennifer and her drug-kingpin's impressive reserves. In contrast to Willie branding God as an accessory to clever Caucasian legal counsel, their pastor's exhortation makes God's inclusion solely sufficient to secure a troubled Christian's solution. Emulating Miss Mildred's theological hopefulness in *Meet the Browns*, Monty's pastor suggests that when you find yourself in deepest trouble, rest assured knowing that such a difficult spot is an indication that your divine breakthrough is imminent. And like Miss Mildred does with Brenda, the preacher transfixes God into the equation not only as the solution, but also as the caretaker of the problem, the providential mediator of Monty's misery. Hence, with its clear directive of God's promise to deliver a believer's breakthrough, some might interpret the sermon as Tyler Perry's takeaway lesson. But the unfolding plot completely disconfirms such a reading of the film.

While Monty is revived by the pastor's message of hope, his daughters continue to endure abusive environs. Living under the dysfunctional guardianship of Jennifer and Joe, they undergo enough stress to give the youngest girl China bad migraines. Joe forces Sierra, the oldest daughter, to take marijuana to her junior high school to sell to her friends in a callous attempt to expand his market share. Similarly upsetting, the girls watch from their bedroom Joe and Jennifer dispense a thrashing to an underling for coming up short on drug sales. But the tragic predicament climaxes when the girls trek to Monty's apartment a few hours after midnight, claiming they can't live with their mother and Joe anymore. They inform Monty that Joe has been beating China because she wouldn't stop crying. Sierra and Lauryn lift up China's shirt to show Monty the bruises on her back. A measured response would be for Monty to contact child welfare services and begin the process of winning custody back from Jennifer because he now has irrefutable evidence of abuse. But his youngest daughter's discolored torso inhibits Monty from acting rationally. After he puts his daughters to bed and promises to resolve the matter, the mechanic irrevocably stops waiting on God and rather recklessly proceeds to secure his own breakthrough.

If his pastor's earlier message on God's interventionist capacities were predictive, we would expect a divine resolution to Monty's tragic dilemma. And the unveiling of the bruises on China's back offers an ideal opportunity for Monty to emit a desperate prayer followed by God's eleventh-hour intervention. But such divine communication and retribution never take place. Even a committed theist has to concede that the film's ending suggests the pastor had it all wrong; it is not God who saves the day but human vengeance. In Monty's lowest moment, facing the painful reality that his girls are in a desperate state of affairs, that their physical wellbeing and existential survival are at stake, the weary mechanic never reaches out to God. What we have instead is a darker and more dangerous response to this tragic situation than Monty's optimistic pastor would have ever conceived of or condoned.

With the girls now asleep, Monty heads over to Joe and Jennifer's apartment building. Looking up, he sees the couple preparing to leave. Knowing they will have to drive by a particular section to exit the complex, Monty lies in wait. The camera cues in on Joe and Jennifer driving and enjoying a loving conversation, but their warm talk is about to confront a cold disruption. When Monty sees their car approaching he steps on the gas and crashes into them. The acceleration sound from Monty's car indicates that this crash is a premeditated vehicular assault rather than an unforeseen coincidence. Monty pulls the dazed and injured drug dealer out of the driver's seat and pummels him, while fellow residents observe from their windows. Also watching from the apartment building are Joe's comrades who rush to the scene to attack Monty. But the same community residents who spent much of the film fearing Joe and his cronies, come to Monty's aid armed with iron skillets and pipes.

The police eventually arrive and, in the process of investigating the crash and melee, find drugs in Joe's car, which gives them reasonable and probable grounds to secure a search warrant for Joe's apartment, which eventually turns up more drugs. The film reveals this chain of discovery when the assistant district attorney makes his case during Joe and Jennifer's preliminary hearing. Securing many volunteers to testify against them, the prosecutor proceeds with the charges and the bailiff takes Joe and Jennifer away for illegal possession of drugs with intent to sell. But next on the docket is Monty who is charged with vehicular assault and inciting a riot. Julia, a corporate attorney who never loses cases, arrives in court to fill in for Willie's aforementioned "two more white people." Standing next to her defiant and unrepentant client, Julia informs the judge that the charges against Monty are baseless, that there isn't any evidence that the crash wasn't simply a random car accident, and that the prosecutor has no proof that Monty had anything to do with the brawl that ensued after the accident. When the judge asks the prosecutor for witnesses to substantiate his charges against Monty, the assistant district attorney, just as he had done moments ago to secure witnesses to testify against Joe and Jennifer, appeals to the spectators in the court, but this time no one stands up because the community is in full support of Monty. So the charges are dropped, and the movie ends with a big celebration in front of Monty's newly purchased auto repair shop.

Nowhere does Monty show a hint of remorse for almost killing Jennifer and Joe by ramming his car into them. And Julia, while implementing a sound defense strategy before the judge, ultimately resorts to subterfuge to get Monty off, for as we know the charges were not baseless, the car accident was in fact premeditated, and the melee was clearly instigated by the raging mechanic. Simply put, Monty was guilty on both charges and would have been convicted and sentenced in a perfect universe. But most importantly, we cannot overlook how Monty's irresponsible actions undermine his pastor's earlier exhortation to wait on God to bring his due season. Monty stopped holding onto the prospect of divine intermediation and took matters into his own hands. And when his negligent ferocity proved fortuitous, Monty didn't thank God for the unforeseen positive outcome. If there is a theodical lesson that we can learn from *Daddy's Little Girls* it is that when the going gets tough, the tough person trusts in his own instincts and acts decisively rather than passively waiting for God to intervene.

So the plot resolutions of *Meet the Browns* and *Daddy's Little Girls* draw attention to an unnoticed aspect of Tyler Perry's cinematic representation of black suffering: God's sidelined status. Perry may infuse his films with Christian protagonists, passionate sermons, and lively gospel music, but his narrative arcs eventually concede credit to human grit rather than to supernatural intervention to resolve black suffering. We can trace this worldly perspective back to his first film, *Diary of a Mad Black Woman* (2005), when Perry's most notable character, Madea, renders her Glock as more reliable than divine justice to punish her enemies. Monty's macho resolution resembles Madea's gun-toting bravado. While some of Perry's characters pray, Monty and Madea understand when it is time to stop praying and start punching.

RED HOOK SUMMER

Set and shot in the Red Hook public housing complexes in South Brooklyn, Spike Lee's *Red Hook Summer* (2012) unfolds layers of black suffering and evil. In addition to underscoring God's inability to solve pesky urban problems like gentrification, environmental exploitation, crime, poverty, and death, Lee's film raises the question of why God would allow a child to endure sexual molestation from his pastor. And instead of demonizing the sexual perpetrator, Lee humanizes him, impelling viewers to ponder whether Christianity has room within its redemptive borders to restore a repentant pedophile to clerical leadership. Hence, *Red Hook Summer* questions not only God's relevance to a struggling community, but also the salvific capacities of Christianity in the context of evil and suffering.

Pastored by Bishop Enoch, Lil' Heaven is a church in the Red Hook project community. When a visitor makes his presence known during an Old-timers' service, the congregants presume he is stepping forward to cure Lil' Heaven's debts with a sizeable donation. The visitor plays into their misconception, introducing himself as the man with the financial contribution that Bishop Enoch prophesied about in an earlier service, a ploy that effectively secures everyone's undivided attention. But the more this mysterious young man talks, the more they learn he does not have a gift to bequeath upon the church but rather disrupting recollections to disclose about their pastor. And we see Bishop Enoch's countenance go from elation to trepidation as he slowly deduces the identity of this visitor as Blessing Rowe, the grown-up version of the adolescent he pastored fifteen years ago in Georgia. After revealing his former pastor's habit of quoting passages from Song of Solomon to seduce, Rowe accuses Bishop Enoch of sexually molesting him as a boy and stealing his faith. This allegation incites mayhem in the church, prompting deacons to remove Rowe from the congregation, while other members cry to God for clarity.

Blessing Rowe drops a bomb that most viewers could not have seen coming. Up to this point in the film, Bishop Enoch's only visible flaws are excessive optimism and imposing his faith on Red Hook residents. Few could have suspected the dedicated cleric is capable of molesting a tween under his pastoral care. Blessing Rowe's revelation and Bishop Enoch's later confession invite viewers to question why a just and sovereign God would allow a trusted servant to exploit scriptures and spiritual leadership to destroy the faith of a vulnerable tween. But beyond the powerful implications of Rowe's revelation for theodicy, Spike Lee's film more comprehensively addresses black suffering in Red Hook.

The backstory that drives the plot involves a boy named Flik leaving his comfortable existence in Atlanta to spend the summer with Bishop Enoch. This trip is not only Flik's first interaction with his grandfather, but also his first experience in church. So the film is as much a coming of age story for a precocious tween as it is a daring treatment of theodicy. Flik, an atheist wrestling with his father's death, navigates new territory regarding life in Brooklyn, and a new relationship with a grandfather who appears as a weird stranger to him. And Flik's exposure to the problems in Red Hook provides the context for some of the movie's most memorable moments, questioning what an omnipotent and loving God has to say and do about the inequality and suffering that Red Hook's black residents endure. In addition to Bishop Enoch, Flik, and Blessing Rowe, the film includes other important characters like Sharon, Chazz, Deacon Zee, and Box.

Sharon is a trustee in Lil' Heaven and mother of Chazz (Flik's sidekick and theodical muse). Sharon is one of three women mentioned in the film who had a child die from AIDS. The other two mothers are tangential characters: Mother Darling, the reinvention of Nola Darling from Spike Lee's earlier classic *She's Gotta Have It* (1986), who appears in this film as a middle-aged proselytizing Jehovah's Witness; and Sister Sweet, a faithful member of Lil' Heaven who, as one character describes, rolls her wheelchair fifteen blocks every day to the subway to go to work. Sharon explains to Bishop Enoch that she did everything to raise her daughter Angel under the auspices of divine influence: "I prayed for my Angel till my knees wore out. Took her to Lil' Heaven every Sunday. But 'the Hook' got her and she died. So this time I ain't just praying for my Chazz. I'm watching her school, her teacher, her friends, her Facebook, her Twitter." Continuing this contrast between the spiritualized way she raised her deceased daughter and the more tactical and vigilant parental mechanics she employs toward raising Chazz, Sharon adds that "I ain't pawning off my responsibility as a parent saying she's in God's hands. She's in my two loving hands and with God's help I will raise this one right." Sharon does not blame God for Angel's demise, only her own parental passivity, as she remains disappointed in herself for putting too much faith in spirituality and not enough effort in preemptive monitoring. Sharon still believes in God but learns to put God in the passenger seat while she takes over the wheel as the driving force in Chazz's life.

Chazz quickly becomes inseparable from Bishop Enoch's grandson Flik, as the two become the youngest African American theodical conversation partners in cinematic history. Their most important confab occurs on Valentino Pier, a dock that makes visible both Red Hook's dilapidated buildings and the elegant Lower Manhattan skyline, thus symbolizing Chazz's demographic contradiction of living near one of the richest environments in the world while remaining far removed from its social capital and liveliness. Chazz informs Flik how she often gazes in wonder at people riding in water taxis to Manhattan, looking so busy and prosperous, while her own life is devoid of meaning and purpose. In Chazz we hear the rare cinematic articulation of dissonance from a young black female Christian who has many questions concerning the inequity that characterizes her existence. She tells Flik, "My mom says, 'Chazz, trust in Jesus,' and I'm trying; I just don't see no light. You see any light?" Chazz struggles to resolve the optimism of her faith against the despondence of her socioeconomic status, admitting that sometimes she just wants to swim to the edge of the world and "go to blackness." She adds, "I want to stop feeling numb. I want to feel pretty, with nice clothes, and a nice house, with nice people that love me."

While Chazz exemplifies theodical ambivalence, one moment pointing to her distress, the next moment encouraging Flik to consider that God feels his pain, Flik maintains a single-minded stance on what he perceives as divine futility. He tells Chazz:

> All this corny yacking about God drives me nuts. My grandfather is a bully and he's got God. The Bloods run everything and jack people's stuff and they had

God. And these white people in these nice houses, they don't want us around, and they have their God. You as loopy as Fruit Loops and you have God too.

Here we see Flik question the point of having God if it does not dramatically impact human affairs or hold people accountable to better ways of living and treating people. When Chazz ends their talk by pretending to execute a suicide jump off the ridge of the pier, Flik falls for the prank and tries to stop Chazz from jumping by cautioning her that God will not catch her. And Flik's final statement on the pier is that he does not believe in God because God lets too much bad stuff happen. Thus, like a young version of Tomas Ericsson, a doubting cleric in Ingmar Bergman's classic film *Winter Light* (1962), Flik questions God's absence. Spike Lee undergirds Flik's skepticism with a mountain of circumstantial evidence of divine inaction: God didn't protect Flik's father during his military tour in Afghanistan; God didn't prevent Blessing Rowe's molestation; God didn't shield Angel from an early demise even though her mother prayed for her every day; God did not step in to relieve Lil' Heaven of its great financial woes; God did not heal Sister Sweet from her disability nor prevent her son from dying of AIDS. In short, God does not appear to offer any kind of help to remedy the destitution, despondence, and death in this troubled Brooklyn community.

Perhaps the most outspoken character in the context of theodical despondence is Deacon Zee, the brother of Sharon and gregarious caretaker of Lil' Heaven. Deacon Zee is a pessimistic alcoholic whose unsolicited soliloquies offer the film's most discerning statements regarding the synchronicity of black suffering, evil, and divine neglect. When Bishop Enoch tells him about his vision of a mysterious former member returning around Old-timers' Day to save Lil' Heaven with a financial gift, Deacon Zee reminds Bishop Enoch that the gift had better be substantial because the church is falling apart and its bills are overwhelming. Unfazed, Bishop Enoch responds by exhorting faith in God's provision, but the deacon counters, "Man plans and God laughs, you know, 'cause He's a jokester!"

But the troubled alcoholic's most cutting comments usually occur when he is alone with Flik and his niece Chazz. It is Deacon Zee who articulates to Flik the hopelessness of African Americans in Red Hook. "The world be goin' round and round, and the white man still ahead," he playfully points out as if to suggest that racial inequality is a persistent disconfirmation of divine governance. Shortly after, he tells Flik a somber story regarding the seriousness of asthma attacks in Red Hook:

There's thirty-one of these project buildings. An EMS brother told me on the low-low that eleven children died of asthma in the last two years. You know why? 'Cause of a light bulb. See, a child has an asthma attack at night, somebody calls 911 and the EMS guys spend fifteen minutes spinning around the projects trying to find that address 'cause they can't see it. By the time they find it, the poor child is dead.

Deacon Zee also estimates that eighty percent of Red Hook residents are unemployed. Flick takes the deacon's gloomy outlook quite seriously. For example, when Bishop Enoch tells his grandson, "Red Hook is a window to God's inspiration," Flik responds, "That's not what Deacon Zee says!" Perhaps Flik is referring to an earlier moment when he was filming a dead rat with his iPad and told Deacon Zee, "Sometimes I like taking pictures of dead things," to which the deacon responded, "Then you're in the right place 'cause everything about this place is dead!"

Deacon Zee acknowledges in his unique way that a substantial part of the suffering he sees in Red Hook is the result of social stratification, and even Bishop Enoch alludes to structural challenges and daunting realities of black urban life in some of his sermons. But Bishop Enoch incorporates divine intervention and personal responsibility into the matrix of misery, suggesting the world can be different if people do not lose hope in God and live healthier lives. Whereas Deacon Zee sees his surroundings as despairing, Bishop Enoch sees human agency and divine intervention as offering possibilities for transcendence. Perhaps Bishop Enoch discerns so much potential and beauty in Red Hook because he arrived there to escape the scandal of his pastorate in Georgia. He tells Flik late in the film that he came to Red Hook to hide, but soon reckoned that life in the struggling Brooklyn community did not seem like punishment. Red Hook has sentimental value for Bishop Enoch because it facilitated his clerical comeback.

The only character who trumps Deacon Zee's despondence is Box, the gang leader of the Bloods. Box attended Lil' Heaven as a child but is now quite hostile to church and God. Box's mother was a devoted member of Lil' Heaven before she died from an illness. Box informs Bishop Enoch that he used to pray with his mother so perhaps he stopped praying the day Augusta Williams stopped breathing. The bleakness that characterizes Box's existence matches his irreverence, as the gang leader does not seem worried about procuring God's wrath. For example, shortly after confiscating Flik's iPad, he issues an unholy warning to Bishop Enoch that exemplifies his defiance:

Wasted my whole childhood in Lil' Heaven. I'm telling you old man, next time I see you or anybody else from your Jesus sect come on this court I'm gonna cut your eyelids off so you can see me clearly before I blast you straight to Big Heaven, understand? And when you get there you can tell God you were sent there by Satan himself.

Here we see Box callously threatening to kill a cleric while rebelliously categorizing himself as the prince of darkness. And later when he learns about Blessing Rowe's revelation, Box and two members of his gang drop in on Bishop Enoch in Lil' Heaven. They find him praying alone and they proceed to beat the cleric mercilessly. To top off this punishing encounter, Box places a tambourine on Bishop Enoch's bloody head and forces his dazed, wounded, and newly crowned former pastor to look at the nearby picture of Jesus wearing a crown of thorns, almost as if to mock both men as delusional suffering servants. Box feels forsaken by God and responds by abandoning all things related to the faith of his youth. He now lives by brute force, imposing his will onto others, while mocking sentimental connections to God.

Much of what happens in *Red Hook Summer* speaks to God's irrelevance in the framework of black suffering and evil. The film's characters are our eyes and ears for venturing into black urban dystopia. It is a despairing Blessing Rowe who loses his faith after being sexually molested by his pastor, while Chazz believes and yet struggles in her faith. Deacon Zee remains a cynical alcoholic, while Box rejects God and the church altogether. Flik looks at all the suffering and inequality in Red Hook as confirmation that God is a useless concept. Sharon sequesters God to the passenger seat of her parenting after Angel dies. Even Bishop Enoch speaks of his "supernatural" deliverance from the grip of pedophilia in the qualified language of theodical secularity, confessing to his grandson that he was a sick man, but God cured him, "And what He didn't do I did with the doctor's help." The Bishop's curative proviso sounds remarkably similar to Willie's aforementioned admonition that Monty will need God plus two more white people to win back his children in Tyler Perry's film *Daddy's Little Girls*. Both annotations are notable for their redundancy and furtive skepticism. *Red Hook Summer* suggests within its own theological formulations that the Christian God does nothing to alleviate systems of inequality, nothing to fend off the agonizing levels of social disadvantage, nothing to relieve the disability of a faithful Christian woman, nothing to prevent children from dying of AIDS and asthma, and nothing to offer a more hopeful future for residents of a struggling community.

CIVIL BRAND

Neema Barnette's film *Civil Brand* (2002) is set in a corporate-sponsored prison where corrupt correctional officers verbally and physically abuse, overwork, and sexually assault black female inmates. After petitions prove ineffective, the film ends with prisoners violently taking matters into their own hands. While prison insurrection is artistically clichéd, the manner in which this film juxtaposes black suffering and God-talk is entirely innovative and relevant to any discussion of theodicy. *Civil Brand* not only exposes the vulnerability of black female inmates but also calls attention to God's disinclination to intervene. If Captain Dease, the head correctional officer and main culprit behind abusing and psychologically terrorizing the inmates, represents evil personified, then the outspoken pregnant Christian inmate known as Lil' Mama signifies God's presence and conscience in the film. In this battle of good against evil, malevolence prevails, as Lil' Mama's prayers prove ineffective toward protecting her fellow inmates and eventually her own body from abuse.

When correctional officers take an inmate named Wet to solitary confinement, Lil' Mama expresses spiritual words of comfort during this chaotic scene, "God is going to keep you, Wet," and then voices a prayer of protection: "Please keep her. Please don't let them hit her. God, please guard Wet." But when Wet returns from solitary confinement, the close-up of her new and nasty facial scar reveals that Lil' Mama's prayer for protection went unanswered. By the same token, when the inmates set forth their plan to organize a peaceful work stoppage on the same day that representatives of Wall Corp, the prison's corporate sponsor, inspect the working conditions of the inmates, Lil' Mama tells her crew, "I been praying on this all night. It's gonna be alright." But their work stoppage and pleas prove unsuccessful, as those executives show no interest in serving as whistle blowers against their own corporate profits. Consequently, the two ringleaders of the work stoppage, Frances and Nikki, receive a long stint in solitary confinement as payback. The cruel duration of their confinement almost drives Nikki to insanity. And while Frances handles her time in "the hole" with more resolve, she returns from the punishing stint and receives the news that her daughter died from a stray bullet.

So once again, Lil' Mama's supplication proves ineffective, even though she prayed all night for the success of their work stoppage. The film's Machiavellian twist on theodicy is clear: power, not prayer, runs the world and prayer can't make powerful people act against their own self interests. Lil' Mama's Christian optimism is ultimately proven to be naïve concerning how the world functions with God sequestered to the sidelines. She keeps hoping for an eleventh-hour intervention that never happens. Meanwhile the female prisoners continue to suffer abuse. But more relevant to the film's treatment of theodicy is how the pregnant Christian warrior herself eventually succumbs to the corruptive power of Captain Dease.

When Lil' Mama's work assignment shifts to Captain Dease's office, he tries to assault her twice by pulling up her skirt while she's standing on a chair to clean a window. But later in the film, Captain Dease more shockingly rapes her. After the violation, Lil' Mama leaves Dease's office in a catatonic state quoting the 27th Psalm: "The Lord is my light and my salvation; whom shall I fear. The Lord is the strength of my life; of whom shall I be afraid." Shortly after, she dies from injuries caused by the violence to her pregnant body. Lil' Mama's dying words inquire about whom she should fear if God is her salvation; her corpse articulates the answer. Saddened by Lil' Mama's death, prisoners decide to fight back in a more purposeful way than praying.

Nikki, Frances, and Wet get the drop on correctional officers, secure guns, and take over the prison while holding Captain Dease as their hostage. During all the commotion, Ayesha steals the videotape of her earlier sexual encounter with Captain Dease, thus securing proof of his corruption and sparking a thorough investigation of the correctional facility. Nikki, Frances, and Wet relish in punishing, torturing, and eventually killing Captain Dease, before facing their own execution by rescuing officers. The rest of the female prisoners are saved, not by Lil' Mama's prayers, but by the barrel of the gun and the cunning of Ayesha, the sly inmate who turned on her former lover as revenge for blackening her eye. Had Captain Dease not been so violent with his once compliant mistress, she would not have had motive to secure the videotape and the entire abusive system would not have been uncovered.

By having the film's hopeful Christian voice discharge failed prayers only later to suffer a fatal sexual assault, Neema Barnette's film ridicules the notion of divine intervention in the context of black female suffering. Captain Dease's oppressive reach is stopped, not by the power of prayer but by the inducement of firearms, suggesting men like Dease can only be blocked by brute force. Another layer of theodicy is revealed in how Frances's daughter dies from a stray bullet and how Frances dies in prison, where she should not have been in the first place because she was wrongfully sentenced for killing her stepfather in self-defense. All is wrong with the universe in this film, as vulnerable women suffer until three of those victims fight back, not with divine firepower to demolish strongholds as suggested by Lil' Mama and Saint Paul (2 Corinthians 10:4), but with carnal weapons of warfare.

EVE'S BAYOU

Kasi Lemmons's directorial debut *Eve's Bayou* (1997) is situated at the crossing point of affliction and cosmic control. While the storyline unfolds from the perspective of a tween named Eve Batiste, the film's theodical relevance centers on Eve's aunt, Mozelle Batiste Delacroix, a psychic counselor who appears to be tragically unlucky in love. Mozelle's past partners all died, including Harry, whose passing at the beginning of the film serves as Mozelle's latest confirmation that she is cursed. She offers revelation to clients, but languishes over her inability to unravel the mystery behind her own bad luck.

Mozelle's first clairvoyant session is with a client named Hilary who is seeking answers about her missing son. Hilary and her husband have been praying for him for two months but have yet to receive divine confirmation of their son's safety. Mozelle gets a vision of Hilary's son using heroin and reports to her client that her son is alive in Detroit at St. Michael's Hospital. Hilary inquires if her son is sick and Mozelle tells her, "Your son's on drugs. Go home and pray for strength. You'll need strength to help you though this." So even as Mozelle purportedly taps into the supernatural realm to track the whereabouts and condition of her client's son, she stops short of summoning supernatural mediation on behalf of the young man's condition. Telling Hilary to pray for her own strength to endure the ordeal rather than instructing her to pray for her son's deliverance highlights divinity's enclosed spaces.

Mozelle is similarly clairvoyant with her next client, revealing that Renard's niece squandered all of her money. This is useful information that nonetheless leaves the client despairing until Mozelle gives Renard a list of instructions that includes securing a bag made of skin of chamois, a piece of moon stone, John Conqueror root, and a sprinkle of holy oil. Whether or not these vestiges of Voodoo prove effective in Renard's situation is left unanswered. After Renard departs, Mozelle tells her niece that such prescriptions were necessary to appease a desperate woman. And when Eve inquires if Voodoo actually works, the psychic counselor replies, "We'll see." Mozelle does not draw upon spiritual power from God to console Renard but rather invokes the individualistic religious system of Voodoo, a numinous competitor of divine justice that empowers the individual to punish evil instead of waiting on God. Perhaps Tyler Perry's subversive character Madea steals a page from Voodoo's theodical handbook in *Diary of a Mad Black Woman* (2005) when she informs Myrtle that God takes too long to secure retribution because her enemies need to "get got" without delay. That Madea's weapon of choice to invoke swift retribution is a gun rather than filaments of chamois and moon stone is no more indicative of agentive action (and sidelining God) than a Voodoo practitioner's tactical deployments to punish her nemesis post-haste. In either case, one trusts her own ability to enact revenge in a timely fashion rather than waiting for divine retribution.

While Mozelle proves useful to both clients by tapping into the spiritual realm to provide new information, such clairvoyance leads viewers to question its source. If God is behind Mozelle's revelatory power, then why did God refrain from offering similar disclosures to protect her past lovers from preventable deaths? Perhaps an unnerving answer to the latter question comes from Mozelle's rival, an elder fortuneteller named Elzora. When Mozelle and her sister-in-law Roz (Eve's mother) visit Elzora, it quickly becomes clear that the two soothsayers have a contentious relationship. Elzora first turns to Roz, discerning that while Roz is currently in pain, she'll be happy in three years. But when it is time to give Mozelle consultation, Elzora takes great pleasure in conveying to her rival, "You are a curse! A black widow! Next man who marries you is a dead man. Like the others. Always be that way," causing Mozelle to run away irate. So Elzora's explanation for why Mozelle has had three partners die confirms Mozelle's own suspicion that she is cursed. But the film doesn't verify the curse or explain its origin and arbiter.

Another salient theodical development unfolds when a bus hits a child in their community and Roz and her children jump for joy when they hear the news. Mozelle's earlier vision of a bus hurting a young child prompted Roz to put her children under virtual house arrest, fearing the child in Mozelle's vision was one of her own. So news of another child's encounter with a bus resolves Roz's anxiety, setting the family free to roam the streets again, while another family is now distressed at the loss of life. The bus prophecy and accident rekindle questions concerning the source of Mozelle's clairvoyance and why those very same powers never helped her foresee (and hence prevent) the deaths of her previous partners. More obviously, one might wonder why Mozelle gets a vision of such a death without the means to prevent it from happening. The film leaves unclear whether the child's death by bus was a coincidence or actually foreseen by Mozelle.

The film's most explicit theodical exchange occurs toward the end when Mozelle laments to her niece:

> Sometimes I feel like I've lost so much I have to find new things to lose. All I know is there must be a divine point to it all and it's just over my head. And when we die, it will all come clear, and we'll say, "So that was the damn point!" And sometimes I think there's no point at all and that's the point.

Mozelle here tries to assess how loss and suffering cohere with any notion of divine order, as her own experience invites her to entertain a nihilistic conclusion. Continuing in the same dialogue, she tells Eve, "No one leaves this Earth without feeling terrible pain. And if there is no divine explanation at the end of it all, well that's sad." Mozelle alludes to the existential absurdity of human suffering and injustice outside the context of a providential scheme. Perhaps Mozelle's ruminations are too ethereal for her niece, who simply responds by asking, "How do you kill someone with Voodoo?" Eve's focus is on punishing her father for allegedly hurting her sister. But Mozelle's philosophical reflections are nonetheless penetrating in terms of how she processes her own pain and loss, and how she articulates the absurdity of the universe if such pain and loss are not grounded in an ultimate principle of meaning.

In contrast to Mozelle's musings, Eve chooses to venture down a more proactive path by visiting her aunt's rival Elzora to pay for a Voodoo curse to kill her father. To echo an earlier point, Voodoo makes supernatural power an impersonal servant to the whims of its draftsperson. It represents the ability to act beyond the presumed contours of fate, making the human the sovereign force in the world. Thus, the practice of Voodoo has immense import for theodicy. Voodoo provides Eve with the belief that she has the power to punish her father, just as earlier in the film it empowers Mozelle's distraught client Renard whose niece allegedly stole all her money. And whether it is through coincidence or the power of Elzora's spell, a jealous husband kills Eve's philandering father soon after, leaving Eve with great guilt and discomfort. And if Elzora's spell is the culprit behind Louis Batiste's demise, then the film resembles Nollywood's modified deistic dualism (discussed in the epilogue) in which Satan worshipers, witchdoctors, and diviners exert paranormal usefulness, while the supreme God remains sidelined.

Toward the end of the film, Mozelle informs Eve, "When I woke up, I told Julian I would marry him. He wouldn't have it any other way. Maybe God will be kind and allow me to go with him. I'm so tired of being left alone." Here for the first time Mozelle brings God into the picture concerning the ramifications of her alleged curse. But does this confirm God is the force behind the curse after all? The film ends without answering this question or clarifying whether Julian becomes the fourth casualty in the psychic counselor's string of slain partners. Nor does the conclusion help us make sense of Eve's guilt behind her father's death. The film in general leaves us with more questions than answers. But what *Eve's Bayou* does reveal is that evil is quite complex, and God's role in allowing or even orchestrating unseemly events is murky at best. Kasi Lemmons's classic film teaches its viewers that no one really knows why tragedy strikes and no one can discern God's role behind tragic events; that even our most prescient diviners are clueless as to the seemingly idiosyncratic workings of spiritual combat in the context of evil and suffering.

WOMAN THOU ART LOOSED: ON THE 7TH DAY

David and Kari Ames seem to be enjoying an idyllic existence in Neema Barnette's *Woman Thou Art Loosed: On the 7th Day* (2012), a film spearheaded and produced by one of the nation's most popular black spiritual leaders, Bishop T. D. Jakes. David is a professor and dean of a humanities department and Kari is a real estate agent. They have a six-year-old daughter Mikayla and a beautiful home. Early in *Woman Thou Art Loosed: On the 7th Day* (*WTAL 7th Day*) Kari's life seems quite enviable. But underneath the veneer of happiness resides a troubled woman with a tragic past. What brings Kari's subterranean turmoil to the surface is the abduction of Mikayla.

The film presents a clever contrast between Kari and another African American mother named Ms. Beckham whose daughter Lynette disappeared shortly before Mikayla. Law enforcement officials and media treat the two abductions quite differently based on each woman's social standing, explicating another theodical stratum to consider: a world in which social privilege and political power can determine whether an innocent child lives or dies. Kari and her husband have powerful connections extending all the way up to the mayor of New Orleans. Ms. Beckham is a working-class woman with no clout, and so Lynette's abduction received no attention until the daughter of the more privileged mother disappears.

The film's final juxtaposition of Kari Ames and Ms. Beckham occurs after law enforcement agents apprehend a man known as MK as their prime suspect for several counts of child abduction. What we learn from the interrogation of MK is that he is guilty and that all his abductees are dead, with Lynette his last victim. We also learn that the disappearance of Kari's daughter is not connected to MK's serial abductions, presenting the hope that Mikayla is still alive. And we can infer from the timeline of events that had law enforcement representatives acted immediately when Lynette Beckham went missing, the same clues would have led them to discover MK as their prime suspect a day before he killed her. Without the backing of familial prestige and political contacts, Lynette was just another urban tragedy to be ignored. This disparity has distressing implications for theodicy, as it implies that a mother's social capital can determine whether or not her daughter survives an abduction.

But beyond class inequities, *WTAL 7th Day* also compels us to question how divine providence resides in conjunction with the elimination of four children by a deranged serial killer. MK killed under the misguided notion of offering human sacrifices to appease God's wrath. The slightest amount of divine mediation could have orchestrated mental health intervention long before MK was able to unleash gratuitous murder and mayhem. Nowhere in *WTAL 7th Day* is there an attempt to make sense of God's absence, even as the film is replete with spiritual messages, moments of preaching, and faith claims. At the end of the day, the deaths of four children appear to be haphazard, quite absurd, and outside of the control and responsibility of a sidelined God.

In Ms. Beckham's final appearance she is crying profusely on the courthouse steps. And Kari Ames, the mother of privilege, who now enjoys renewed hope that Mikayla is still alive, makes her first physical contact with Ms. Beckham to hug her less privileged counterpart, while Ms. Beckham utters, "He killed my child," to which Kari can only respond, "I'm sorry." Ms. Beckham's tears and anguish mock the idea that human suffering and engagement with evil are redemptive. Kari confirms this point and summarizes the film's tacit theodical leitmotif when she tells David, "There's no reason for anything. God is like Mikayla's blankie: just because it made her feel secure doesn't mean it had any power."

Early in the movie when Kari tells Mikayla that God will never let her down, she is not speaking from experience but merely projecting what she feels a Christian parent should say to her daughter at bedtime. We know this because the film later reveals how, during her childhood, God did let her down as the victim of rape by her father, which led to a downward spiral and stint as a prostitute and drug addict until she received help at the Survivor's Abuse Center. Wil Bennett, the FBI special agent and childhood friend of Kari, witnessed her recovery at the Survivor's Abuse Center. And so while working the case of Mikayla's abduction, when the special agent discerns that stress has propelled Kari back to drinking, he takes her to the very same institution that empowered her previous recovery. And it is a professional counselor, not a preacher, who helps Kari overcome her childhood trauma, advising Kari to heal herself by forgiving her deceased father. While the counselor does tell Kari that God is there for her, the film shows no evidence that this is the case. Even though the movie ends with Kari having an earnest conversation with her pastor and claiming that her faith is restored, we see no indication of God's intervention behind getting Mikayla back. Finding out that her husband's teaching assistant and former lover Beth abducted Mikayla, Kari doesn't pray, instead she steals Wil Bennett's gun to rescue her daughter. There is no divine resolution, only brute force, anger, and the lethal power of a special agent's stolen firearm, as Kari shoots Beth in the back and takes her daughter home.

While *WTAL 7th Day* articulates evangelical ideals, the film does not attempt to offer Christianity as a panacea for human tragedy. It points to God as the source of meaning and guidance but does so while unleashing rational limitations on God's provisional capabilities. Evil is in no way thwarted or mediated by God; rather, justice is administered in the most provincial fashion, as those with more resources like David and Kari enjoy more support from law enforcement, and those lacking social capital must suffer the consequences of life's tragedies. A young girl like Lynette Beckham dies because her mother can't leverage law enforcement officials to marshal the necessary resources in time to find the abductor. The film invites viewers to conclude that God resides on the sidelines of human history to offer coaching, comfort, and encouragement but no direct intervention.

MORE CONTEMPORARY FILMS

Perhaps it is fitting to include in our discussion of contemporary films a selection that offers an enchanting reprieve from vertical boundaries. Penny Marshall's *The Preacher's Wife* (1996), set in a struggling church called St. Matthews, opens with the voice of a boy named Jeremiah Biggs: "Sometimes I think about what we must sound like to God. How does He know who's in trouble and needs help? How did he know to come to us?" The person in trouble is the young narrator's father, Henry Biggs, the pastor of St. Matthews whose church is besieged with a litany of problems including rising bills and declining donations. Jeremiah's questions and the refrain of the opening song of St. Matthew's choir, which introduces a God who "may not come when you want Him, but He'll be right there on time," foreshadow the film's salute to a supernatural God. But the distressed look on Reverend Biggs's face suggests that the pastor does not believe his own choir's repeated exhortation, "Help is on the way." Despite his lack of faith, God does respond to the reverend's desperation by sending an angel named Dudley. As the plot unfolds, the struggling pastor overcomes doubt and grows in confidence through the angel's guidance and intervention. *The Preacher's Wife* offers more paranormal activity than one will see in the entire oeuvre of Christian filmmaker Tyler Perry and most Christian dramas.

Two years later, Hype Williams's urban drama *Belly* (1998) appears to emulate *The Preacher's Wife* by hinting at the prospect of supernatural intervention until its bait-and-switch tactic sends God flying back to the sidelines. The sequence occurs during the end of *Belly* when a troubled thug named Tommy strategically positions himself to snuff out a religious luminary called the Minister moments before the new millennium commences. Unsurprised by Tommy's abrupt gun-toting presence in his office, the Minister offers his would-be killer a long speech that begins with a depiction of the dire situation that black youth face on streets plagued with drugs and violence. The Minister shifts his message to divine justice by asking if Tommy thinks God will allow such hatred and evil to go unpunished before intervening. He then informs Tommy, "Tonight with this new millennium God will begin to overcome this evil," giving the impression that God has had enough and is ready to stop evil with firepower from heaven. But the more the Minister talks, the more his suggestion of God's power to harness evil takes the form of a humanist mission armed with truth and love, which he petitions Tommy to join:

> Help me to stop the slaughter of our children. Help me to put an end to the disrespect and dishonor of our most valuable resource, the black woman. Help me to put an end to the destruction of the young mind through the use of drugs, alcohol. Help me to build up a population of great thinkers, people who create

change through thoughtfulness and spirituality. Will you choose that truth? Will you? Will you choose light over the darkness?

Moved by his speech, Tommy surrenders his gun and embraces the Minister, whose film-ending speech raises the prospect of divine retribution only moments later to clarify that God is totally dependent on human hands to fulfill such a mission. Beginning as an apocalyptic edict, the Minister's speech morphs into a pedestrian appeal for activism.

In Gary Harvey's movie *Taken From Me: The Tiffany Rubin Story* (2011), the protagonist's six-year-old son Kobe is abducted and taken to South Korea by his Korean-American father. When Tiffany's mother tells her, "We said a special prayer for you at church today," Tiffany responds, "What good is another prayer gonna do? I've been on my knees every night. Kobe's still not back and I don't have the money to get him back." Tiffany eventually receives crucial help from an advocate named Mark Miller who has a successful track record retrieving abducted children and reuniting them with their families. Mark provides vital consultation and tactical assistance, not only toward preparing Tiffany to retrieve her son, but also in accompanying her to South Korea to execute the strategy. The same Christian mother who urged her daughter to have faith in God for Kobe's return now is suddenly troubled by the prospect of Tiffany traveling to South Korea to play a direct role toward securing Kobe's return. Perhaps Tiffany's mother expected God to miraculously bring Kobe back with no risk to her daughter. To her mother's chagrin, Tiffany decides she is not going to wait around for a miracle and puts her faith in the implementation of a rational plan under the professional guidance of Mark Miller. Thus the movie, even with its intermittent spiritual discourse and Christian perspectives, ultimately advocates a modern message of self-reliance and professionalization.

Before heading off to Asia, Tiffany invites her mother's pastor and church members over the house. The pastor promises to surround Tiffany and her family with prayer until she brings Kobe back. But faith in this film is construed as support and comfort rather than as a mechanism to release God's intervening power. Tiffany and Mark carry out a perfectly timed plan using grit and guile, while breaking a few laws to achieve their goal. And whereas one could claim that God ultimately sanctioned their plan, such a conclusion still places God on the sidelines while humans make all the big plays to change outcomes. The pastor and congregants provide prayer and comfort, but it is agentive tactical action that eventually brings Kobe home.

Films like *New Jack City* (1991), *Juice* (1992), *Poetic Justice* (1993), *Sugar Hill* (1994), *Dead Presidents* (1995), *Paid in Full* (2002), and a host of other contemporary urban dramas present drugs and violence in black communities in such a way as to inevitably broker the topics of suffering and evil. Two additional films stand out for their brief but important allusions to God in the context of black tragedy. In a crucial scene in *Boyz N the Hood* (1991), Doughboy scans the abundance of people hanging out on Crenshaw Boulevard and asserts, "Goddamn, there's a lot of motherfuckers out here," prompting his friend Chris to reprimand him for using God's name in vain. Chris then asks their friend Dooky if he believes in God and Dooky responds by pointing to the wonders of nature as proof of God's existence. Doughboy counters Dooky's "intelligent-design" apologetic by inserting the problem of evil as a pervasive part of contemporary black life: "There ain't no God! If there was a God then why He be letting motherfuckers get smoked every night?" Two years later, *Menace II Society* (1993) offers a similar theodical take after Caine's grandfather preaches from the Bible to Caine and his friend O-Dog, and O-Dog responds, "Sir, I don't think God really care too much about us. Or he wouldn't have put us here. I mean look where we stay at. It's all fucked, it's messed up around here." Caine's narration tops off the scene by revealing that his grandfather's continuous preaching would go through one ear and out the other. Both urban dramas present the harrowing conditions of violence, poverty, drugs, and death as challenges against neatly packaged presumptions about a divinely governed universe. If God intervenes in time and space, Doughboy, Caine, and O-Dog don't see any evidence of that intervention in the tragic environs they inhabit. But if one expects to see gritty street films convey theodical skepticism, the fact that the following Christian dramas also set their sails to secular currents is less foreseeable.

Early in Rob Hardy's film *The Gospel* (2005), Bishop Taylor's teenage son David rushes to the hospital to visit his ailing mother. Sensing the seriousness of her condition, David kneels at her bed and prays, "Dear Lord, please don't let my mother die. She's done so much for people and we need her here with us Lord. I'll do anything you ask, anything, please!" But God does not answer David's prayer and so his mother dies. The film jumps fifteen years and we see David as a rising star in the music industry having long abandoned the clerical aspirations of his youth. Bishop Taylor's diagnosis with prostate cancer brings David home and the prodigal son begins warming up to church again. In a poignant scene, David rushes to the hospital to see Bishop Taylor, as it appears his cancer has reached its culmination. David learned something from his earlier experience at his mother's deathbed: that God is not in the business of healing. So this time the concerned son does not attempt to make any deals with God. Whereas the death of his mother rocked his faith, Bishop Taylor's death does not shake his restored faith, as David has accepted God's sidelined status.

In Shavar Ross's film *Lord Help Us* (2007), Reverend Henry Thomas and his wife Dorinda enjoy forty-two years of marriage before Dorinda expires from ovarian cancer, leaving the pastor of Mt. Moriah Baptist Church disheartened. A flashback reveals the couple's last conversation in which Dorinda attempts to prepare her husband for her pending death, while the reverend assures her, "You're already healed in my eyes," claiming that God has never let him down. But Dorinda does die, and less than a week after her funeral Reverend Thomas shocks his congregation by stepping down as pastor. Six months later we see the reverend drinking to numb the pain of missing his wife. He speaks disparagingly of God to his maid Kayla, "Didn't expect the Good Lord to take her away from me like He did. I don't know why He let me down. I had all the faith in the world. Just don't know why He let me down." Kayla responds by reminding him, "She's in a better place now. She doesn't have to suffer anymore." Kayla then offers Reverend Thomas advice she learned from a friend, "Sometimes God will let someone you love die just so they don't suffer anymore." Reverend Thomas accepts this counsel and concludes that he's been selfish in his anger at God instead of realizing that his wife had suffered enough. Kayla's soothing words help him reconnect with God and make steps toward regaining control over his church. It is important to note how Kayla's encouragement only makes sense to a person who has learned to take for granted God's sidelined status. In proposing that God shows mercy by letting sick people die to end their suffering, Kayla overlooks how an omnipotent God can show even more mercy by healing Dorinda of ovarian cancer so that she could both be alive and pain-free.

David Kane Garcia's film *The Prayer Circle* (2013) balances its explicitly evangelical perspective with the constraints of a sidelined God. The film is set in the aftermath of the robbery of a convenience store. Annie, Tony, Michelle, and Will are the four victims who served as hostages in the incident. Tony was pistol-whipped by the perpetrators and suffered a severely damaged arm that ended his military career. The masked armed robbers used Annie as a bargaining chip during their standoff with the police, such that she was held at gunpoint for the duration of the hostage event. Will and Michelle were also used as pawns. Even though the police eventually succeeded in apprehending the culprits, the incident traumatized each victim, necessitating that they meet regularly as a support and Bible study group to heal themselves and each other.

Annie invites Wood, the recently paroled get-away driver of the robbery, to one of their meetings for him to offer an apology for his participation in the incident. While Wood's presence initially spawns hostility, they eventually work out their differences and accept his apology. But oddly enough, the meeting allows for Wood to discover that Annie's son Barry was the teen who killed Wood's mother in a car accident. Hence the film unfolds multiple levels of forgiveness and conflict and two contexts to see divine passivity at play. Not only did God allow Annie, Will, Tony, and Michelle to endure life-changing trauma as hostages, but God also allowed Wood's Christian mother to die in a car accident generated by Barry's careless drag racing. *The Prayer Circle* demonstrates the vulnerability of Christians to the turning tides of fate. God functions as a source of inspiration and comfort but is absent when people seem most needful of direct intervention.

In Stephen Tolkin's film *A Day Late and a Dollar Short* (2014), the protagonist Viola, the matriarch of a troubled Christian family, learns from her doctor that she has a fatal illness. She spends her last moments trying to prepare her adult children for her absence and repair their own familial troubles. Paradoxically, the one occasion Viola is in church she spends more time urging her daughter to give make-up fellatio to Viola's son-in-law than seeking God's healing. In fact, the only time Viola addresses God is in her dying words to say, "This is it Lord, remember, I just want my kids to be happy. I want them to find their place in the world." Throughout the duration of her illness, Viola never offers a hint of confidence that God could restore her health. Like Viola, a Christian woman named Shirley suffers a fatal illness in Tyler Perry's film *Madea's Big Happy Family* (2011). At Shirley's deathbed, Tammy begs her mother to pray for God's healing, but the longsuffering Christian informs Tammy and the rest of the family that her healing will come on the other side in heaven. Shirley's faith in God's existence provides great meaning and comfort and yet her trust in God's healing power is absent throughout her ordeal.

CONCLUSION

In her analysis of Tyler Perry's films, Andrea White (2014) links Perry's humanist project of self-cultivation and emphasis on personal wellbeing with the prosperity gospel's individualist deployment of spirituality. White classifies any causal link between faith and prosperity as a naïve theological understanding of grace. But perhaps White underestimates or altogether misses the pessimism in Perry's filmic outlook that contradicts the theological dynamism of prosperity teachings. Whereas proponents of the prosperity gospel proffer an active and interventionist God who is ready and able to prevent or relieve financial and physical hardship among faith-filled Christians, Perry's plot resolutions point to human activity as the only feasible remedy for black suffering. In *Meet the Browns*, while Miss Mildred endorses a theological perspective and urges Brenda to wait on the Lord for her breakthrough out of poverty, the plot unfolds carnal solutions to Brenda's problems, thus minimizing space for divine intervention and maximizing recognition of human achievement. And in *Daddy's Little Girls*, it is human vengeance via a premediated vehicular assault and not divine intervention that solves

Monty's problem. The weary mechanic stops waiting on God and takes matters into his own hands. Perry's movies indulge in gospel music and preaching moments that give lip service to God's benevolence, but none of his plot resolutions ultimately point to divine intervention as the crucial mechanism to set situations straight.

Spike Lee is even more deliberate in depicting the Christian God as detached from widespread suffering, racial inequality, and personal tragedy. In *Red Hook Summer*, God does not heal Sister Sweet of her crippled state; God does not intervene to prevent the children of Sister Sweet, Sharon, and Mother Darling from dying of AIDS; God does not relieve Lil' Heaven of its financial problems; God does not heal Box's mother Augusta Williams from a fatal illness; God does not prevent a cleric from sexually abusing a vulnerable boy under his care; and God does nothing radical to mitigate the misery within the impoverished black environs of Red Hook. And so, like Voltaire's *Candide*, Spike Lee offers a philosophical tale with tremendous import for theodicy in depicting Red Hook as a domain that in no way can be construed as the best of all possible worlds that God could create and govern.

In Neema Barnette's prison film *Civil Brand*, Captain Dease rapes Lil' Mama, the film's most prominent Christian. His recompense for the fatal rape and other evil deeds against prisoners comes from three angry victims of his abuse. *Civil Brand* suggests that God's protective powers are null and void and that in this unjust and ungoverned universe, humans must fend for themselves and meet violence with violence. The Christian film *Woman Thou Art Loosed: On the 7th Day* could have easily offered an interventionist role for God to prevent a deranged man's abductions and murders of young children. But instead Bishop Jakes's film is much like *Civil Brand* in how it connects human depravity with a modern understanding of human vulnerability, while offering intermittent sprinkles of religious discourse. In doing so the movie demonstrates how economically privileged people survive and thrive, while vulnerable people suffer due to their lack of social standing. Similarly indicative of vertical boundary work is the way in which the film's protagonist progresses. We learn that Kari overcame her tragic childhood and downward spiral into drugs and prostitution, not by a religious conversion but via the help of a professional counselor. And surprisingly the movie ends with Kari reaffirming her faith to her pastor in a conversation that serves as the context for retelling the events of the movie. Kari's faith is restored, not because God intervenes to save Kari's daughter, but because Kari finally accepts her own personal power to forgive her dead father and move on with her life. Even the erratic move in which Kari steals a gun from special agent Bennett and rushes over to Beth's house to rescue her daughter is reminiscent of Monty (*Daddy's Little Girls*) ignoring his pastor's promise of divine intervention to unleash an assault against his enemies. Like the three angry prisoners in *Civil Brand*, Kari and Monty refuse to wait for God to solve their problems.

This chapter reveals how even films that lay claim to God's intervening hand do so in ways that raise more questions than answers. In this regard, two additional examples are worth noting. Spike Lee's documentary *When the Levees Broke: A Requiem in Four Acts* (2006) features Hurricane Katrina survivors attempting to make sense of the preventable levee breach that devastated so many families in New Orleans and surrounding areas. Act III opens with a prayer by a cleric, Mother Audrey Mason:

> Father, in the name of Jesus we come at you, our Lord, saying thank you. Thanking you for being so kind with your mercy, your love, and your grace. Father, as we wade through the water, my mind thought about the song that my old ancestors used to sing, what I was raised up on. Father, as I walked through that water all I could say was Lord wading in the water, wading in the water, God's gonna trouble the water. Father, you troubled that water for our protection, and I want to thank you, Lord. I want to thank you for bringing us through that water and as we wade, God, you was there bringing us over to destiny.

While Mother Mason's prayer alludes to God's protective intervention in the flooded streets, Spike Lee ends Act III with the voice of another mother, not a cleric like Mother Mason, but the parent of a five-year-old girl who drowned in those divinely protected Katrina flood waters Mother Mason alluded to in her prayer. With tears streaming down her face, Kimberly Polk laments the fact that she never had an opportunity to say goodbye to her daughter. Act III concludes with Serena Polk's funeral and her distraught mother walking off in the distance. Mother Mason's opening prayer and Act III's closing memorial confirm how many filmic attempts to project an interventionist God in the midst of black suffering and human tragedy ultimately end up presenting God as inscrutably disengaged when black bodies need God most. Mother Mason's claims on God's protective intervention seem discordant with the fact that hundreds of children like Serena Polk died in those allegedly troubled waters of Hurricane Katrina.

The prospect of divine intervention is even more out of sync in Haile Gerima's *Ashes and Embers* (1982), so much so that one can safely suppose satirical intentionality behind its inclusion, especially when considering Gerima's hostile treatment of Christianity in his later film *Sankofa* (1993). Nate Charles's grandmother informs the recently returned Vietnam veteran that she prayed for him every day while he was at war and insists her prayers are the reason he made it back alive. She reiterates this claim when testifying at her church, perceiving the protagonist's safe return as confirmation that God answered her prayers. But such an assertion does not come without its own absurdist implications. For the notion of God intervening in time and space to bring one man home safely from the horrors of war pales in comparison to the destruction of life and torment that the same man experienced in Vietnam, some of which viewers confront in vivid flashbacks. If God is active in protecting the protagonist's body, as his grandmother claims, then God is incongruously passive regarding the protection of the same man's mind, as Nate Charles can't shake recollections of fields replete with bones of women and children killed by American bombs, along with images of an exploding child, headless bodies, and comrades turned into corpses. His grandmother would have a tough time explaining why God saved her grandson but did not intervene to help tens of thousands of soldiers and civilians who suffered brutal deaths in the war. The film also exposes his grandmother's own suffering and how she laments having to sell off her family's land to pay delinquent property taxes. The grandmother's early claims of divine intervention are overshadowed by more potent suggestions of nonintervention within the film's bleak depiction of war and the misfortunes that black people face in the United States. Hence, *Ashes and Embers* confirms how those rare filmic plots that endorse divine interventionist capacities to remove black suffering or balance the scales of justice usually end up as fuel for Anthony Pinn's (2002: 9) fiery query: "If history is so designed and God is concerned with the welfare of all human beings because they contribute to civilization and the divine plan, why do African Americans suffer more than most?" The simplest answer rests with the notion of a modern God.

Epilogue

Africa

The New Cinematic Holocaust

In a 2006 public trial, representatives of African countries accused the World Bank and the International Monetary Fund of ratifying crippling provisions that perpetuate African insolvency as a ploy to facilitate multinational corporations' lucrative extractions of the continent's natural resources. Since no African court possesses the jurisdictional capacity to indict such powerful institutions, filmmaker Abderrahmane Sissako dramatizes this legal confrontation in his experimental film *Bamako* (2006). Set in the capital of Mali, *Bamako* features real lawyers questioning an assortment of witnesses on how the vicious cycle of debt and the stringent adjustment policies imposed to ensure its payment hinder Africa's ability to provide basic civil services to its people and handle challenges like the spread of HIV/AIDS. In her closing statement, one of the prosecuting attorneys offers a statistical snapshot of the continent's vulnerable trajectory: the life expectancy for Africans has dropped to forty-six; fifty million children are scheduled to die over the next five years; three million children will die of malaria in the next year. Any report compiled around the date of her closing statement could augment those alarming integers with additional indicators of Africa's forlorn future: the continent is responsible for less than five percent of global production; nearly fifty percent of Africa's population lives in abject poverty; Africans make up more than sixty percent of the world's HIV/AIDS cases (Sparks 2003).

Bamako balances the bleakness of the trial with intermittent forays into Malian life. One of these ethnographic breaks occurs in a church and features a preacher exhorting his congregation to trust in God to straighten all that is crooked in African lives. Viewers counting effective strikes between the trial's disconsolate diagnosis of African deprivation and the preacher's theological sanguinity might concede that the latter is so remarkably outmatched by the former that *Bamako*'s theistic intrusion merely functions as Sissako's method of satirizing divine intervention as only an alleged solution to African suffering. The film's meticulous itemization of African scarcity suggests that if evil exists, it does not manifest in demonic forces but rather through the decrees of powerful institutions, and if there is a credible solution to straighten all that is crooked in African lives, as the preacher infers, it will not come in the form of a spiritual breakthrough but rather by means of decisive assaults against exploitative structures that afflict African nations. There is little doubt that *Bamako*'s theodical blueprint is biased against the optimism of the preacher's sermon. And thus the film is quite overt in how it sidelines God and signifies black suffering with modern tools of analysis.

A year after the release of *Bamako*, another film contrasts African tragedy and claims of divine efficacy. *Without the King* (2007), a documentary on the social problems in Swaziland, offers a distressing scene depicting ravished bodies in the AIDS ward of Mbabane Government Hospital. As the camera closes in on a sign that says, "Jesus Takes Away Sin and Diseases in Our Bodies," we hear the sounds of a man preaching in his Swazi native tongue. The camera finally catches up with the mysterious voice, exposing a man with Bible in hand. This scene breaks from the film's sociological analysis of black suffering to offer a spiritual elucidation of the problem and solution to said suffering. The optics of dying bodies and a sign claiming Jesus's primacy over diseases offer an eerie apposition of tragic suffering and supernatural intervention. If Jesus does in fact take away diseases, as the sign suggests, then viewers of the documentary will be hard pressed to find evidence of this manifest in Mbabane's AIDS ward or, indeed, in any film on the devastating impact of HIV/AIDS in African countries. *Bamako* and *Without the King* present Africa as a context for examining secularizing capacities of cinematic theodicy that incorporate stochastic claims of divine solutions to black African suffering.

This epilogue explores how cinematic integrations of black African suffering and God-talk arouse viewers to consider what God and religion have to say in the face of great tragedies and wanton human destruction. It assesses theodical import in dozens of films covering the vicious display of human waste in the Rwandan genocide, the cruelty of South African apartheid, the heinous decimation of citizens in Central Africa, and other ethnic cleansings and national tragedies to elucidate how cinema provides an interpretive lens through which to experience and perceive historical events of great trauma and evil as they relate to God or religion. This epilogue introduces Nollywood's brand of deistic dualism where occultic powers and dark forces exert supernatural sway over outcomes, while the supreme God of the universe remains stunningly passive and detached from individual suffering.

For much of the twentieth century, Auschwitz signified the cinematic breeding ground for representations of God and the problem of evil. But toward the end of the century, Africa emerged as the hotspot for cinematic contemplations on theodicy. Like treatments of the Holocaust, films covering black suffering in Africa display the theodical work of ascribing boundaries to God. But while doing so they accomplish the exegetical work of: exposing the material costs of genocide, oppression, and other forms of trauma; coding and narrating evil deeds and actors; and situating black sufferers within symbolic resources of collective identities of trauma. The epilogue's coverage of theodicy in numerous films set in African regions exposes conundrums and contradictions within attempts to place side by side God's interventionist capacities and the slings and arrows of misfortune. And perhaps no other artistic undertakings more conspicuously sideline God in the context of human tragedy than filmic treatments of the most compressed killing spree in human history, the Rwandan genocide.

RWANDAN GENOCIDE

Ousmane Sembène made an astounding assertion in an interview: "Since 1960, Africans have killed more Africans than a hundred years of slavery and colonization" (Gadjigo 2008: 195). No occurrence in recent African history better corroborates Sembène's calculation than the Rwandan genocide. Cinema accomplished much to awaken world consciousness concerning the savagery that slayed almost a million (mostly Tutsi) Rwandans in less than a hundred days. Fused within these filmic representations are moments when God-talk and religion accompany the carnage and genocidal cruelty. In Raoul Peck's *Sometimes in April* (2005), the priest of a Catholic boarding school tells a schoolteacher named Marti that he can't stop Hutu rebels from killing their Tutsi girls, even as Marti reminds him these are students he has raised as if they were his own daughters. The priest responds to Marti, "What can I do, my child? We cannot protect all of them. I do not have the power to change the situation. We must pray." The priest remains concerned yet powerless when Hutu rebels enact his worst fears and take over the school, demanding the ethnic separation of students to spare the Hutus. But rather than abandoning their Tutsi peers, the Hutu students refuse to be separated—and thus are killed with them. So the priest's prayers are unable to save any of his girls from the massacre.

Nick Hughes's *100 Days* (2001) offers a far more hurtful depiction of a Catholic cleric. For context, it should be noted that an overwhelming majority of the Rwandan population at the time of the genocide identified as Christians or members of a Christian church, implying that the mass murder campaign was organized and implemented almost entirely by people who call themselves Christians (Locke 2004). The film *100 Days* offers Father Kennedy as a clerical representation of this striking demographic reality. The

Hutu priest lures desperate Tutsis seeking sanctuary only to call militias to kill every man, woman, and child residing in the church. Father Kennedy not only aids and abets genocide, but rapes young Tutsi women he keeps under bondage as his concubines. In a crucial sequence, Father Kennedy imprisons and rapes Josette and then takes her back to the church to see thousands of Tutsi corpses including members of her family. Later in the film we see Tutsi children locked in a shack, which is then filled with gasoline and ignited to burn these children alive. *100 Days* also offers poignant scenes that signify the disinformation campaign that convinces regular Hutu citizens to kill their Tutsi neighbors. In doing so, the film codes and narrates the Rwandan genocide not as a spontaneous break with civility, but rather as a carefully planned and well-organized deployment of propaganda, skilled leadership, and clerical craftiness to harness Hutu aggression—in other words, as quite the modern massacre.

A decade later, the film *Kinyarwanda* (2011) reveals how Muslim clerics gave refuge to thousands of vulnerable Tutsis and how a Tutsi priest worked with these Muslim clerics to provide spiritual leadership and counsel. It is perhaps the only treatment of the genocide that offers a semblance of hope that competing religious institutions can work together to serve the better interests of human survival. But even as *Kinyarwanda* captures clerical ecumenical courage, it in no way offers divine intervention as an option to protect vulnerable Rwandans from the machete. The film shows human efforts mitigating the impact of murderous campaigns rather than divine interposition. And the film exposes how many people were murdered, thus generating questions crucial to theodicy similarly raised during the Holocaust concerning why some people suffer and die, while others are saved. *Kinyarwanda* ends with the protagonist's narration:

> The Rwandan genocide lasted about one hundred days. It was long enough for the seasons to change. Long enough for over one million women, children, and men to die. Long enough for some to question their faith. Long enough to question God. Some faith was restored, some even strengthened. Long enough for us to share our stories.

Like most filmic portrayals of the genocide, *Kinyarwanda* makes no attempt to erase God but rather sequesters God to the sidelines. If faith is restored and strengthened through the ordeal, it is the kind of faith that understands God's renegotiated contract as cosmic coach. While the above three films exhibit intermittent moments relevant to any discussion of theodicy, the intensive interface of genocidal evil and God-talk in Michael Caton-Jones's 2005 biopic *Beyond the Gates* (titled *Shooting Dogs* outside the United States) warrants more careful consideration.

Set on the campus of a Catholic secondary school in Kigali that doubles as a military base for the United Nations peacekeepers, *Beyond the Gates*'s theodical dynamism manifests mostly via the dialogues and actions of Father Christopher, the school's European headmaster, and Joe Connor, the younger and more theologically liberal new English teacher from Britain, as the two colleagues deal with escalating killings in Kigali. Early on while Father Christopher is teaching students doctrinal fundamentals like transubstantiation and the meaning behind Jesus's salvific act on the cross, Hutu rebels within the same city are organizing lists of Tutsi families to target for butchery. The presence of the UN peacekeepers provides protection, so the campus quickly morphs into an asylum for more than 2,000 Tutsis fleeing Hutu militias throughout Kigali. But as the film unfolds, Father Christopher, Joe, and others gradually lose trust that the UN peacekeepers will come through for vulnerable Rwandans seeking sanctuary.

Joe tells the priest, "It's really weird out there Christopher," alluding to the militias he saw enforcing roadblocks during his brief trip off campus. Shortly after, a former Rwandan government official comes to the school to explain to the captain of the UN peacekeepers that the violence that is brewing throughout the city is not random but planned. The captain responds by reminding the official that theirs is a peacekeeping mission and the frustrated governmental official responds: "Captain, you are no doubt aware what the Nazis attempted to do with the Jews? This is what we're facing here. These Hutu extremists who have taken control even call this a Tutsi problem. They plan to wipe the Tutsis out, do you understand me? All of them!" The official's allusion to the Shoah serves as a symbolic reference point from which to interpret the brewing genocidal activities in Rwanda and perhaps will continue to serve as a referent for all genocidal campaigns in the future. But such a discursive deployment of Nazi aggression fails to convey to the captain (and to the world community) the seriousness of what is brewing in Kigali; that it is a crime against humanity like the Holocaust.

As things are getting desperate, Father Christopher dresses for Mass when Joe asks, "Do you think this is the best time for that?" Father Christopher replies, "Times of stress people need to commune with God," to which Joe answers, "I think maybe they'd prefer some food, water, instead of reassurance." This exchange echoes a brewing conflict between the English teacher who is consumed with meeting the practical needs of Rwandans housed on their campus and the priest who prioritizes spiritual disciplines in this taxing moment. We see this bifurcation of urgencies spill into the next scene with Father Christopher presiding over Mass, while Joe is outside helping men create fortifications and prepare food.

As time passes, Father Christopher learns that ten Belgian soldiers are missing and deduces that if militias can target UN peacekeepers then the city's situation is quite desperate. Joe's student Marie translates a radio broadcast that alerts everyone about the genocidal danger that is looming, "Who will fill the empty graves? The cockroaches are hiding in the churches; they are hiding in the schools." Later we see Joe driving with a BBC reporter and cameraperson to capture footage of bloody slaughtered children on the side of the road. Father Christopher also learns how his clerical colleague, Father John, and all his parishioners were hacked to death in church.

When Father Christopher leaves campus to go to the pharmacy to get medicine for a newborn Tutsi baby, the pharmacist puts him in a quandary by asking if the prescription is for a Hutu or a Tutsi. The priest lies and tells the pharmacist that the prescription is for a Hutu baby. And while waiting for the pharmacist to get the medicine, Father Christopher notices a trail of blood that eventually leads to the corpse of a slaughtered man. The shocked cleric receives the medicine and drives off and must employ deceit again when he reaches a roadblock where one of the militiamen tries to confiscate his medicine. The priest pretends he is sick, claiming the medicine is for himself and not for a Tutsi. During this exchange, another militiaman recognizes Father Christopher and directs the priest's attention to corpses of women and children near him like a proud artist drawing attention to his masterwork.

Father Christopher visits a convent and quickly discovers the source of a terrible stench, inducing him to cover his nose: three slaughtered nuns. He surmises from the positioning of their bodies and elevated dresses that the nuns were raped and then killed. Still in shock and utter despair from viewing the corpses of the nuns, Father Christopher returns to campus expressing sentiments and directives that sound more like Joe. For example, when Marie informs him they have no more firewood, the priest instructs her, "Use the Bibles," a provocative solution that signifies he has seen enough evil in one day to render Bibles useful only for providing warmth. As Father Christopher collects his makeshift fuel, he ponders if he's made a difference before telling Joe, "I spent thirty years on this bloody continent. The only thing we ever had that ever stayed the same was hope. We always had hope Joe. Fact is that's all we ever had. Now I think we're running dry."

Just when things appear as if they cannot get worse, a battalion of French troops arrives on campus with its trucks and weapons. Sounds of cheers from desperate Rwandans greet the newly arrived soldiers from Europe. But the hopeful Rwandans learn that those French troops are commissioned to evacuate Europeans and non-Rwandans from the school, leaving more than two thousand Rwandans to fend for themselves against the Hutu militiamen patiently waiting beyond the gates for the French troops and UN peacekeeping soldiers to leave. While others are now deflated, Marie is in chapel with a few young people and they recite the Apostle's Creed in a dispassionate way as if it's a rote exercise. Marie stops to ask Father Christopher a question most relevant to theodicy, "Does He love everyone? Does He even love those men on the roads outside?" Father Christopher responds, "God doesn't always like everything we do, that's our choice, but He loves all His children."

In the next scene, a few despondent families decide to leave the compound and are swiftly murdered when the militia catches up to them. The audience must witness these murders in real time in contrast to how corpses signified most of the film's previous deaths. Joe watches as militiamen use axes, machetes, and guns to kill their Tutsi prey. In perhaps the most shocking scene, a woman is hiding in the bush with her baby and the baby starts crying, alerting Hutus who in turn hack the woman and the baby to death. Later a disheartened Joe asks Father Christopher if humans have a cutoff valve that shuts down when they experience too much pain. Since the priest has no answer, Joe facetiously tends to his own question: "God knows. Maybe we should ask Him, if He's still around." With the French troops already removed, the remaining UN peacekeepers disclose their orders to leave the campus as well. While Joe is despairing about leaving the people, especially after seeing what militiamen were capable of doing to Tutsi families after a few wandered off campus after the French troops left, he ultimately decides to evacuate with the UN peacekeepers, leaving his students and two thousand Rwandans to face brutal deaths.

Father Christopher is resolute that the Rwandans should not die before receiving Holy Communion and so the next filmic sequence goes back and forth between Father Christopher's Mass and the UN troops packing up their gear to leave the compound, a daunting juxtaposition between a salvific spiritual exercise and physical abandonment of epic proportion. It is important to note Father Christopher's own sidelining of God throughout the film, as at no moment does the priest pray to God for protection from the ensuing onslaught. Thus, the priest's lack of prayer for an eleventh-hour intervention is itself a form of vertical boundary work that pervades many cinematic representations of the genocide and black African suffering more generally. It is as if many desperate people know in advance that God won't intervene to save them.

Before Joe leaves with the UN troops, he asks Father Christopher why he is staying with the Rwandans to face certain death, and the priest answers a different question, "You ask me Joe, 'Where is God in everything that is happening here in all this suffering?' I know exactly where He is. He's right here with these people suffering. His love is here more intense and profound than I ever felt." Father Christopher's statement resembles sentiments of the liberation theologians discussed in chapter 2, which place God's presence and loyalty on the side of sufferers, even as such priority warrants no divine intervention on behalf of those vulnerable people. While God's love might be with Father Christopher and the Tutsis on campus, God's protection is not with them and, therefore, immediately after the UN troops leave, the militia leader blows his whistle and shouts, "Begin the work!" Father Christopher and thousands of remaining Rwandans are slaughtered, and in the aftermath the camera pans over a sea of dead men, women, and children.

Beyond the Gates pits cruel statistics of black carnage against the backdrop of religion's salvific interactions with humans through rituals and God-talk. Ultimately God and religious rituals provide existential exuberance but prove ineffective toward stopping and explaining genocidal impulsion. God and religion function as symbolic vehicles, offering meaning and comfort but no cogent narrative to illuminate why God allows genocidal activity against innocent people. *Beyond the Gates'* tacit message for theodicy resonates with other filmic treatments of the genocide: God may offer love and comfort, but will offer no intervention on behalf of vulnerable victims expiring in evil's grip. Father Christopher dies with his flock and Joe is safe as a result of his European privilege. The difference between living and dying is judged by French troops and UN peacekeepers based on the color of one's skin and one's nationality. As with Jewish Holocaust films, treatments of the genocide tacitly promote a central tenet of theodical secularity: God offers no protection against the truculent forces of human depravity.

The shocking depth and breadth of human suffering depicted in cinematic treatments of the Holocaust as well as in Rwanda and more recent genocidal developments in Africa challenge confidence in a sovereign playbook guiding human history. But unlike how movies that address the horrors of Auschwitz have intellectual traditions to inform and undergird them in the interpretive process of narrating evil, the more recent horrors documented in films about the Rwandan genocide and other forms of terror in Africa are too current to be reinforced by a longstanding intellectual architecture of post-genocidal reflection. Put differently, filmic treatments of the Shoah are built on cultural work already in motion to universalize Jewish suffering, while movies in the context of African evil and suffering play a more immediate role in alerting world populations to the barbarity of genocidal attacks against suffering black bodies. Cinema provides the ritualistic performances to elevate the Rwandan genocide to the status of a universal Holocaust event and plays a direct role toward humanizing victims, coding and narrating evil, and generating intercontinental solidary throughout its poignant significations of African suffering. Cinema persuades world populations not to perceive the Rwandan genocide as just another demographically differentiated ethnic squabble, but as a crime against all humanity.

SOUTH AFRICA

The South African television mini-series *Shaka Zulu* (1986) tells the story of the legendary nineteenth-century warrior and king whose military leadership transformed the Zulu nation from a small tribe into a regional dynasty. The historical Shaka reigned over the Zulus from 1818 to 1828 (Chalk and Jonassohn 1990), and much of the history retold in this mini-series about Shaka's supremacy, as one of its characters, Henry Fynn, describes, "hinges on witchcraft and tales of the supernatural." Despite all the supernatural pronouncements and prophecies about Shaka's magnitude, the end of the story is tragically human with his mother's unexpected death and Shaka's ensuing madness. The dark windup of the mini-series is merely a microcosm of the calamity black South Africans would suffer in subsequent generations. And no artform interconnects God-talk and religious representation with the terror and tragedy of South African apartheid better than cinema.

Richard Attenborough's film *Cry Freedom* (1987) is loosely based on the real-life friendship between the black activist martyr Steve Biko and a white newspaper editor named Donald Woods. Their rapport gives the editor a new lens through which to view his racial and economic privilege and the repressive South African government. In an early scene with the two men visiting a black township, the activist offers the editor insight on the depressive dimensions of social stratification:

> It's a miracle a child survives here at all. Most of the women who have work permits are domestic maids so they only get to see their kids for a couple of hours on Sundays. The place is full of drunks, thuggery, people so desperate for anything they'll beat a kid bloody if they thought he had five pounds.

Biko informs Woods how the apartheid system perpetuates inequality and humiliation, causing black South Africans to question the value of their humanity.

In another scene, Biko's wife Ntsiki gives the editor a quick tour of their church, while explaining the hustle and bustle of social activity that Woods observes: "We're trying to make a kind of community center where black people can meet, maybe have classes." The camera captures how the political and practical community interests have literally commandeered the worship and theological components of the church. Positioning the church as the fulcrum for cultural awareness and black activism, *Cry Freedom* replaces a theological prism through which to assess the sins of apartheid with a political one. By cleansing Biko's church of all remnants of a spiritual function, the film offers a secular religion that collapses the difference between praxis and metaphysical allegiances. Its message for theodicy is clear: God is removed from Biko's church just as God is nowhere to be found in the South African black struggle. In God's place we find cultural awareness, consciousness raising, and other agentive human efforts. Even Father Kani, the heroic black priest who helps Donald Woods and his family escape South Africa, appears more as an activist than a spiritual leader. The film doesn't show him praying or offering spiritual counsel, but only tactically engaged in his political mission, even when it requires lying and falsifying documents. All throughout the film and up to the point of his death, Biko's faith is not in God but in the kind of country South Africa can become through heroic activists like himself. The only time Biko refers to clergy or anything remotely spiritual is in jest after Woods teasingly accuses the activist of being a dirty rugby player. Biko responds, "I was taught by a Catholic priest. What do you expect?" From Biko's vantage point, the church is not a house of God, nor a theological force against the problem of evil, but simply brick and mortar to house political and cultural activities. Similarly, the masked men who break into Biko's church and destroy everything within reach of their swinging bats (culprits we later find out are white police officers) obviously do not think of the church as having sacred significance.

While lyrics of a song intoned at Biko's funeral call for God to bless Africa, the overall tenor of the film concedes that God has already abandoned black South Africans in general and Biko in his martyrdom. But the best summation of God's sidelined status is uttered by Donald Woods in a dispute with his wife Wendy over the costs and merits of his choice to write Biko's biography. Considering how South African officials harassed, tortured, and murdered Biko for subverting white supremacy, it is obvious to Woods that writing Biko's biography necessitates leaving his homeland with his wife and four children, a move that brings Wendy to a state of great unease. Woods tells his wife, "Steve died for nothing if we let them just bury his name." Wendy responds, "Who do you think you are, God?" to which the editor responds, "I'm not God. But we know what this country is like now. And we can't accept it and we can't wait for God to come and change it." All three heroic figures in this film—Biko, Woods, and Father Kani—accentuate human action as the remedial force to extirpate the structures and strictures of South African apartheid. None of these heroes promote or place any faith in God's ability to provide solutions to black South African suffering.

Darrell Roodt's film *Cry, the Beloved Country* (1995) is a remake of a 1951 British film with the same title and is similarly set in 1946. The film's protagonist, Stephen Kumalo, is a black pastor in Natal who travels to Johannesburg on a quest to find missing members of his family. Reverend Kumalo's brother-in-law first went missing, and his sister went to Johannesburg to look for her husband but never found him and then also went missing. Kumalo's son Absalom combed the same city looking for his aunt and, in doing so, also disappeared, so the reverend travels to Johannesburg to find answers concerning his missing brother-in-law, sister, and son. Once in Johannesburg, escorted by his young black host, Reverend Msimangu, Kumalo's first move is to visit his brother John, a politician who has no use for the church anymore. Kumalo first encounters his brother delivering a fiery speech about the white man's power being rooted in the gold mines:

> Everything is in the mines. Everything the white man has is built with the gold from the mines. The hospital for Europeans, the biggest hospital south of the equator is built with gold from the mines. But go to our [black] hospital and see our people lying on the floors. They lie so close you cannot step over them. Everything is built on our labor and we get poorer and the white man gets richer.

When John articulates his mantra, "What God has not done for South Africa, men must do," a surprised Kumalo mutters to his host, "My brother has greatly changed." But Msimangu responds that John "has some truth on his side," and presses Kumalo to bear in mind how black people's lives in South Africa are replete with suffering and pain, as the young priest confesses, "Sometimes it is hard even for me to keep faith!"

The film projects three vantage points from which to view the notion of faith and black suffering: a young cleric like Msimangu negotiating racial inequality with his Christian faith, an older political figure like John Kumalo addressing problems with solutions rooted in political action devoid of faith, and Stephen Kumalo's faith that lacks a cogent explanation for the coexistence of black oppression and theological hope. John and Msimangu challenge the protagonist's conservative sensibilities which can't offer theological clarity concerning the racial inequality that plagues the country.

Later in the film a white South African activist named Arthur Jarvis offers an even harsher critique of Christianity in a letter he was writing moments before Kumalo's son Absalom murdered him. Jarvis's letter states, "We call ourselves a Christian people. When posterity comes to judge us it will consign us to the sewers of history, as tyrants, oppressors, criminals." So *Cry, the Beloved Country* not only projects God's inability to disrupt racial inequality and oppression, it also indicts white Christians for their participation in the perpetuation of such oppressive racial conditions. Of note, this film is set two years before apartheid authorizes an era of state-sanctioned campaigns against black freedoms. Toward the end of the film, after Kumalo finds out Absalom has been tried and convicted of murdering Arthur Jarvis, another cleric describes Stephen Kumalo as "the only truly good man I've ever met." Msimangu responds to the cleric's statement with a theodical inquiry: "Then why, I wonder, does God not show him any mercy?"

Despite its many allusions to the Reverend Kumalo's enduring faith, the film's main message for theodicy comes through its triangulation of divine inefficacy: God as powerless to balance the scales of justice, God as unable to alleviate black poverty and pain in Johannesburg, and God as incapable of offering resolution and peace to the faithful cleric Stephen Kumalo. But even while the film reinforces theodical secularity, it serves a moralizing and memorializing function in its depiction of inequities that perpetuate suffering for many black South Africans.

Mandela: Long Walk to Freedom (2013) covers Nelson Mandela's early years as a lawyer and freedom fighter for the African National Congress (ANC), his long stint in prison, and his post-apartheid presidency. In an early scene, young Mandela is diligently working and his wife Evelyn tells him, "Nelson, you can't work all night. I'm going to bed now." Mandela insists on continuing to work and she responds, "You need to give yourself a rest. You can't do everything, give some things to God." Outraged by Evelyn's allusion to a divine aspirant to which he can outsource political struggle, Mandela responds, "Does your God want our children to go hungry? I don't see your God caring for our people. It seems to me that He's looking after the Boers." Mandela responds to his wife's notion of a divine support system by suggesting that divine patronage seems to bypass black South Africans. Mandela's claim captures the notion of divine racism (Jones 1973) through his insinuation that God must not like black people as much as the Boers, the descendants of the Dutch-speaking settlers in South Africa who enjoy all of their society's power, wealth, and social stability. Mandela's theodical retort is incommensurate with black liberationist claims (discussed in chapter 2) on God's partiality toward black people in terms of explicating blacks' disadvantaged status in comparison to whites.

After Mandela's first wife Evelyn divorces him, the ANC activist meets his new love interest, Winnie, whose theological perspective seems more in line with her future husband's outlook. Early in their courtship, while walking in the hills of the countryside, Winnie recalls, "When I was seven years old my little sister started coughing blood and my mother, she begged God to save her. But she died. So ever since then I've known we have to save ourselves and we have to live while we can." If Mandela's first wife Evelyn believes God can intervene to relieve black African suffering and pain, the reflection of Mandela's future second wife, Winnie, resonates with the modern message of the film: South Africans can't rely on divine intervention but must save themselves. But above and beyond its sidelining of God, the film is even more explicit in signifying the corrupting legacy, aggressive tactics, and taken-for-granted notions of white supremacy embedded within the struggles of black South Africans under apartheid. An early scene portrays Nelson Mandela in court questioning a white woman on the witness stand who accuses his client of theft. Rather than responding to his inquiries, an outraged Mrs. De Kock asks the judge, "Am I to be spoken to like this by a native?" After the judge reminds her that the native in question is counsel for the defendant and Mandela continues his interrogation, Mrs. De Kock finally reaches her limit and blurts out, "I will not be spoken to like this. It's disgusting. If I'd known I was going to be so insulted in a court of law, I would never have come!" and exits the witness stand and courtroom. Later scenes offer more gruesome displays of racist contempt when the apartheid government guns down protesting black South Africans in Orlando Township and Sharpeville; tragedies that clarify for viewers the extent to which the white South African power structure was willing to sacrifice the safety of the majority population to preserve the minority's dominance.

But what is more noteworthy is the fact that *Mandela: Long Walk to Freedom* captures and condones Mandela and the ANC's terrorist turn. The film not only builds a convincing case for the ANC's terrorist activity, but also allows Nelson Mandela to remain unapologetic throughout his prison sentence for his active participation in sabotage. It codes the terrorist activity as the inevitable result of vulnerable victims being provoked to adopt a more aggressive solution than non-violence. The film tosses a theodical curveball toward its end when President De Klerk brokers Mandela's prison release and a peaceful exchange of power to the ANC under De Klerk's presumption that God used his presidency to save South Africa. Such a divine calling still has secular undertones in confirming that God can only operate through human hands and rational means rather than through supernatural impositions into history. De Klerk's claim also raises inquiries about God's inefficiency in allowing apartheid to ruin so many generations of South Africans before finding a pragmatic solution to the problem through the office of the presidency. This offers another example of how when cinema raises the notion of divine intervention to relieve black suffering, it not only almost exclusively circumscribes divine mediation as functionally dependent on human hands, but also generates pressing new questions and conundrums about God's intermittent (or perhaps inscrutable) intervention. And if one is keeping score concerning the ways in which black South Africans suffer, one need not look further than cinema's portrayal of their vulnerability to AIDS.

The documentary *Motherland* (2008) reveals that HIV/AIDS has reached pandemic proportions in Africa, taking millions of lives every year. Focusing its attention on South Africa, one of the continent's hardest hit countries by the pandemic, *Motherland* covers mothers from the United States who, to cope with the recent death of a child, take a trip to South Africa to do volunteer work with children and families affected by poverty and AIDS. The trip is designed to offer these American mothers healing through their own acts of compassion. One of *Motherland*'s most memorable scenes occurs in a church where the preacher claims, "Where there is no God there is pain and suffering. When God is with us, we are not threatened. When God is with us, we are not afraid. Because God will not fail us." Shortly after this sermonic interlude the film cuts to another volunteer facility where a South African woman explains, "There's hardly a family that I know that has not been affected by AIDS or by poverty or by some disaster. So together people have borne a lot." That the documentary pitches both claims consecutively highlights an absurd disparity that is relevant to any discussion of theodicy, in the way that the preacher's assertion that "God will not fail us" seems incongruous with the pain and suffering all around him. In a country ransacked by the deadliest disease since the Black Death, and in a documentary that features children so poor that the only time many of them can eat is at school, the claim that God's presence shields people from pain and suffering is a difficult theodical pill to swallow. A South African mother coping with the death of her daughter to AIDS utters the film's telling coda: "Sometimes you feel as though you've been punished by God."

NOLLYWOOD

Akin to how Bollywood signifies India's bustling film industry, the term Nollywood distinguishes a profusion of filmmakers and films from Southern Nigeria since the late 1980s. Most early Nollywood projects were shot on VHS and sold on the streets, prompting a Nigerian journalist's claim that it takes less effort to remove water from a stone than to secure trustworthy data on the country's home-video industry (Oladunjoye 2008). While precise audits of video sales are unattainable, by the turn of the century Nollywood symbolized a dramatic democratization of the movie-making industry, as Onookome Okome confirms:

> Nollywood is not only a huge industry in Nigeria; it is an exceptional field of cultural production, the kind that is difficult to ignore, one that has crossed national boundaries, creating what is akin to a sub-region expression of culture and society. Suffused with recognizable sentiments of the poor and vulnerable in the Nigerian postcolonial economy of want and deprivation, and keenly aware of the massive acceptance that it enjoys, Nollywood has articulated the popular consciousness of the African continent and its diasporas in a form unprecedented here or in cinematic practice anywhere in the world. (Okome 2010: 27)

By 2010, the Nollywood landscape shifts from humble video dramas to large-scale productions, as some filmmakers secure corporate investment and government funding to deliver works on par with Hollywood films (Witt

2017). Many of these so-called "New Nollywood" productions enjoy international casts, large budgets, greater technical sophistication, and worldwide distribution (Austen and Saul 2010; Haynes 2016). Accordingly, Nigeria has fashioned one of the largest film industries in the world, one that flaunts its own distinctive genres and aesthetic patterns, while integrating religious and political artifacts from local, continental, and global cultural-conduits and contexts (Haynes 2016; Witt 2017).

Whether they are crafting small-scale videos screened in the homes of patrons, or large-scale celluloid productions shot in multiple countries and debuted in posh theaters, Nollywood filmmakers are the most visible artistic purveyors of indigenous African expressionism (Krings and Okome 2013). As scholars assess how Nollywood films capture dynamic dimensions of Nigerian spirituality (Tsika 2015), exhibit a syncretic overlaying of Christian and Igbo cultural forms and intersections between supernatural elements and social problems (Haynes 2016), and exude Christian theological undercurrents that vitiate traditional African cultural forms (Pype 2013), their theodical nuances remain unexplored in terms of how Nollywood characters give lip service to God's supremacy and ultimate moral authority, while leaving it up to lower-level spiritual prognosticators to impose change in the world. Despite Nollywood's frequent use of explicitly Christian rhetoric about divine justice and governance, God remains above the fray while only Satan, demons, ghosts, or human mediators of animistic power can affect change in negative or positive ways for black sufferers. No film demonstrates this deistic dualism better than Nollywood's first blockbuster video, Chris Obi Rapu's *Living in Bondage* (1992) and its sequel *Living in Bondage* 2 (1993).

Living in Bondage opens with its protagonist Andy crying out in frustration, "My God, did you bring me into this world to suffer? Am I bewitched or is this my destiny?" Andy's wife Merit hears him and interjects, "Andy, I've told you this before: no one has bewitched you. God has not said that you won't ever be rich." But Andy continues to complain about God's inaction, while comparing himself to thriving peers. This juxtaposition with successful men becomes more critical when we learn that some of them achieved their triumphs not through faith in God but via sacrifices to Lucifer. So early in the film, theodical discourse expresses doubt in a divine solution to Andy's lack of success and foreshadows a more effective spiritual path to achievement.

After squandering his wife's savings on a failed business venture, Andy tells one of his successful colleagues that he is willing to do anything to become rich. This colleague, Paul, senses Andy's urgency and invites him to participate in a money cult that offers sacrifices to Lucifer. During Andy's initiation ceremony, the chief priest asks him to offer his wife up for sacrifice at their next meeting. When Andy protests, Paul reminds him of his earlier claim that he would do anything to be successful and wealthy, and other cult members testify how when they sacrificed their wives Lucifer rewarded them with enormous wealth. Andy barks back that such an act would condemn him to hell, to which the chief priest responds: "The church tells us falsely that there is hell fire. The Holy Bible proclaims God's kindness. Let me ask you, would you condemn your beloved to hell fire? Yes we will wrong Him but He will forgive us." The chief priest then prays for Lucifer to reveal to Andy everything "he is supposed to see, and we will unite in your paradise to end the feast." For Christian viewers, I imagine it must be astonishing to hear the chief priest transition from assuring Andy of God's forgiveness to beseeching revelation from Lucifer in one fell swoop. The fluidity with which Andy and the chief priest go back and forth from affirming Christianity's greatest foe to referencing God and the Bible demonstrates one of Nollywood's earliest and most peculiar forays into deistic dualism. Lucifer is presented as a spiritual ruler not only independent of God but also as more reliable at providing followers with great wealth. But rather than jettisoning the notion of God and projecting Lucifer as the ultimate sovereign of the universe, the chief priest still acknowledges God's supremacy and the Bible as an epistemological foundation for understanding God. And oddly enough, Andy worries that sacrificing his wife will send him to hell but expresses no hesitation about worshipping Lucifer. With the chief priest and other cult members alleging Lucifer's efficacy, we should expect to hear them denounce God, but they don't. This duality remains a staple of Nollywood's unique brand of deism where God is billed as the supreme deity but remains ultimately sidelined, while other spiritual sources outperform the allegedly sovereign ruler in terms of manifesting material rewards.

Andy attempts to fool the cult members by bringing a prostitute in place of his wife to the next ceremony, but Paul exposes the deception. Displeased with Andy's trickery, the chief priest promises Andy that if he doesn't bring his wife to the next meeting, he will die in her place. Andy heeds the chief priest's warning and brings Merit to the ceremony where the cult members extract and drink her blood while she lays in a catatonic state. The chief priest petitions Lucifer to honor Andy's diligence by sharing his kingdom with him, which confirms that Lucifer, despite God's existence and alleged supremacy, has his own jurisdictional authority to endow humans with blessings and power. In the next scene Merit is in a hospital uttering words of shock at her husband's betrayal followed by a prayer for God's kingdom to be her reward—and then dies. Andy quickly prospers as promised and decides to remarry, to the chagrin of his parents who are still mourning their daughter-in-law's death. At the wedding ceremony Paul tells Andy, "You see you've forgotten your wife now. Money is the emperor of this world. There's no business you can't venture into now." Andy's punishment comes when Merit's ghost haunts him during the wedding ceremony and the film ends with Andy collapsing. The sequel *Living in Bondage 2* begins by showing that Andy did not die at his wedding ceremony but his new bride used his hospitalization as an opportunity to steal his money and leave him. Andy is also still haunted by Merit's ghost, another syncretic layer confirming the film's (and Nollywood's) penchant for supplementing a Christian sacred cosmos with otherworldly analogues. Merit was a Christian so it seems weirdly out of place that her ghost would haunt Andy as opposed to her soul being received by heaven into fellowship with God and the angels. Dualism aside, Andy endures other troubles and doesn't find relief until he confesses to the murder. The sequel ends with Andy repenting and becoming a Christian.

Living in Bondage is no doubt a Christian cautionary tale about the deficits of selling one's soul to Satan, or better yet, the problems that come with compromising one's standards to achieve worldly gain. Making a mockery of the desperate greed that leads men to sacrifice their own spouses just to receive material success, the film's moral message can be summed up in one of Jesus's most notable inquiries: What will it profit a person if he gains the whole world and yet loses his soul (Matthew 16:26)? Andy did receive remuneration, but he did not gain fulfilment, only more problems, including being haunted by his wife's ghost. But while the takeaway lesson of *Living in Bondage* is clearly in support of mainstream Christian doctrine, warning would-be cultists that tapping into dark powers will ultimately corrupt one's soul and haunt one's life, the theodical talking point does in fact suggest that Lucifer, not God, can turn an underdog like Andy into a successful businessman. God demands faith and loyalty and in return provides believers with peace and moral stability, while Lucifer demands human sacrifice and in return offers the ability to secure wealth. If *Living in Bondage* and its sequel offer a theodical memorandum for a struggling continent, it is one that presses Africans to look to God for salvation and moral stability and look to Lucifer to relieve financial suffering and deprivation. The great popularity and success of *Living in Bondage* set the stage for future Nollywood productions to offer a similar kind of deistic dualism in which God is billed as the moral fulcrum of the universe but does nothing supernatural while other forces change outcomes on earth via supernatural intervention.

A four-part filmic series, Ernest Obi's *Freedom in Chains* (1 & 2) followed by *The Power of the Tongue* (1 & 2), demonstrates the populist potential of Nollywood films to extend feminist challenges to patriarchy while tackling the topic of theodicy. The opening film of the series, *Freedom in Chains* 1, begins with a father threatening to skin his daughter alive, setting the tone for what the movie focuses on as the marginalization of women in a small Nigerian village. In this locality, a gender double standard abounds in the form of a curse on Nigerian women who cheat on their husbands, while no such curse exists for the preponderance of unfaithful male spouses. Three families are the focus of gendered marginalization and concomitant suffering. In one family, the father provides funds for the son to pursue college while his smarter daughters are denied such an opportunity simply because they are females. In another family, a young widow is pressured to go back to the house of her late husband to marry her middle-aged brother-in-law to fulfill tradition. The woman would much rather pursue her education than marry a man older than her father, but tradition compels her to do so. The third family involves a woman who, because of the village's infidelity curse on women, goes insane after cheating on her husband, even though it was her husband's serial unfaithfulness that prompted her to do so.

These three familial situations expose the suffering of women under sexist precepts of African tradition. The notion of divine governance is interfaced with sexism such that God appears incapable of alleviating the women's pain and balancing the scales of gender justice. For example, the mother's solution to help her daughter avoid marrying against her wishes is to pray for another man to come and marry her daughter. The mother presents her daughter with younger but no less unimpressive men and orders her daughter to choose one of them as the solution to her problem. So the mother's petition for divine intervention limits prospective solutions to those who conform to the gender strictures of African tradition. If the daughter is to be saved, it is through marriage, not through divine disruption of the oppressive constellation of options. The presumption is that God can only work within African culture; God can't transcend African tradition on behalf of suffering women in the village. Similarly, in the scenario with the unfaithful wife who has gone mad, the husband feels guilty and tries to get her help, but the village "ghost" that enforces the sexist marital mandate makes the man go mad just like his wife. So the only spiritual power we see in this film comes from a ghost rather than from God. The wife and husband are now out of their right minds and no divine intervention can help them. The film's theodical implication is that African tradition constrains divine governance.

In the film's three sequels *Freedom in Chains 2* and *The Power of the Tongue* (1 & 2), the women continue to suffer from male domination and never get a fair break. Chroma, one of the two sisters denied an education by their chauvinist father, attempts to resolve her predicament through beseeching divine intervention: "I just pray God will send me a man that will send me to school as his wife." Once again, the petition presupposes that God must work within African culture to intervene. Instead of supporting her in school, the man she marries ends up physically abusing her to the point where she has to leave him. *The Power of the Tongue 2* ends the four-part series with women of the village demanding that the village king do something to establish a more equitable existence along gender lines. The king claims he does not have authority to challenge the village's tradition and hence passes the buck to the chief priest to weigh in on the women's demands. At the conclusion of the film and series, tradition wins out, with the women in tears listening to the chief priest's story about the origin and irrevocability of the gender constraints. This despondent verdict delivered by the village's spiritual leader brings into greater focus the film's modern message for suffering women: God cannot transcend the oppressive elements of African tradition.

By 2010, the New Nollywood phase emerges with its producers and directors incorporating the populist dynamism of earlier video films toward the goal of making better films with larger budgets and international appeal (Haynes 2016; Witt 2017). For example, Tony Abulu's film *Doctor Bello* (2012) enjoyed funding by the Nigerian government to secure international marketing and a cast of American and Nigerian prominent actors. The film premiered at The Kennedy Center in Washington, D.C. (Tsika 2015). Chineze Anyayene's *Ije: The Journey* (2010) also employed an international crew of actors and support staff, was shot in two countries, and was showcased in international film festivals. If Abulu's and Anyayene's films represent a new era of international celluloid films for Nollywood, then Jeta Amata's *Black November* (2012) codifies the era's vertical boundary imputations.

Black November is shot and set in Los Angeles and Nigeria, exposing the danger and corruption the Nigerian government and multinational corporations inflict on residents of the Niger Delta. Early in the movie, a Western oil pipeline explodes, killing over a thousand women and children. Unlike earlier Nollywood films, *Black November* does not present suffering black Africans turning to Lucifer or any form of mysticism or pagan spirit as a means by which to right the wrongs of history or alleviate the pains caused by corrupt oppressive forces. Instead, heroes of the film turn to acts of sabotage in attempts to end the oppressive practices of the Nigerian government and Western oil companies. Ultimately, *Black November* ends with its most moral and courageous character, Ebiere being executed shortly after Nigerian freedom fighters are apprehended. We can see how Jeta Amata's vision for this new era of Nollywood depicts a Sembènesque truism: that in the context of black African suffering, the gods of traditional religion and the God of world religions are not capable of creating a level playing field for the vulnerable black African masses. Amata is a child of the Niger Delta, and hence knows all too well the vulnerabilities Nigerians suffer due to the oil industry. So while the film represents Nollywood's newfound political power to bring international awareness to the wreckage caused by the petroleum industry, its realism offers a new layer of theodical secularity for Nollywood, presenting God and the gods as sidelined forces in the black African struggle for a healthy and peaceful existence.

Robert Peters's *30 Days in Atlanta: The Adventures of Akpors* (2014) is another New Nollywood contribution that was shot on two continents, utilizing mainstream U.S. and Nigerian actors. The film's premise is a Nigerian named Akpos wins a trip to Atlanta and takes his cousin Richard with him after which the two fall into mayhem during their thirty-day excursion before falling in love with American women. *30 Days in Atlanta* makes no attempt to frame penetrating problems from a theological vantage point, and instead uses spirituality for comedic interludes, like when Akpos's mother forces a pre-trip prayer on her son and nephew, or when Akpos is praising God in the shower and Richard orders his cousin to keep his voice down. But the romantic comedy does incorporate traditional Nollywood moralism in the form of an acute message that doesn't look to God or spiritual power but rather to Nigerians themselves to take responsibility for actions and to stop misrepresenting their country to the world. If *Black November* and *30 Days in Atlanta* demonstrate toned-down spirituality, then the latest iteration of a Nollywood classic confirms that "New Nollywood" filmmakers have not completely abandoned the inimitable brand of deistic dualism featured in earlier ventures into theodicy.

Ramsey Nouah's *Living in Bondage: Breaking Free* (2020) is the last chapter to the abovementioned *Living in Bondage* film that popularized Nollywood videos three decades earlier. Nouah's aerial shots of Lagos and technical proficiency prove Nollywood has come a long way since videotapes of the original low-budget films hit Nigerian homes in 1992 and 1993. But what remains consistent with the original story is the new sequel's dualistic treatment of evil and spiritual efficacy where God does nothing remarkable to relieve suffering and ward off evil, while Lucifer unleashes spiritual and material efficacy. The film opens with Obinna, a member of the Brotherhood of the Six cult, brutally killing his adorable young daughter with a machete to ensure his wealth and success via satanic power. Obinna's career accomplishments are contrasted against the protagonist Nandi's flailing business and complaint that God has neglected him. When Nandi finally joins the Brotherhood of the Six, his career skyrockets under the mentorship of the cult's leader, Richard. Once again, God may have ultimate authority, but it is the lower and darker powers of Satan that impact change on Earth. Andy Okeke, the protagonist of the original *Living in Bondage* series who sacrificed his wife to enjoy great career success, is now a middle-aged pastor teaming up with a journalist to take down the same powerful cult he pledged allegiance to almost three decades earlier.

In a crucial scene indicating the film's deistic dualism, Andy is alone praying when Richard, the leader of the Brotherhood of the Six, ventures into Andy's church, and his mere presence causes the cross hanging on the wall to mysteriously turn upside down. In this battle between the servant of God and the servant of Satan, the latter is the only one armed with supernatural firepower. Andy quotes scripture and an unimpressed Richard responds by zapping Andy with a spiritual chokehold that levitates his torso several feet off the ground leaving Andy suspended in air gasping for breath until Richard releases spiritual energy sending Andy crashing to the floor. Andy reminds Richard that God is above Satan and that every knee shall bow at the name of Jesus, but it is Richard's dark power that offers the only supernatural efficacy throughout the film, as Richard and his followers see spiritual and material manifestations from their sacrificial allegiance to Satan. While *Living in Bondage: Breaking Free*'s moral message conveys that God is the ultimate source of salvation and truth and that service to Satan is objectionable and destined for self-destruction, the film's subtle but no less salient theodical message is in line with the boundary work we see in countless Nollywood films and modern cinema in general: that when it comes to impacting life outcomes, fighting evil, or reducing suffering, God remains sequestered to the sidelines.

THE CONGO AND OTHER COUNTRIES

Raoul Peck's historical drama *Lumumba* (2000) is set around the events preceding and succeeding the Democratic Republic of the Congo's independence from Belgium in 1960. Peck's film begins with Patrice Lumumba's ascendance as prime minister of the newly independent republic, but after this triumphant moment, postcolonial life quickly goes awry, as Lumumba tries to rein in his reckless military and maneuver around the machinations of foreign agitators. In one scene, the prime minister confronts his military general Joseph Mobutu for crimes his troops committed against Congolese civilians, including locking up women, children, and old people in a church and slaughtering them, an atrocity that foreshadows the abuse of power that will characterize Mobutu in relation to his country and his superiors. Lumumba could have deduced from Mobutu's church slaughter that the coldhearted general would have no qualms about eventually turning on his prime minister. And indeed, not long after the church massacre, Lumumba is betrayed by his military, removed from his position, and imprisoned.

In the film's most melancholy moment, we see a beaten Lumumba in the backseat of a car with a Belgian official who offers him an opportunity to pray before his pending execution. Lumumba rejects the Belgian official's offer and chooses instead, through the film's first and only use of magical realism, to narrate his last moments alive, informing us that he was born fifty years too early, and that what he wanted for the Congo others didn't want. Lumumba's final words, coming seconds before bullets perforate his body, clarify the prime minister's tragic situation better than any priestly last rites could have offered. With Lumumba's execution accomplished, the film cuts back to the Congo's new leader General Mobutu at a public ceremony offering an ironic moment of silence for the man he betrayed and executed in a power grab. Peck's closing scene and venture into magical realism inspires contemplation on how Lumumba's assassination paved the way for three decades of Mobutu's terrifying reign in the young country he renamed Zaire. In summing up Mobutu's impact as the country's long-term dictator, journalist Michela Wrong writes that "no other president had been presented with a country of such potential, yet achieved so little. No other leader had plundered his economy so effectively or lived the high life to such excess" (Wrong 2001: 4). Similarly, Thierry Michel's documentary *Mobutu King of Zaire* (1999) offers a chilling depiction of the murder campaigns and destruction of the Zaire economy and infrastructure resulting from the dictator's control. The real victims, Michel shows, were the Congolese people.

Turning to a more recent epoch in Congolese history, the documentary *Lumo* (2007) reveals how the bodies of black women bear the brutality of war, as Congolese militias readily employed sexual assault as a technique of terror. The film intersects black suffering and divine representation through the eyes of a young woman named Lumo Sinai who was gang raped by so many soldiers she was unable to provide a precise count of the perpetrators. The attack caused a traumatic fistula, which the documentary reveals is a common injury to sexual assault victims that makes them incontinent and unable to give birth to children. The rape and injury resulted in Lumo's fiancé and family members shunning her. *Lumo* showcases the efforts of a hospital (HEAL Africa) devoted to helping victims of rape receive corrective surgery, and in the process offers many occasions for theodical discourse concerning God's relationship to women who have suffered life-altering tragedy.

Early in the documentary one of the African counselors greets the new arrivals to the hospital with warmth and encouragement: "All of you will be healed. All of you will be healed in Jesus's name." The counselor envisions the psychological and Christian empowerment of these victims as one and the same, and portrays God as playing an active role in the victim's healing. But not long after this counselor's declaration of God's interventionist power, we learn of a rape victim who, after six surgeries, is still not healed. A counselor comments on her distress, "Her genital organs are destroyed. She must wash all the time or flies will follow her." But perhaps surprising to some, we see the same victim praying with a counselor in the name of Jesus Christ. Claims on God's healing capabilities followed by the reality of continual suffering are, in and of themselves, theodical statements, suggesting either a sidelined God or recalcitrant hope in God's future intervention, an interpretive binary we encounter throughout the film.

In one sequence, a counselor offers spiritual encouragement to all the victims during a campus worship service: "All of the suffering you are going through, don't be astonished. Many others have been through the same situation. If you have left home to come here, that is the will of God. We will pray for those who have been operated on." If, as this counselor suggests, God wills for victims to receive treatment, one is left to ponder why God did not correspondingly will for the women not to be brutally raped. Similarly, the above quote from the counselor alludes to anticipation of a miraculous healing from God, when the hospital secures results quite commensurate with any modern medical institution, whereby some patients gradually convalesce after surgery, while others never get better. The documentary authenticates no miracles, only some successful surgeries and a commensurate number of unsuccessful ones. If God is part of this process, as several counselors proclaim, then divine power is relegated to the limits of modern surgical procedures.

The documentary's focus quickly turns to Lumo, whose own tragic story of victimization has theodical relevance. After being attacked, she reveals, "Most of the time, I cried and prayed to God. I thought it must be God's will for me to suffer." So the first question her tragic circumstance poses is why in fact did an all-powerful and loving God allow her to be so viciously gang-raped? One could exert great time and energy wrestling with Lumo's initial presupposition that her suffering was divinely sanctioned. If true, then what does that say about Lumo's loving and just God? If not, then what does that suggest about divine governance if something so horrific can happen outside of God's will? Lumo's tragic fate affords few theodical answers that make sense in terms of triangulating divine omnipotence, benevolence, and governance.

Lumo experiences four unsuccessful surgeries and goes through various emotions from trust in God's providence to almost complete despondence. While she is bedridden with a catheter after her fifth surgery, Lumo exhibits theodical variance. Initially we see her singing a song with such lyrics as, "In my heart I want to be like Jesus," and immediately afterwards praying:

> Father, in the name of Jesus, I ask your forgiveness for being arrogant and selfish. You know, Father, that I am a sinful person in need of your wisdom. My Lord, you see that I have been operated on. Surely, you will do something for my body. Whatever you do, nobody can contest it. In the name of Jesus, Amen.

In this prayer Lumo is humble and repentant and demonstrates trust in God—even though, up to this point, God has not intervened on her behalf to remove her incontinence and suffering. She asks God for forgiveness for her pride and egoism, an exegetical tactic discussed in earlier chapters as indicative of a theodicy of sin. Under this logic, the sufferer concludes that she must be doing something wrong not to receive divine intervention and perhaps as a pragmatic concession she repents to get right with God to receive mediation. A theodicy of sin explains God's lack of intervention and keeps the door open for an eventual reversal of fate under God's jurisdictional edict, a more hopeful alternative to the sidelining of God we see throughout black liberation theology, the God-talk of modern Americans (Ammerman 2014b) and many filmic treatments of black suffering. One might inquire what exactly Lumo could have done to deserve such a harsh ordeal, but such penitent thinking preserves God's sovereignty while providing new answers that uphold hope in God's interventionist power and justice.

But not long after rendering a remorseful overture to secure divine healing, Lumo appears dejected, telling her friends, "I don't feel like I owe thankfulness to anybody. Why thank God? I can't do it." Hearing these words, one of her friends playfully slaps Lumo and tells her she's talking like a fool. Lumo amends her position to say, "If I am healed, I will thank the Lord. If I don't [heal], I won't thank Him." Similarly ambivalent, when a male interviewer brings up her rapists and reminds her, "You know that Jesus was also beaten," Lumo reproaches the interviewer for comparing her gratuitous pain and suffering to Christ's sacrificial act for humanity. Lumo's conversations and the counselors' claims on God's will and intervention demonstrate the complications of fitting divine providence into the context of tragic suffering.

Lumo's fifth reconstructive surgery eventually proves successful and she is finally able to return to her family after two years of living in the hospital. When Lumo says goodbye to the counselors, one of them hugs the departing patient and tells her, "You resemble God. Now do you see how the devil wanted you to become worse? See how you beat the devil? Be safe and go with God, Mama! Go with God completely." The counselor's last sentence elicits the question: Was God not with Lumo completely when the soldiers raped her two years earlier? And with Lumo's release from the hospital and return to her village, a locality that is still occupied by rebel soldiers, does the counselor's exhortation, "Go with God completely," insinuate that God will prevent rebel soldiers from raping her again? By placing the theological hopes of women against the severity and consequences of their victimization, the documentary raises profound questions concerning the seemingly inscrutable will of God in the context of evil and suffering. Even Lumo's recuperation happens gradually after her fifth surgery rather than as the result of an abrupt display of supernatural efficacy. If God is acting on *Lumo*'s behalf, it appears as if such intervention comes solely through human hands and modern medical procedures. But *Lumo* differs from many contemporary cinematic features that more explicitly sideline God in that in this documentary, you have people expressing belief in God's supernatural power to mitigate suffering.

Turning eastward, *The Last King of Scotland* (2006) is a fictional drama inspired by the real reign of Idi Amin over Uganda. The film unfolds from the perspective of the dictator's personal physician from Scotland, Nicholas Garrigan. After General Amin's successful coup, he promises a government that will build new schools, roads, and houses, while remaining attentive to the needs of the people. Dr. Garrigan is a metaphor for Ugandan citizens and world observers who were initially naïve concerning Amin's new headship, considering the bold leader as a herald of hope. Garrigan finally discovers that Amin is no man of the people but a mercurial tyrant who incessantly and systematically eliminates potential opposition to his reign. The key moment addressing theodicy occurs after Amin's men have captured and tortured Garrigan. Dr. Junju rescues his medical colleague and facilitates his travel out of the country. When an appreciative Garrigan asks Junju what will happen to him for facilitating his escape, Junju responds, "My fate is in God's hands." The next scene shows Amin's minister of operations shooting Junju in the head. *The Last King of Scotland* makes a theological statement in killing off its only hero, shortly after Dr. Junju places his fate in God's hands: To be in God's hands is not to be protected from a maniacal despot, a contention also confirmed by the film-ending caption declaring that 300,000 Ugandans were killed during Amin's reign.

Set in the same country, the documentary *War Dance* (2006) features the story of three children in a war-zone displacement camp who participate in a music and dance competition while negotiating their pain and suffering from losing parents killed by a rebel group called the Lord's Resistance Army. The film is as hopeful in portraying the children's resilience as it is gloomy in disclosing what these young victims and their families endured. Rose reveals how the rebels killed her father with a machete and then ordered her mother to bury the corpse and then return so that the rebels could rape her. Rebels abducted Dominic when he was nine and he describes how for two weeks, "The deaths I saw were terrifying!" The rebels also abducted Dominic's brother who never made it back. Perhaps the most touching moment is when Nancy visits the grave where her father is buried and becomes hysterical, wishing the rebels had killed her alongside her father. Still crying, Nancy calms down enough to say a prayer at the grave:

> Dear God, I'm so sad. You took him away from me. My brother and sisters did not get to know him. You took him away. Daddy, I will never see you again. You have gone for good. Maybe one day God will bring you back so I can see you one more time and keep you in my heart forever. I have nothing more to say.

Nancy frames God's refusal to protect her father as tantamount to God's culpability in her father's death, twice claiming, "You took him away." God-talk reappears in the documentary during the competition, when the leader of one of the teams prays, "Oh Mighty God, we pray for your servants. May you be with them, guide them, protect them, until we meet again." Such a prayer seems appropriate in most Christian contexts but unnervingly discordant in this documentary. For one can only imagine what such a petition for divine protection sounds like to a young girl like Rose whose mother was raped and beheaded. Such an entreaty itself can unwittingly serve as a reminder of the ways in which God did not intervene to protect many of their family members from far worse tragedy than what derived from a music and dance competition.

Turning to Liberia, *Pray the Devil Back to Hell* (2008) documents how an activist movement called Women of Liberia Mass Action for Peace successfully mobilized protest efforts to end the country's long and bloody civil war. The movement morphed out of the desperation that Liberians experienced after watching their loved ones killed or wounded in conflicts. Realizing that prayer was not enough to end urban combat, Leymah Gbowee organized Christian women to protest for peace, which sparked the attention of Muslim women who then joined the movement. At the onset, interfaith tensions challenged the initiative, but activist Vaiba Flomo reveals how two simple questions quickly quashed their theological quarrels: "Can a bullet pick and choose? Does the bullet know Christians from Muslims?" Hence, the reality that both Muslims and Christians were dying in absurd proportions was enough for women of Liberia to put aside their theological differences and unite. But in acknowledging that bullets can't distinguish between Muslim and Christian collateral damage, Flomo and other Liberian women concede that God does not protect Muslim and Christian bystanders from the destructive power of the bullets. Such an admission has theodical relevance in the manner in which it inadvertently discards the presumption of divine protection for believers.

When considering the political mission of the movement, the film's title *Pray the Devil Back to Hell* becomes indubitably misleading. If the documentary teaches one thing, it is that ending a destructive civil war requires intensive social activism rather than supplication. The women's success suggests that the best nonviolent work people can unleash to combat evil is to organize and meet at regular intervals, share information and resources, and, most importantly, to stage tactical demonstrations of power in the public square that pressure leaders to act in ways for which they were initially reluctant. In other words, the documentary's signifying potency reveals how the women of Liberia were organized, persistent, tactical, loud, and quite visible toward achieving their objectives. They demanded to be heard, and when they were heard they offered persuasive pleas for peace. They leveraged their numbers to pressure opposing forces to attend peace talks in Ghana, and when those peace talks stalled, they staged a powerful protest in the conference halls of those meetings, demanding that delegates from warring forces continue to meet and broker a peace agreement. Such actions generated worldwide media attention that pressured warring factions to negotiate an end to the conflict. And when a solution was finally codified, the women of Liberia did not relinquish their activism, but instead marshalled their clout and resources toward electing Liberia's new leader, the first woman president of any African nation. So the film verifies how black suffering in Africa can be relieved: not by praying the devil back to hell as the film's title suggests, but through the activist energies of courageous African people.

God Grew Tired of Us (2006) is another documentary that displays a title with great import for filmic discussions of theodicy. It explores the progress of the so-called "lost boys" of Sudan, parentless boys who were separated from families during vicious civil-war conflicts that killed more than two million people. Muslim Sudanese militias massacred their villages, forcing many of them to flee on foot for hundreds of miles as part of a year-long trek to a refugee camp in Kakuma, Kenya. The film focuses on three of the boys—Daniel, John, and Panther—as they relocate to the United States to begin new lives while attempting to extract meaning out of their complicated pasts. The film's title is inspired by a quote from John shortly after he relocates to Syracuse, New York. John describes how the brutality of war in the Sudan convinced him that "God got tired of us and He wanted to finish us." At another juncture in the film, John ponders, "The place that I am now is very good. But those whom I left in Kakuma, I left them in a very bad place. So, if I get a good place, why not them? That's my first question." John here wrestles with a timeless question of theodicy concerning why some innocent people succumb to evil and suffering while others are spared. But John's questions and concerns do not damper his faith, as he insists that God ordained the lost boys' relocation to the United States for a special purpose. So John has the difficult task of harmonizing his belief in divine intervention with the realities he and his comrades experienced in the aftermath of tragedy: separation from family, death of millions of Sudanese citizens, and the fact that many more lost boys won't get the chance to relocate to a prosperous country.

John receives a letter from his brother informing him that his family is alive and residing in a refugee camp in Uganda. Up until that point, John was unaware of what happened to the rest of his family after he fled the Sudan. So hearing from his family is a great boon. In the correspondence, John's brother credits God for protecting and preserving John, and then John comments on how his family's survival is the answer to his prayers. But even as the letter offers much to rejoice about, John's brother also informs him that their family is suffering in the Ugandan refugee camp and that government troops killed their uncle and his five children. So while crediting God for familial preservation and nourishment, the letter also insinuates that God did not intervene to save their uncle and his children, or to stop the rest of their clan from being wiped out by government troops. The film's cheeriest moment questions why God saves some and not others.

CONCLUSION

God Grew Tired of Us and other documentaries and feature films demonstrate that while cinematic theodicy focuses great attention on characters and plots expressing doubt, disinterest, or reticence about God's transcendent capacities, one must not overlook how some dramas and documentaries include black people trusting in God to fight evil or relieve their suffering. Thus, our investigation of the filmic interface of black suffering and divine representation is not only interested in boundary work that sidelines God, but also in theodical questions and concerns that surface when characters credit supernatural involvement toward the alleviation of suffering. Two additional films are worth mentioning for their more explicit allusion to spiritual firepower or divine intervention.

In Souleymane Cisse's film *Yeelen* (1987), a father named Soma beseeches divine help to locate his son Niankoro so he can kill him. Every time we see Soma he is making celestial appeals, such as: "God of the swamps! God of the sands and of the rocks, search the plains and mountains. Almighty Mari, dry the lakes! Bring him from Earth or sky that all may see him." Niankoro and his mother suffer greatly as a result of dodging Soma's pursuit, until Niankoro hones his own spiritual power. And in David Hickson's *Beat the Drum* (2003), a South African orphan named Musa looks beyond the hopelessness of his daily struggle on the streets to imagine a new existence. He explains to his street companion Letty, "Before my mother got sick she taught me how to pray. I'll pray for a new home for both of us. So we can have as much food as we can eat. And it will be safe so we won't have to hide." After Letty is brutally attacked in the street and Musa overcomes his own frightful challenges, both tweens eventually end up in an orphanage with plenty of food and protection, an occurrence that Musa clarifies to Letty as God answering his earlier prayer.

Yeelen and *Beat the Drum* offer cinematic scenes and characters alluding to or utilizing divine power in the context of black suffering. *Yeelen*, in particular, like a considerable number of Nollywood films, depicts a world in which supernaturalism does impact human events. But part of any assessment of cinematic theodicy should identify the ways in which infusions of supernatural proclivities engender conundrums and contradictions that surface in any attempt to reconcile how God's teleological reach encompasses lingering forms of black suffering. For example, while we hear about and observe supernatural power throughout *Yeelen*, we later learn through the prophetic utterance of Djigui, the uncle of Niankoro, that a dark fate awaits their Malian people: "What I foresee promises nothing good for the Bambaras. The country's future hangs by a thread." Djigui adds that Niankoro's successors "will undergo a great change. They'll be slaves, and deny their race and faith." Djigui here is prefiguring Mali's future in the transatlantic slave trade, as the film is set two centuries before chattel slavery changes the fate of millions of West Africans. Djigui forecasts Mali's future as dark, implying that none of the supernatural power demonstrated by Niankoro and his father Soma will save their descendants from the horrors to come when they are forced into the transatlantic slave trade. And we must consider that both Soma and his son die at the film's ending. So *Yeelen*'s presentation of divine power only reveals the problem of theodicy more dramatically by generating a pressing question: What good are such impressive displays of spiritual power if they fail to help black Africans overcome their greatest threat and source of tragedy and suffering—European slavers?

And in *Beat the Drum*, while young Musa believes his prayers for Letty and himself were answered with their new life of sustenance and protection in the orphanage, the great theodical challenge the film implicitly negotiates by signifying the harrowing effects of AIDS does in fact raise more questions about why God allows the virus to kill millions of black people in Musa's country, South Africa. *Beat the Drum* may end on a positive note for the young protagonist and his friend Letty who no longer have to rummage dangerous streets for daily sustenance, but that offers no consolation to the thousands of other orphans the film acknowledges will continue to suffer cruel fates on those same streets. The film-ending caption notifying viewers that "AIDS has already orphaned more than 12 million African children" is congruently bleak; even as the film allocates divine intervention, it poignantly invites the viewer to consider the quandary of that very same intervention: If God can provide Musa and Letty a reprieve from scavenger life on the harrowing streets, why couldn't that same God have done something to prevent the vast spread of AIDS to millions of black Africans? Robert Wuthnow (2012: 113) offers a salient question that can serve as a fitting response to claims of divine intervention like the one made by young Musa:

> If hundreds or thousands of people are killed, does it really make sense to say that some people were spared because they prayed? A moment's thought shows that either the people who died did not pray (unlikely) or that God chose to kill them anyway. The arguments quickly get into logical quicksand that thoughtful people are likely to steer clear of.

The "thoughtful people" Wuthnow alludes to are more inclined to sideline God altogether rather than interject salutary intermittent forays of supernaturalism to a coterie of fortunate people. And the world of cinema is replete with such thoughtful people who employ vertical boundaries at almost every turn to avoid the conundrum that young Musa's claim necessitates.

If Auschwitz once inspired the most cinematic treatments of theodicy, the continent of Africa represents a new destination for filmic intersections of God and vast human suffering. The films discussed in this epilogue provide only a sample in terms of what cinematic theodicy's secularizing and signifying capacities offer toward the negotiation and exegesis of black African suffering. A few additional films are worth noting. *The Constant Gardener* (2005) features fraudulent drug trials, conspiracies, and murders in Kenya to demonstrate how black Africans are exploited to test dangerous drugs before they are deemed safe for Westerners. Similarly depressive, *Blood Diamond* (2006) represents the heartbreaking loss of life that comes with the mining of diamonds in war zones in Sierra Leone, while *Attack on Darfur* (2009) depicts the rampant raping and killing of Sudanese villagers by the Janjaweed. In both its signifying and secularizing faculties behind representing black African suffering, cinema draws a line in the sand, clearly separating victims from perpetrators, leaving little room for a divine plan overlooking historical events. Such horizontal and vertical displays of boundary work expose how cinema is not only an effective artistic medium to awaken attention to inconceivable atrocities committed against communities, but also an effective mechanism to spark theodical contemplation on the role of God or religion in protecting humankind from the consequences of human depravity. And such deliberation most often results in relegating God to the sidelines of human history. Even as Nollywood's depictions of satanic or African traditional religious sources of supernatural efficacy offer an alternative religious vision to theodical secularity, Nollywood's recurring sidelining of the supreme God is quite consistent with cinematic theodicy's vertical boundary work. One can leave many Nigerian films wondering if God is capable of doing anything on Earth to alleviate suffering among black African people. Even the works of devout Christian Nollywood filmmakers confirm that ultimately God can't revoke the residual effects of tradition and patriarchy in African societies.

Journalistic depictions of the Holocaust helped to convert the extermination of Jewish life into a universally recognized crime against humanity (Alexander 2003) in a similar fashion that films like *Hotel Rwanda*, *Kinyarwanda*, *Sometimes in April*, *100 Days*, and *Beyond the Gates* helped to humanize the Tutsi victims and make the depths of the pain and destruction of the Rwandan genocide known to a world audience. Hence this work's focus on theodicy is sensitive to the role cinema plays as a modern ritual toward the generation of intercontinental solidarity by coding and narrating evil deeds and oppressive social processes, crafting interpretive frameworks to contextualize suffering, humanizing victims while identifying perpetrators, and, most importantly, moralizing and memorializing genocidal tragedy. Along these lines of highlighting cinematic theodicy's signifying capacities, we have explored how cinema depicts the personal nature of Rwandan mass murders: how they occupied public spaces and how ordinary Hutu patriots attacked their Rwandan neighbors with machetes and other weaponry. In contrast to the Holocaust, where death camps and the mechanistic killing arrangements were most often secluded from mainstream public spaces and killers employed impersonal industrial implementations of death (Mamdani 2001), films reveal that Christian schools and churches, places where vulnerable Tutsis sought refuge and divine protection, were converted into slaughterhouses. Thus cinema shapes interpretations of real-life accounts of how thousands of victims were hacked to death in places where they sought sanctuary and how some religious leaders aided and abetted the identification of Tutsi populations for elimination. But most importantly, the scope of participation by the overwhelmingly Christian populace in Rwanda makes the genocide even more relevant to any discussion of theodicy.

Apartheid offers another remarkably useful cinematic context for exploring the sociological underpinnings of evil. Cinema not only sidelines God in the midst of South African brutality, but also signifies the dehumanizing effects of apartheid and how the white South African government was willing to pull out all the stops to maintain its domination over black bodies and consciousness. An additional film like *Sarafina* (1992) reveals how hundreds of black South African activists were murdered and thousands more protesters were either shot down in marches or brutally tortured when detained by the police. And we discussed how *Mandela: Long Walk to Freedom* offers the most provocative theodical treatment of apartheid through its sanctification of Nelson Mandela's terrorist past. While other films gloss over Mandela's efforts at armed resistance against the apartheid regime, *Mandela: Long Walk to Freedom* devotes considerable attention dramatizing young Nelson and the ANC's transition from nonviolent tactics of civil disobedience to deliberate acts of sabotage. And more importantly, the film does little to atone for the ANC's terrorist turn, instead making a persuasive case that Mandela and his comrades were left with little choice when dealing with a violent government that was set on dehumanizing and exterminating innocent black Africans. The film even offers a surprising scene with Nelson and his ANC associates standing around a technician teaching them how to make bombs; and we see the effects of such training in successive scenes when they blow up buildings while hiding from the authorities until their eventual capture. During his trial, Mandela offers a speech in which he acknowledges sabotage and still takes the moral high ground. And after almost three decades in prison, when

Mandela is released and emerges as a savior of South African civility, he still remains as defiant against the historical legacy of white South African repressive tactics and policies as he is unapologetic for his earlier armed resistance. The film signifies South African apartheid as so evil, so destructive in its willingness to dehumanize and exterminate black bodies, that sabotage is a viable solution that enjoys the moral high ground in the process. Here cinema recodes terrorism as an acceptable response to state-sanctioned murder and mayhem, the morally upright thing to do when an oppressed group has no other recourse.

Equally demonstrative of cinematic theodicy's signifying relevance to the social construction of evil and the exegesis of black human suffering is *Tsotsi* (2011), which features the life of a poor black petty criminal named Tsotsi whose existence is limited to a desperate sprint for survival in the streets of Johannesburg. If *Cry Freedom* captures the social injustice and economic inequality black South Africans endured during the apartheid era, then *Tsosti* reveals a post-apartheid world in which blacks are poor and suffer and whites are prospering while desperately maintaining their dominance over blacks. And if *Mandela: Long Walk to Freedom* clarifies the deep level of corruption it took for the white minority to maintain repressive rule over the black majority, then *Tsotsi* reminds us that the era of South African apartheid was a complex system of racial, social, and economic inequality that still affects millions of black South Africans in its aftermath. The film contextualizes the protagonist's life of crime within his diminished (if not depressing) post-apartheid possibilities. Cinema raises profound questions concerning the destructive capacities of South African apartheid that were prolonged without divine mediation, while signifying the social and economic costs of systemic black oppression.

But even as we appreciate cinema's accomplished role behind the social construction of evil and the portrayal of systemic inequality that perpetuates contemporary black African suffering, we can acknowledge cinema's greater theodical attentiveness to how Janjaweed decimations of Sudanese villages, civil wars in the Congo, a terrifying despot in Uganda, and other contexts and perpetrators of black African suffering have the potential to shake the most fervent believer's trust in any notion of divine intervention in human events. Cinema presses people to consider how a maniacal despot can engage in murderous campaigns against hundreds of thousands of his own citizens; how South African apartheid can dehumanize millions for multiple generations; how Congolese soldiers can commit gang-rape without fear of reprisal; how cities can be decimated by coups, factions, and ethnic cleansings; and how a seemingly preventable virus like AIDS can prematurely end the lives of millions of black Africans under the watchful eye of a divine governor. Thus, we learn in impressive detail how cinematic theodicy's representation of African tragedy exerts secularizing import on three levels: a social level intended to arouse solidarity and collective identity of impoverished patriots of black African countries; a moral level framing of the West, international agencies like the IMF, colonialism, patriarchy, Islam, Christianity, and black African tradition as harmful or, at best, unsympathetic to Africa's systemic deprivations; and a theodical level by which thoughtful people trade in the once accepted wisdom of divine governance for the more acceptable notion of a modern God.

Filmography

The Confederate Spy (1910)
The Birth of a Nation (1915)
Mammy's Rose (1916)
Within Our Gates (1920)
Uncle Tom's Cabin (1927)
The North Star (1943)
Rome, Open City (1945)
Adventures of Huckleberry Finn (1955)
Band of Angels (1957)
The Seventh Seal (1957)
Ana Lucasta (1959)
The Adventures of Huckleberry Finn (1960)
Through a Glass Darkly (1961)
Winter Light (1962)
Borom Sarret (1963)
Black Girl (1966)
Mandabi (1968)
Emitai (1971)
Goodbye Uncle Tom (1971)
The Legend of Nigger Charlie (1972)
Huckleberry Finn (1974)
Mandingo (1975)
Xala (1975)
The Last Supper (1976)
The River Niger (1976)
Ceddo (1977)
Roots (1977)
A Woman Called Moses (1978)
Ashes and Embers (1982)
Adventures of Huckleberry Finn (1986)

Shaka Zulu (1986)
She's Gotta Have It (1986)
Cry Freedom (1987)
Yeelen (1987)
Camp de Thiaroye (1988)
Glory (1989)
Romero (1989)
Boyz N the Hood (1991)
New Jack City (1991)
Guelwaar (1992)
Juice (1992)
Living in Bondage (1992)
Sarafina (1992)
Living in Bondage 2 (1993)
Menace II Society (1993)
Poetic Justice (1993)
Sankofa (1993)
Schindler's List (1993)
Race to Freedom: The Underground Railroad (1994)
Sugar Hill (1994)
Cry, the Beloved Country (1995)
Dead Presidents (1995)
Nightjohn (1996)
Amistad (1997)
Eve's Bayou (1997)
Mobutu King of Zaire (1999)
Lumumba (2000)
100 Days (2001)
Faat Kiné (2001)
Civil Brand (2002)
The Crime of Padre Amaro (2002)
Paid in Full (2002)
Beat the Drum (2003)
Brother to Brother (2004)
Hotel Rwanda (2004)
Moolaade (2004)
Submission (2004)
500 Years Later (2005)
Beyond the Gates (2005)
The Constant Gardener (2005)
The Gospel (2005)

Lackawanna Blues (2005)
Sometimes in April (2005)
Amazing Grace (2006)
The Amazing Grace (2006)
Bamako (2006)
Blood Diamond (2006)
God Grew Tired of Us (2006)
The Last King of Scotland (2006)
Rag Tag (2006)
War Dance (2006)
When the Levees Broke: A Requiem in Four Acts (2006)
Daddy's Little Girls (2007)
Lord Help Us (2007)
Lumo (2007)
Without the King (2007)
Family (2008)
Gangster Paradise: Jerusalema (2008)
Meet the Browns (2008)
Motherland (2008)
Pray the Devil Back to Hell (2008)
Attack on Darfur (2009)
Mississippi Damned (2009)
Precious (2009)
Children of God (2010)
Ije: The Journey (2010)
Kinyarwanda (2011)
Life, Above All (2010)
Mooz-Lum (2010)
A Screaming Man (2010)
Madea's Big Happy Family (2011)
Pariah (2011)
Taken from Me: The Tiffany Rubin Story (2011)
Tsotsi (2011)
Black November (2012)
Call Me Kucho (2012)
Django Unchained (2012)
Doctor Bello (2012)
Lincoln (2012)
Red Hook Summer (2012)
Woman Thou Art Loosed: On the 7th Day (2012)
The African Americans: Many Rivers to Cross (2013)
God Loves Uganda (2013)

Mandela: Long Walk to Freedom (2013)
The Prayer Circle (2013)
A Day Late and a Dollar Short (2014)
Thirty Days in Atlanta: The Adventures of Akpos (2014)
Timbuktu (2014)
Harriet (2019)
Living in Bondage: Breaking Free (2020)

FILMS LACKING IDENTIFIABLE RELEASE DATES

Freedom in Chains 1
Freedom in Chains 2
The Power of the Tongue 1
The Power of the Tongue 2

References

Abu-Lughod, Lila. 2013. *Do Muslim Women Need Saving?* Cambridge, MA, and London: Harvard University Press.

Adams, Marilyn McCord. 1999. *Horrendous Evils and the Goodness of God*. Ithaca, NY, and London: Cornell University Press.

Alexander, Jeffrey. 2001. "Toward a Sociology of Evil: Getting beyond Modernist Common Sense about the Alternative to the Good." In *Rethinking Evil: Contemporary Perspectives*, edited by Maria Pia Lara, 153–172. Berkeley and London: University of California Press.

———. 2003. *The Meanings of Social Life: A Cultural Sociology*. Oxford and New York: Oxford University Press.

———. 2010. *The Performance of Politics: Obama's Victory and the Democratic Struggle for Power*. New York: Oxford University Press.

———. 2011. *Performative Revolution in Egypt: An Essay in Cultural Power*. London and New York: Bloomsbury Academic.

———. 2012. *Trauma: A Social Theory*. Cambridge, UK, and Malden, MA: Polity Press.

———. 2013. *The Dark Side of Modernity*. Cambridge, UK, and Malden, MA: Polity Press.

Alexander, Torin Dru. 2016. "The Black Messiah and Black Suffering." In *Albert Cleage Jr. and the Black Madonna and Child*, edited by Jawanza Eric Clark, 77–95. New York: Palgrave Macmillan.

Allen-McLaurin, Lisa M. 2014. "Jesus Will Fix It, After While: The Purpose and Role of Gospel Music in Tyler Perry Productions." In *Womanist and Black Feminist Responses to Tyler Perry's Productions*, edited by LeRhonda S. Manigault-Bryant, Tamura Lomax, and Carol Duncan, 57–72. New York: Palgrave Macmillan.

Ammerman, Nancy T. 2014a. "Response by Nancy T. Ammerman: Modern Altars in Everyday Life." In *The Many Altars of Modernity: Toward a Paradigm for Religion in a Pluralistic Age*, by Peter Berger, 94–110. Boston and Berlin: Walter de Gruyter.

———. 2014b. *Sacred Stories, Spiritual Tribes: Finding Religion in Everyday Life*. New York: Oxford University Press.

Armes, Roy. 2011. "African Cinema and Postmodernist Criticism." In *Symbolic Narratives/African Cinema: Audiences, Theory, and the Moving Image*, edited by June Givanni, 134–135. London: British Film Institute.

Asad Talal. 2003. *Formations of the Secular: Christianity, Islam, Modernity*. Stanford, CA: Stanford University Press.

Austen, Ralph, and Mahir Saul. 2010. "Introduction." In *Viewing African Cinema in the Twenty-First Century: Art Films and the Nollywood Revolution*, edited by Mahir Saul and Ralph Austen, 1–8. Athens: Ohio University Press.

Baker-Fletcher, Karen. 1998. *Sisters of the Dust, Sisters of Spirit: Womanist Wordings on God and Creation*. Minneapolis, MN: Fortress Press.

Baldwin, James. 1963. *The Fire Next Time*. New York: Dial Press.

Barnette, Henlee H. 1967. *The New Theology and Morality*. Philadelphia, PA: Westminster Press.

Barth, Karl. 1978. *The Humanity of God*. Atlanta, GA: John Knox Press.

Bauman, Zygmunt. 1989. *Modernity and the Holocaust*. Ithaca, NY: Cornell University Press.

Becker, Ernest. 1968. *The Structure of Evil: An Essay on the Unification of the Science of Man*. New York: George Braziller.

Bellah, Robert. 1970. *Beyond Belief: Essays on Religion in a Post-Traditional World*. New York and London: Harper & Row Publishers.

Berger, Peter L. 1961a. *The Noise of Solemn Assemblies: Christian Commitment and the Religious Establishment in America*. Garden City, NY: Doubleday & Company.

———. 1961b. *The Precarious Vision: A Sociologist Looks at Social Fictions and Christian Faith*. Garden City, NY: Doubleday & Company.

———. 1967. *The Sacred Canopy: Elements of a Sociological Theory of Religion*. Garden City, NY: Doubleday.

———. 1969. *A Rumor of Angels: Modern Society and the Rediscovery of the Supernatural*. Garden City, NY: Doubleday.

———. 1977. *Facing Up to Modernity: Excursions in Society, Politics, and Religion*. New York: Basic Books.

———. 1979. *The Heretical Imperative: Contemporary Possibilities of Religious Affirmation*. Garden City, NY: Anchor Press/Doubleday.

———. 2004. *Questions of Faith: A Skeptical Affirmation of Christianity*. Malden, MA, and Oxford: Blackwell Publishing.

———. 2007. "Foreword." In *Everyday Religion: Observing Modern Religious Lives*, edited by Nancy T. Ammerman, v–viii. New York: Oxford University Press.

———. 2014. *The Many Altars of Modernity: Toward a Paradigm for Religion in a Pluralistic Age*. Boston and Berlin: Walter de Gruyter.

———, and Anton C. Zijdervelf. 2009. *In Praise of Doubt: How to Have Convictions without Becoming a Fanatic*. New York: HarperOne.

———, Brigitte Berger, and Hansfried Kellner. 1973. *The Homeless Mind: Modernization and Consciousness*. New York: Random House.

———, Grace Davie, and Effie Fokas. 2008. *Religious America, Secular Europe: A Theme and Variations*. London and New York: Routledge.

Bergesen, Albert J., and Andrew M. Greeley. 2000. *God in the Movies*. New Brunswick, NJ, and London: Transaction Publishers.

Berkovits, Eliezer. 2001. "Faith after the Holocaust." In *A Holocaust Reader: Responses to the Nazi Extermination*, edited by Michael Morgan, 96–101. New York and Oxford: Oxford University Press.

Best, Wallace. 2005. *Passionately Human, No Less Divine: Religion and Culture in Black Chicago, 1915–1952*. Princeton, NJ: Princeton University Press.

Binder, Amy. 1999. "Friend and Foe: Boundary Work and Collective Identity in the Afrocentric and Multicultural Curriculum Movements in American Public Education." In *The Cultural Territories of Race: Black and White Boundaries*, edited by Michele Lamont, 221–248. Chicago and London: University of Chicago Press.

Blum, Edward J. 2007. *W. E. B. Du Bois, American Prophet*. Philadelphia: University of Pennsylvania Press.

———, and Jason R. Young. 2009. "The Forgotten Spiritual Power of W. E. B. Du Bois." In *The Souls of W. E. B. Du Bois: New Essays and Reflections*, edited by Edward J. Blum and Jason R. Young, vii–xxii. Macon, GA: Mercer University Press.

Blumenthal, David. 1993. *Facing the Abusing God: A Theology of Protest*. Louisville, KY: Westminster/John Knox Press.

Bonino, José Miguez. 1975. *Doing Theology in a Revolutionary Situation*. Philadelphia, PA: Fortress Press.

Braiterman, Zachary. 1998. *(God) after Auschwitz: Tradition and Change in Post-Holocaust Jewish Thought*. Princeton, NJ: Princeton University Press.

Brown, Callum. 1992. "A Revisionist Approach to Religious Change." In *Religion and Modernization: Sociologists and Historians Debate the Secularization Thesis*, edited by Steve Bruce, 31–58. Oxford, UK: Clarendon Press.

Brown, Vincent. 2008. *The Reaper's Garden: Death and Power in the World of Atlantic Slavery*. Cambridge, MA: Harvard University Press.

Bruce, Steve. 1996. *Religion in the Modern World: From Cathedrals to Cults*. Oxford, UK, and New York: Oxford University Press.

———. 2011. *Secularization: In Defence of an Unfashionable Theory*. Oxford, UK, and New York: Oxford University Press.

Bryson, Bethany. 1996. "'Anything but Heavy Metal': Symbolic Exclusion and Musical Dislikes." *American Sociological Review* 61: 884–899.

Buhring, Kurt. 2008. *Conceptions of God, Freedom, and Ethics in African American and Jewish Theology*. New York: Palgrave Macmillan.

Burke, Kenneth. 1970. *The Rhetoric of Religion: Studies in Logology*. Berkeley and London: University of California Press.

Burrell, David B. 2008. *Deconstructing Theodicy: Why Job Has Nothing to Say to the Puzzled Suffering*. Grand Rapids, MI: Brazos Press.

Burton, Tara Isabella. 2020. *Strange Rites: New Religions for a Godless World*. New York: PublicAffairs.

Butler, Judith. 2011. "Is Judaism Zionism?" In *The Power of Religion in the Public Sphere*, edited by Eduardo Mendieta and Jonathan VanAntwerpen, 70–91. New York: Columbia University Press.
Cannon, Katie Geneva. 1995. *Katie's Canon: Womanism and the Soul of the Black Community*. New York: Continuum.
Casanova José. 1994. *Public Religions in the Modern World*. Chicago and London: University of Chicago Press.
———. 2006. "Secularization Revisited: A Reply to Talal Asad." In *Powers of the Secular Modern: Talal Asad and His Interlocutors*, edited by David Scott and Charles Hirschkind, 12–30. Stanford, CA: Stanford University Press.
Chalk, Frank, and Kurt Jonassohn. 1990. *The History and Sociology of Genocide*. New Haven, CT, and London: Yale University Press.
Charney, Leo, and Vanessa Schwartz. 1995. "Introduction." In *Cinema and the Invention of Modern Life*, edited by Leo Charney and Vanessa Schwartz, 1–12. Berkeley and Los Angeles: University of California Press.
Chopp, Rebecca S. 1986. *The Praxis of Suffering: An Interpretation of Liberation and Political Theologies*. Eugene, OR: Wipf & Stock.
Clark, Jawanza Eric. 2012. *Indigenous Black Theology: Toward an African-Centered Theology of the African American Religious Experience*. New York: Palgrave Macmillan.
Cleage, Albert. 1989. *The Black Messiah*. Trenton, NJ: Africa World Press.
Cohen, Arthur. 1993. *The Tremendum: A Theological Interpretation of the Holocaust*. New York: Continuum.
Coleman, Monica A. 2008. *Making a Way Out of No Way: A Womanist Theology*. Minneapolis, MN: Fortress Press.
———. 2013. "Introduction: Ain't I a Womanist Too? Third Wave Womanist Religious Thought." In *Ain't I a Womanist Too? Third Wave Womanist Religious Thought*, edited by Monica A. Coleman, 1–31. Minneapolis, MN: Fortress Press.
Coleman, Will. 2000. *Tribal Talk: Black Theology, Hermeneutics, and African/American Ways of "Telling the Story."* University Park: Pennsylvania State University Press.
Collins, Randall. 2004. *Interaction Ritual Chains*. Princeton, NJ, and Oxford: Princeton University Press.
Cone, Cecil Wayne. 1975. *The Identity Crisis in Black Theology*. Nashville, TN: AMEC.
Cone, James. 1969. *Black Theology and Black Power*. Maryknoll, NY: Orbis Books.
———. 1970. *A Black Theology of Liberation*. Maryknoll, NY: Orbis Books.
———. 1984. *For My People: Black Theology and the Black Church*. Maryknoll, NY: Orbis Books.
———. 1989. "Black Theology as Liberation Theology." In *African American Religious Studies: An Interdisciplinary Anthology*, edited by Gayraud Wilmore, 177–207. Durham, NC, and London: Duke University Press.
———. 1992. *The Spirituals and the Blues: An Interpretation*. Maryknoll, NY: Orbis Books.

———. 1999. *Risks of Faith: The Emergence of a Black Theology of Liberation, 1968–1998*. Boston: Beacon Press.

———. 2011. *The Cross and the Lynching Tree*. Maryknoll, NY: Orbis Books.

Connolly, William. 1999. *Why I Am Not a Secularist*. Minneapolis and London: University of Minnesota Press.

Cooper, John. 1967. *The Roots of the Radical Theology*. Philadelphia, PA: Westminster Press.

Cooper, John C., and Carl Skrade. 1970. "Preface." In *Celluloid and Symbols*, edited by John C. Cooper and Carl Skrade, vii–x. Philadelphia, PA: Fortress Press.

Copeland, M. Shawn. 2010. *Enfleshing Freedom: Body, Race, and Being*. Minneapolis, MN: Fortress Press.

Cox, Harvey. 1965. *The Secular City: A Celebration of Its Liberties and an Invitation to Its Disciplines*. New York: Macmillan.

Crawford, Elaine Brown. 2002. *Hope in the Holler: A Womanist Theology*. Louisville and London: Westminster/John Knox Press.

Cripps, Thomas. 1996. "The Making of The Birth of a Race: The Emerging Politics of Identity in Silent Movies." In *The Birth of Whiteness: Race and the Emergence of U.S. Cinema*, edited by Daniel Bernardi, 38–55. New Brunswick, NJ: Rutgers University Press.

Crumpton, Stephanie. 2014. *A Womanist Pastoral Theology against Intimate and Cultural Violence*. New York: Palgrave Macmillan.

Cupitt, Don. 1976. *The Leap of Reason*. London: Sheldon Press.

Damico, Linda. 1987. *The Anarchist Dimension of Liberation Theology*. New York: Peter Lang.

Davis, David Brion. 2003. *Challenging the Boundaries of Slavery*. Cambridge, MA, and London: Harvard University Press.

Davis, Natalie Zemon. 2000. *Slaves on Screen: Film and Historical Vision*. Cambridge, MA: Harvard University Press.

Day, Keri. 2012. *Unfinished Business: Black Women, the Black Church, and the Struggle to Thrive in America*. Maryknoll, NY: Orbis Books.

———. 2014. "Doctrine of God in African American Theology." In *The Oxford Handbook of African American Theology*, edited by Katie G. Cannon and Anthony Pinn, 139–152. New York: Oxford University Press.

Deacy, Christopher. 2007. "Faith in Film." In *The Religion and Film Reader*, edited by Jolyon Mitchell and S. Brent Plate, 306–311. New York and London: Routledge.

Deeb, Lara. 2006. *An Enchanted Modern: Gender and Public Piety in Shi'I Lebanon*. Princeton, NJ, and Oxford: Princeton University Press.

Detweiler, Craig. 2008. *Into the Dark: Seeing the Sacred in the Top Films of the 21st Century*. Grand Rapids, MI: Baker Academic.

Diallo, Siradiou. 2008. "African Cinema Is Not a Cinema of Folklore." In *Ousmane Sembène: Interviews*, edited by Annett Busch and Max Annas, 52–62. Jackson: University Press of Mississippi.

Diawara, Manthia. 2011. "The Iconography of West African Cinema." In *Symbolic Narratives/African Cinema: Audiences, Theory, and the Moving Image*, edited by June Givanni, 81–89. London: British Film Institute.

Dillon, Michele. 2018. *Postsecular Catholicism: Relevance and Renewal*. New York: Oxford University Press.

DiMaggio, Paul. 1992. "Cultural Boundaries and Structural Change: The Extension of the High Culture Model to Theater, Opera, and the Dance, 1900–1940." In *Cultivating Differences: Symbolic Boundaries and the Making of Inequality*, edited by Michele Lamont and Marcel Fournier, 21–57. Chicago and London: University of Chicago Press.

Dorrien, Gary. 2015. *The New Abolition: W. E. B. Du Bois and the Black Social Gospel*. New Haven, CT, and London: Yale University Press.

Douglas, Kelly Brown. 1999. *The Black Christ*. Maryknoll, NY: Orbis Books.

———. 2012. *Black Bodies and the Black Church: A Blues Slant*. New York: Palgrave Macmillan.

———. 2015. *Stand Your Ground: Black Bodies and the Justice of God*. Maryknoll, NY: Orbis Books.

Dunn, Stephane. 2008. *"Baad Bitches" and Sassy Supermamas: Black Power Action Films*. Urbana and Chicago: University of Illinois Press.

Durkheim, Emile. [1912] 1995. *The Elementary Forms of Religious Life*. New York: Free Press.

———. 2004. "The Relationship between God and the World (Conclusion): Providence, Evil, Optimism, and Pessimism." In *Durkheim's Philosophy Lectures: Notes from the Lycee de Sens Course, 1883–1884*, edited by Neil Gross and Robert Alun Jones, 311–314. Cambridge, UK, and New York: Cambridge University Press.

Dyson, Michael Eric. 2015. "God Complex, Complex Gods, or God's Complex: Jay-Z, Poor Black Youth, and Making 'the Struggle' Divine." In *Religion in Hip Hop: Mapping the New Terrain in the U.S.*, edited by Monica Miller, Anthony Pinn, and Bernard "Bun B" Freeman, 54–68. London and New York: Bloomsbury.

Eagleton, Terry. 2010. *On Evil*. New Haven, CT, and London: Yale University Press.

Edmondson, Mika. 2017. *The Power of Unearned Suffering: The Roots and Implications of Martin Luther King Jr.'s Theodicy*. Lanham, MD: Lexington Books.

Equiano, Olaudah. 1999. *The Life of Olaudah Equiano: Or Gustavvus Vassa, the African*. Mineola, NY: Dover Publications.

Evans, Curtis. 2008. *The Burden of Black Religion*. New York and Oxford, UK: Oxford University Press.

Evans, James, Jr. 1987. *Black Theology: A Critical Assessment and Annotated Bibliography*. New York and Westport, CT: Greenwood Press.

———. 1992. *We Have Been Believers: An African American Systematic Theology*. Minneapolis, MN: Fortress Press.

Eyerman, Ron. 2001. *Cultural Trauma: Slavery and the Formation of African American Identity*. Cambridge, UK, and New York: Cambridge University Press.

Fackenheim, Emil. 1968. *Quest for Past and Future*. Boston: Beacon Press.

———. 1970. *God's Presence in History: Jewish Affirmations and Philosophical Reflections*. New York and London: New York University Press.

———. 2001. "Jewish Faith and the Holocaust: A Fragment." In *A Holocaust Reader: Responses to the Nazi Extermination*, edited by Michael Morgan, 115–121. New York and Oxford, UK: Oxford University Press.
Feuerbach, Ludwig. [1841] 1989. *The Essence of Christianity*. Amherst, NY: Prometheus Books.
Field, Allyson Nadia. 2015. *Uplift Cinema: The Emergence of African American Film and the Possibility of Black Modernity*. Durham, NC, and London: Duke University Press.
Floyd-Thomas, Juan. 2014. "Liberation in African American Theology." In *The Oxford Handbook of African American Theology*, edited by Katie G. Cannon and Anthony Pinn, 200–211. New York: Oxford University Press.
Floyd-Thomas, Stacey M. 2006. "Introduction: Writing for Our Lives—Womanism as an Epistemological Revolution." In *Deeper Shades of Purple: Womanism in Religion and Society*, edited by Stacey M. Floyd-Thomas, 1–16. New York and London: New York University Press.
———. 2008. "From Embodied Theodicy to Embodied Theos." In *Being Black, Teaching Black: Politics and Pedagogy in Religious Studies*, edited by Nancy Lynne Westfield, 125–135. Nashville, TN: Abingdon Press.
Foster, Benjamin R. (ed.). 2001. *The Epic of Gilgamesh: A Norton Critical Edition*. New York: W. W. Norton & Company.
Frederick, Marla. 2003. *Between Sundays: Black Women and Everyday Struggles of Faith*. Berkeley and London: University of California Press.
Fukuyama, Francis. 1992. *The End of History and the Last Man*. New York: Free Press.
Fuller, Steve. 2006. *The New Sociological Imagination*. London: Sage.
Gadjigo, Samba. 2008. "Interview with Ousmane Sembène." In *Ousmane Sembène: Interviews*, edited by Annett Busch and Max Annas, 190–196. Jackson: University of Mississippi Press.
Garrett, Greg. 2007. *The Gospel According to Hollywood*. Louisville, KY, and London: Westminster/John Knox Press.
Ghali, Noureddine. 2008. "Interview with Ousmane Sembène." In *Ousmane Sembène: Interviews*, edited by Annett Busch and Max Annas, 72–81. Jackson: University of Mississippi Press.
Gieryn, Thomas F. 1983. "Boundary-Work and the Demarcation of Science from Non-Science: Strains and Interests in Professional Ideologies of Scientists." *American Sociological Review* 48: 781–795.
Giesen, Bernhard. 1998. *Intellectuals and the Nation: Collective Identity in a German Axial Age*. Cambridge, UK, and New York: Cambridge University Press.
Gillespie, Michael Allen. 2008. *The Theological Origins of Modernity*. Chicago and London: University of Chicago Press.
Glaude, Eddie S., Jr. 2000. *Exodus: Religion, Race, and Nation in Early Nineteenth-Century Black America*. Chicago and London: University of Chicago Press.
———. 2007. *In a Shade of Blue: Pragmatism and the Politics of Black America*. Chicago and London: University of Chicago Press.

Goffman, Erving. 1967. *Interaction Ritual: Essays on Face-to-Face Behavior*. New York: Pantheon Books.
Gordon, Richard. *Cinema, Slavery, and Brazilian Nationalism*. Austin: University of Texas Press.
Grant, Jacquelyn. 1989. "Womanist Theology: Black Women's Experience as a Source for Doing Theology with Special Reference to Christology." In *African American Religious Studies: An Interdisciplinary Anthology*, edited by Gayraud Wilmore, 208–227. Durham, NNC, and London: Duke University Press.
Guerrero, Andres G. 1993. *A Chicano Theology*. Maryknoll, NY: Orbis Books.
Gunning, Tom. 2006. "Modernity and Cinema: A Culture of Shocks and Flows." In *Cinema and Modernity*, edited by Murray Pomerance, 297–315. New Brunswick, NJ, and London: Rutgers University Press.
Gutierrez, Gustavo. 1973. *A Theology of Liberation: History, Politics, and Salvation*. Maryknoll, NY: Orbis Books.
———. 1987. *On Job: God-Talk and the Suffering of the Innocent*. Maryknoll, NY: Orbis Books.
———. 1999. "The Task and Content of Liberation Theology." In *The Cambridge Companion to Liberation Theology*, edited by Christopher Rowland, 19–38. Cambridge, UK, and New York: Cambridge University Press.
———, and Gerhard Ludwig Muller. 2015. *On the Side of the Poor: The Theology of Liberation*. Maryknoll, NY: Orbis Books.
Habermas, Jürgen. 1984. *Theory of Communicative Action. Volume 1: Reason and the Rationalization of Society*. Boston: Beacon.
———. 1987. *The Philosophical Discourse of Modernity: Twelve Lectures*. Cambridge, MA: MIT Press.
———. 2002. *Religion and Rationality: Essays on Reason, God, and Modernity*. Cambridge, UK: Polity Press.
———. 2006. "Prepolitical Foundations of the Democratic Constitutional State?" In *The Dialectics of Secularization: On Reason and Religion*, edited by Florian Schuller, 19–52. San Francisco, CA: Ignatius Press.
———. 2011. "The Political: The Rational Meaning of a Questionable Inheritance of Political Theology." In *The Power of Religion in the Public Sphere*, edited by Eduardo Mendieta and Jonathan VanAntwerpen, 15–33. New York: Columbia University Press.
Hackett, Rosalind, and Benjamin Soares. 2015. "Introduction: New Media and Religious Transformations in Africa." In *New Media and Religious Transformations in Africa*, edited by Rosalind Hackett and Benjamin Soares, 1–16. Bloomington and Indianapolis: Indiana University Press.
Haley, Alex. 1976. *Roots: The Saga of an American Family*. New York: Doubleday.
Hardy, Clarence, III. 2003. *James Baldwin's God: Sex, Hope, and Crisis in Black Holiness Culture*. Knoxville: University of Tennessee Press.
Harris, Fredrick. 1999. *Something Within: Religion in African American Political Activism*. Oxford, UK: Oxford University Press.
Hart, David Bentley. 2013. *The Experience of God: Being, Consciousness, Bliss*. New Haven, CT, and London: Yale University Press.

Hart, William David. 2011. *Afro-Eccentricity: Beyond the Standard Narrative of Black Religion*. New York: Palgrave Macmillan.
Hayes, Diana. 2011. *Standing in the Shoes My Mother Made: A Womanist Theology*. Minneapolis, MN: Fortress Press.
Haynes, Jonathan. 2016. *Nollywood: The Creation of Nigerian Film Genres*. Chicago and London: University of Chicago Press.
Hennebelle, Guy. 2008. "We Are Governed in Black Africa by Colonialism's Disabled Children." In *Ousmane Sembène: Interviews*, edited by Annett Busch and Max Annas, 18–23. Jackson: University Press of Mississippi.
Hernandez, Jill Graper. 2016. *Early Modern Women and the Problem of Evil: Atrocity and Theodicy*. New York and London: Routledge.
Heyward, Isabel Carter. 2010. *The Redemption of God: A Theology of Mutual Relation*. Eugene, OR: Wipf & Stock.
Hick, John. 1963. *Philosophy of Religion*. Englewood Cliffs, NJ: Prentice-Hall.
———. 1966. *Evil and the God of Love*. New York: Harper & Row.
Hickman, Jared. 2017. *Black Prometheus: Race and Radicalism in the Age of Atlantic Slavery*. New York: Oxford University Press.
Hicks, Derek. 2012. *Reclaiming Spirit in the Black Faith Tradition*. New York: Palgrave Macmillan.
Higgins, Kathleen Marie. 1987. *Nietzsche's Zarathustra*. Philadelphia, PA: Temple University Press.
Hochschild, Adam. 1998. *King Leopold's Ghost: A Story of Greed, Terror, and Heroism in Colonial Africa*. Boston and New York: Houghton Mifflin Company.
Hopkins, Dwight. 2000. *Down, Up, and Over: Slave Religion and Black Theology*. Minneapolis, MN: Fortress Press.
———. 2001. "Black Theology on God: The Divine in Black Popular Religion." In *The Ties That Bind: African American and Hispanic American/Latino/a Theologies in Dialogue*, edited by Anthony Pinn and Benjamin Valentin, 99–112. New York and London: Continuum.
———. 2009. "W. E. B. Du Bois on God and Jesus." In *The Souls of W. E. B. Du Bois: New Essays and Reflections*, edited by Edward J. Blum and Jason R. Young, 18–40. Macon, GA: Mercer University Press.
Hurley, Neil P. 1970. *Theology through Film*. New York and London: Harper & Row.
Hutchison, William. 1976. *The Modernist Impulse in American Protestantism*. Cambridge, MA, and London: Harvard University Press.
Isasi-Diaz, Ada Maria. 1996. *Mujerista Theology: A Theology for the Twenty-First Century*. Maryknoll, NY: Orbis Books.
———. 2004. *En la Lucha/In the Struggle: Elaborating a Mujerista Theology*. Minneapolis, MN: Fortress Press.
Jackson, Sherman A. 2009. *Islam and the Problem of Black Suffering*. Oxford, UK, and New York: Oxford University Press.
Jakelic, Slavica. 2016. *Collectivistic Religions: Religion, Choice, and Identity in Late Modernity*. New York: Routledge.
Jedlowski, Alessandro. 2013. "From Nollywood to Nollyworld: Processes of Transnationalization in the Nigerian Video Film Industry." In *Global Nollywood:*

The Transnational Dimensions of an African Video Film Industry, edited by Matthias Krings and Onookome Olome, 25–45. Bloomington and Indianapolis: Indiana University Press.

Jelks, Randal Maurice. 2012. *Benjamin Elijah Mays, Schoolmaster of the Movement: A Biography*. Chapel Hill: University of North Carolina Press.

———. 2019. *Faith and Struggle in the Lives of Four African Americans: Ethel Waters, Mary Lou Williams, Eldridge Cleaver, and Muhammad Ali*. London and New York: Bloomsbury Academic.

Jewett, Robert. 1993. *Saint Paul at the Movies: The Apostle's Dialogue with American Culture*. Louisville, KY: Westminster/John Knox Press.

———. 1999. *Saint Paul Returns to the Movies: Triumph over Shame*. Grand Rapids, MI, and Cambridge, UK: William B. Eerdmans.

Jonas, Hans. 1996. "The Concept of God after Auschwitz: A Jewish Voice." In *Mortality and Morality: A Search for the Good after Auschwitz*, edited by Lawrence Vogel, 131–143. Evanston: Northwestern University Press.

Jones, Major J. 1971. *Black Awareness: A Theology of Hope*. Nashville, TN, and New York: Abingdon Press.

———. 1987. *The Color of God: The Concept of God in Afro-American Thought*. Macon, GA: Mercer University Press.

Jones, William R. 1973. *Is God a White Racist? A Preamble to Black Theology*. Boston: Beacon Press.

———. 1978. "The Case for Black Humanism." In *Black Theology II: Essays on the Formation and Outreach of Contemporary Black Theology*, edited by Calvin E. Bruce and William R. Jones, 215–31. Cranbury, NJ, and London: Associated University Presses.

Kahn, Jonathon S. 2009. *Divine Discontent: The Religious Imagination of W. E. B. Du Bois*. Oxford, UK, and London: Oxford University Press.

Kant, Immanuel. [1793] 1960. *Religion within the Limits of Reason Alone*. New York: Harper & Row.

Kaplan, E. Ann. 2005. *Trauma Culture: The Politics of Terror and Loss in Media and Literature*. New Brunswick, NJ, and London: Rutgers University Press.

Katz, Elihu, and Michael Gurevitch. 1976. *The Secularization of Leisure: Culture and Communication in Israel*. London: Faber & Faber.

Kayes, D. Christopher. 2006. "Organizational Corruption as Theodicy." *Journal of Business Ethics* 67: 51–62

Key, Andre Eugene. 2011. *What's My Name: An Autoethnography of the Problem of Moral Evil and Ethnic Suffering in Black Judaism*. PhD diss., Temple University, Philadelphia, PA.

Kirk-Duggan, Cheryl A. 2001. *Refiner's Fire: A Religious Engagement with Violence*. Minneapolis, MN: Fortress Press.

———. 2014. "Signifying Love and Embodied Relationality: Toward a Womanist Theological Anthropology. In *Womanist and Black Feminist Responses to Tyler Perry's Productions*, edited by LeRhonda S. Manigault-Bryant, Tamura Lomax, and Carol Duncan, 41–56. New York: Palgrave Macmillan.

Kourouma, Ahmadou. 2006. *Allah Is Not Obliged*. New York: Anchor Books.

Krings, Matthias, and Onookome Okome. 2013. "Nollywood and Its Diaspora: An Introduction." In *Global Nollywood: The Transnational Dimensions of an African Video Film Industry*, edited by Matthias Krings and Onookome Okome, 1–24. Bloomington and Indianapolis: Indiana University Press.

Lackey, Michael. 2007. *African American Atheists and Political Liberation: A Study of the Sociocultural Dynamics of Faith*. Gainesville: University Press of Florida.

Lamont, Michele. 1992. *Money, Morals, and Manners: The Culture of the French and the American Upper-Middle Class*. Chicago and London: University of Chicago Press.

———. 2000. *The Dignity of Working Men: Morality and the Boundaries of Race, Class, and Immigration*. Cambridge, MA, and London: Harvard University Press.

———, and Lauren Thevenot. 2000. "Introduction: Toward a Renewed Comparative Cultural Sociology." In *Rethinking Comparative Cultural Studies: Repertoires of Evaluation in France and the United States*, edited by Michele Lamont and Laurent Thevenot, 1–22. Cambridge, UK, and New York: Cambridge University Press.

Lane, Christopher. 2011. *The Age of Doubt: Tracing the Roots of Our Religious Uncertainty*. New Haven, CT, and London: Yale University Press.

Leab, Daniel J. 1975. *From Sambo to Superspade: The Black Experience in Motion Pictures*. Boston: Houghton Mifflin Company.

Leaman, Oliver. 1995. *Evil and Suffering in Jewish Philosophy*. New York: Cambridge University Press.

Lee, Shayne. 2015. *Tyler Perry's America: Inside His Films*. Lanham, MD: Rowman & Littlefield.

———, and Phillip Sinitiere. 2009. *Holy Mavericks: Evangelical Innovators and the Spiritual Marketplace*. New York and London: New York University Press.

Leibniz, Gottfried. [1710] 2015. *Theodicy: Essays on the Goodness of God the Freedom of Man and the Origin of Evil*. Createspace Independent Publishing Platform.

Lena, Jennifer C., and Richard Peterson. 2008. "Classification as Culture: Types and Trajectories of Music Genres." *American Sociological Review* 73: 697–718.

Litch, Mary M. 2010. *Philosophy Through Film*, 2nd ed. New York and London: Routledge.

Lloyd, Vincent. 2018. *Religion of the Field Negro: On Black Secularism and Black Theology*. New York: Fordham University Press.

Locke, Hubert. 1999. "The Death of God: An African-American Perspective." In *The Death of God Movement and the Holocaust: Radical Theology Encounters the Shoah*, edited by Stephen R. Haynes and John K. Roth, 91–97. Westport, CT, and London: Greenwood Press.

———. 2004. "Religion and the Rwandan Genocide: Some Preliminary Considerations." In *Genocide in Rwanda: Complicity of the Churches?* edited by Carol Rittner, John Roth, and Wendy Whitworth, 27–35. St. Paul, MN: Paragon House.

Luckmann, Thomas. 1996. "The Privatization of Religion and Morality." In *Detraditionalization: Critical Reflections on Authority and Identity*, edited by Paul

Heelas, Scott Lash, and Paul Morris, 72–86. Cambridge, MA, and Oxford, UK: Blackwell Publishers.

Lyden, John C. 2003. *Film as Religion: Myths, Morals, and Rituals*. New York and London: New York University Press.

Mahmood, Saba. 2015. *Religious Difference in a Secular Age: A Minority Report*. Princeton, NJ: Princeton University Press.

Mamdani, Mahmood. 2001. *When Victims Become Killers: Colonialism, Nativism, and the Genocide in Rwanda*. Princeton, NY: Princeton University Press.

Marsh, Clive. 1997. "Film and Theologies of Culture." In *Explorations in Theology and Film*, edited by Clive Marsh and Gaye Ortiz, 21–34. Malden, MA, and Oxford, UK: Blackwell Publishers.

Massood, Paula J. 2003. *Black City Cinema: African American Urban Experiences in Film*. Philadelphia, PA: Temple University Press.

Mast, Jason L. 2013. *The Performative Presidency: Crisis and Resurrection during the Clinton Years*. Cambridge, UK, and New York: Cambridge University Press.

Mays, Benjamin E. 1938. *The Negro's God: As Reflected in His Literature*. Boston: Chapman & Grimes.

Mays, Milton A. 1964. "Frankenstein, Mary Shelley's Black Theodicy." *Southern Humanities Review* 3: 146–153.

Medina, Nestor. 2013. "Rethinking Liberation: Toward a Canadian Latin@ Theology." In *The Reemergence of Liberation Theologies: Models for the Twenty-First Century*, edited by Thia Cooper, 77–87. New York: Palgrave Macmillan.

Meldau, Robert, and Stan Knapp. 2013, June 28. "Sociology as Theodicy." *BYU Journal of Undergraduate Research*.

Mendieta, Eduardo, and Jonathan VanAntwerpen. 2011. "Introduction: The Power of Religion in the Public Sphere." In *The Power of Religion in the Public Sphere*, edited by Eduardo Mendieta and Jonathan VanAntwerpen, 1–14. New York: Columbia University Press.

Metz, Johannes. 1969. *Theology of the World*. New York: Herder & Herder.

Moltmann, Jürgen. 1967. *Theology of Hope: On the Ground and the Implications of a Christian Eschatology*. New York and Evanston, IL: Harper & Row.

———. 1999. *God for a Secular Society: The Public Relevance of Theology*. Minneapolis, MN: Fortress Press.

Morgan, David, and Iain Wilkinson. 2001. "The Problem of Suffering and the Sociological Task of Theodicy." *European Journal of Social Theory* 4: 199–214.

Morris, Aldon. 1984. *The Origins of the Civil Rights Movement*. New York: Free Press.

Morrison, Toni. 1970. *The Bluest Eye*. New York: Holt, Rinehart, and Winston.

———. 1987. *Beloved: A Novel*. New York: Alfred A. Knopf.

Murphy, David, and Patrick Williams. 2007. *Postcolonial African Cinema: Ten Directors*. Manchester, UK: Manchester University Press.

Neal, Ronald. 2012. *Democracy in Twenty-First Century America: Race, Class, Religion, and Region*. Macon, GA: Mercer University Press.

Neiman, Susan. 2002. *Evil in Modern Thought: An Alternative History of Philosophy*. Princeton, NJ, and Oxford, UK: Princeton University Press.

Nichols, Bill. 2010. *Engaging Cinema: An Introduction to Film Studies*. New York and London: W. W. Norton & Company.
Niebuhr, H. Richard. 1951. *Christ and Culture*. New York: Harper & Brothers Publishers.
Nietzsche, Friedrich. [1887] 2014. *On the Genealogy of Morals*. New York: Penguin Classics.
Nippert-Eng, Christena E. 2008. *Home and Work: Negotiating Boundaries through Everyday Life*. Chicago and London: University of Chicago Press.
Northup, Solomon, and David Wilson. 1853. *Twelve Years a Slave*. Auburn, NY: Orton and Mulligan.
Okome, Onookome. 2010. "Nollywood and Its Critics." In *Viewing African Cinema in the Twenty-First Century: Art Films and the Nollywood Revolution*, edited by Mahir Saul and Ralph Austen, 26–41. Athens: Ohio University Press.
Oladunjoye, Tunde. 2008. "Jumping on the Bandwagon." In *Nollywood: The Video Phenomenon in Nigeria*, edited by Pierre Barrot, 62–69. Bloomington: Indiana University Press.
Palmer, Colin. 1975. "Religion and Magic in Mexican Slave Society, 1570–1650." In *Race and Slavery in the Western Hemisphere: Quantitative Studies*, edited by Stanley Engerman and Eugene Genovese, 311–328. Princeton, NJ: Princeton University.
Paoletti, Giovanni. 2008. "Some Concepts of 'Evil' in Durkheim's Thought." In *Suffering and Evil: The Durkheimian Legacy*, edited by W. S. F. Pickering and Massimo Rosati, 63–80. New York and Oxford, UK: Durkheim Press/Berghahn Books.
Paris, Peter. 1995. *The Spirituality of African Peoples: The Search for a Common Moral Discourse*. Minneapolis, MN: Fortress Press.
Parsons, Talcott. 1952. "Sociology and Social Psychology." In *Religious Perspectives in College Teaching*, edited by Hoxie N. Fairchild, 286–337. New York: Ronald Press Company.
———. 1974. "Religion in Postindustrial America: The Problem of Secularization." *Social Research* 41: 193–225.
Pattillo, Mary. 1998. "Church Culture as a Strategy of Action in the Black Community." *American Sociological Review* 63: 767–784.
Pfaff, Francoise. 1984. *The Cinema of Ousmane Sembène: A Pioneer of African Film*. Westport, CT, and London: Greenwood Press.
Phillips, D. Z. 2001. "Theism without Theodicy." In *Encountering Evil: Live Options in Theodicy*, edited by Stephen Davis, 14–60. Louisville, KY: Westminster/John Knox Press.
Pickering, W. S. F. 1980. "Theodicy and Social Theory: An Exploration of the Limits of Collaboration between Sociologist and Theologian." In *Sociology and Theology: Alliance and Conflict*, edited by David Martin, John Orme Mills, and W. S. F. Pickering, 59–79. New York: St. Martin's Press.
———. 2009. *Durkheim's Sociology of Religion: Themes and Theories*. Cambridge, UK: James Clarke & Co.

Pinn, Anthony B. 1995. *Why, Lord? Suffering and Evil in Black Theology*. New York: Continuum.

———. 2002. "Introduction." In *Moral Evil and Redemptive Suffering: A History of Theodicy in African American Religious Thought*, edited by Anthony B. Pinn, 1–20. Gainesville: University Press of Florida.

———. 2004. *African American Humanist Principles: Living and Thinking Like the Children of Nimrod*. New York: Palgrave Macmillan.

———. 2010. "Black Theology." In *Liberation Theology in the United States: An Introduction*, edited by Stacey M. Floyd-Thomas and Anthony Pinn, 15–36. New York and London: New York University Press.

———. 2012. *The End of God-Talk: An African American Humanist Theology*. New York and Oxford, UK: Oxford University Press.

———. 2015. "Zombies in the Hood: Rap Music, Camusian Absurdity, and the Structuring of Death." In *Religion in Hip Hop: Mapping the New Terrain in the U.S.*, edited by Monica R. Miller, Anthony B. Pinn, and Bernard Freeman, 183–197. London and New York: Bloomsbury Academic.

Plantinga, Alvin. 1967. *God and Other Minds: A Study of the Rational Justification of Belief in God*. Ithaca, NY, and London: Cornell University Press.

———. 1977. *God, Freedom, and Evil*. Grand Rapids, MI: Eerdmans.

Prentiss, Craig R. 2014. *Staging Faith: Religion and African American Theater from the Harlem Renaissance to World War II*. New York and London: New York University Press.

Pype, Katrien. 2013. "Religion, Migration, and Media Aesthetics: Notes on the Circulation and Reception of Nigerian Films in Kinshasa." In *Global Nollywood: The Transnational Dimensions of an African Video Film Industry*, edited by Matthias Krings and Onookome Okome, 199–222. Bloomington and Indianapolis: Indiana University Press.

Raboteau, Albert. 1995. *A Fire in the Bones: Reflections on African American Religious History*. Boston: Beacon Press.

———. 2004. *Slave Religion: The "Invisible Institution" in the Antebellum South*. Oxford, UK, and New York: Oxford University Press.

Rael, Patrick. 2000. "Black Theodicy: African Americans and Nationalism in the Antebellum North." *The North Star: A Journal of African American Religious History* 3: 1–24.

Raphael, Melissa. 2003. *The Female Face of God in Auschwitz: A Jewish Feminist Theology of the Holocaust*. London and New York: Routledge.

Redding, J. Saunders. 1951. *On Being Negro in America*. Indianapolis, IN, and New York: Bobbs-Merrill Company.

Reder, Michael, and Joseph Schmidt. 2010. "Habermas and Religion." In *An Awareness of What Is Missing: Faith and Reason in a Post-Secular Age*, edited by Ciaran Cronin, 1–14. Cambridge, UK, and Malden, MA: Polity Press.

Rediker, Marcus. 2007. *The Slave Ship: A Human History*. New York: Viking.

Reed, Teresa L. 2003. *The Holy and Profane: Religion in Black Popular Music*. Lexington: University Press of Kentucky.

Roberts, J. Deotis. 1971. *Liberation and Reconciliation: A Black Theology*. Philadelphia, PA: Westminster Press.
———. 1987. *Black Theology in Dialogue*. Philadelphia, PA: Westminster Press.
———. 1989. "Religio-Ethical Reflections upon the Experimental Components of a Philosophy of Black Liberation." In *African American Religious Studies: An Interdisciplinary Anthology*, edited by Gayraud Wilmore, 249–266. Durham, NC, and London: Duke University Press.
———. 2003. "A Christian Response to Evil and Suffering." In *Black Religion, Black Theology: The Collected Essays of J. Deotis Roberts*, edited by David Emmanuel Goatley, 169–178. Harrisburg, PA: Trinity Press International.
Robinson, Cedric J. 2007. *Forgeries of Memory and Meaning: Blacks and the Regimes of Race in American Theater and Film before World War II*. Chapel Hill: University of North Carolina Press.
Robinson, Zandria. 2014. *This Ain't Chicago: Race, Class, and Regional Identity in the Post-Soul South*. Chapel Hill: University of North Carolina Press.
Rodriguez, Ruben Rosario. 2008. *Racism and God-Talk: A Latino/a Perspective*. New York and London: New York University Press.
Rorty, Richard. 2005. "Anticlericalism and Atheism." In *The Future of Religion*, edited by Santiago Zabala, 29–41. New York: Columbia University Press.
Rosati, Massimo. 2008. "Suffering and Evil in the Elementary Forms." In *Suffering and Evil: The Durkheimian Legacy*, edited by W. S. F. Pickering and Massimo Rosati, 49–62. New York and Oxford, UK: Durkheim Press/Berghahn Books.
Roth, John K. 2001. "A Theodicy of Protest." In *Encountering Evil: Live Options in Theodicy*, edited by Stephen Davis, 1–20. Louisville, KY: Westminster/John Knox Press.
Rubenstein, Richard L. 1966. *After Auschwitz: Radical Theology and Contemporary Judaism*. Indianapolis, IN, and New York: Bobbs-Merrill Company.
Ryan, Judylyn. 2005. *Spirituality as Ideology in Black Women's Film and Literature*. Charlottesville: University of Virginia Press.
Saffari, Siavash. 2017. *Beyond Shariati: Modernity, Cosmopolitanism, and Islam in Iranian Political Thought*. Cambridge, UK: Cambridge University Press.
Salvatore, Armando. 2007. *The Public Sphere: Liberal Modernity, Catholicism, Islam*. New York: Palgrave Macmillan.
Salvatore, Nick. 2005. *Singing in a Strange Land: C. L. Franklin, the Black Church, and the Transformation of America*. New York and Boston: Little, Brown and Company.
Sands, Kathleen. 1994. *Escape from Paradise: Evil and Tragedy in Feminist Theology*. Minneapolis, MN: Fortress Press.
Savage, Barbara Dianne. 2008. *Your Spirits Walk Beside Us: The Politics of Black Religion*. Cambridge, MA, and London: Belknap Press of Harvard University Press.
Schmidt, Leigh Eric. 2006. *Restless Souls: The Making of American Spirituality*. New York: HarperOne.

Schweid, Eliezer. 2005. "Is There a Religious Meaning to the Idea of a Chosen People after the Shoah?" In *The Impact of the Holocaust on Jewish Theology*, edited by Steven T. Katz, 5–12. New York and London: New York University Press.

Scott, Mark. 2011. "Theodicy at the Margins: New Trajectories for the Problem of Evil." *Theology Today* 68: 149–152.

Sinclair, Charlene. 2013. "Toward a Twenty-First Century Black Liberation Ethic: A Marxist Reclamation." In *The Reemergence of Liberation Theologies: Models for the Twenty-First Century*, edited by Thia Cooper, 165–170. New York: Palgrave Macmillan.

Sophocles. 2007. *Four Tragedies: Ajax, Women of Trachis, Electra, Philoctetes*. Cambridge, MA: Hackett Publishing.

Sorett, Josef. 2016. "Secular Compared to What? Toward a History of the Trope of Black Sacred/Secular Fluidity." In *Race and Secularism in America*, edited by Jonathon S. Kahn and Vincent W. Lloyd, 43–73. New York: Columbia University Press.

Sorkin, David. 2008. *The Religious Enlightenment: Protestants, Jews, and Catholics from London to Vienna*. Princeton, NJ, and Oxford: Princeton University Press.

Sotiropoulos, Karen. 2006. *Staging Race: Black Performers in Turn of the Century America*. Cambridge, MA, and London: Harvard University Press.

Sparks, Allister. 2003. *Beyond the Miracle: Inside the New South Africa*. Chicago and London: University of Chicago Press.

Stark, Rodney. 1996. *The Rise of Christianity: How the Obscure, Marginal Jesus Movement Became the Dominant Religious Force in the Western World in a Few Centuries*. New York: HarperOne

Stewart, Jacqueline Najuma. 2005. *Migrating to the Movies: Cinema and Black Urban Modernity*. Berkeley and London: University of California Press.

Stowe, Harriet Beecher. 1852. *Uncle Tom's Cabin*. Boston: John P. Jewett & Company.

Swinburne, Richard. 1977. "The Problem of Evil." In *Reason and Religion*, edited by Stuart C. Brown, 81–102. Ithaca, NY: Cornell University Press.

Taylor, Charles. 1989. *Sources of the Self: The Making of Modern Identity*. Cambridge, MA: Harvard University Press.

———. 1999. "A Catholic Modernity?" In *A Catholic Modernity: Charles Taylor's Marianist Award Lecture*, edited by James Heft, 13–37. New York and Oxford, UK: Oxford University Press.

———. 2007. *A Secular Age*. Cambridge, MA, and London: Belknap Press of Harvard University Press.

———. 2011. "Why We Need a Radical Redefinition of Secularism." In *The Power of Religion in the Public Sphere*, edited by Eduardo Mendieta and Jonathan VanAntwerpen, 34–59. New York: Columbia University Press.

Taylor, Mark C. 1998. "Introduction." In *Critical Terms for Religious Studies*, edited by Mark C. Taylor, 1–19. Chicago and London: University of Chicago Press.

———. 2007. *After God*. Chicago and London: University of Chicago Press.

Terrell, JoAnne Marie. 2005. *Power in the Blood? The Cross in the African American Experience*. Eugene, OR: Wipf & Stock.

Townes, Emilie. 2006. *Womanist Ethics and the Cultural Production of Evil*. New York: Palgrave Macmillan.
Tsika, Noah. 2015. *Nollywood Stars: Media and Migration in West Africa and the Diaspora*. Bloomington and Indianapolis: Indiana University Press.
Turner, Bryan S. 1992. *Regulating Bodies: Essays in Medical Sociology*. London and New York: Routledge.
Twain, Mark. 1885. *Adventures of Huckleberry Finn*. Hartford, CT: Charles L. Webster & Co.
Ukadike, Nwachukwu Frank. 1994. *Black African Cinema*. Berkeley and London: University of California Press.
Urban, Martina. 2012. *Theodicy of Culture and the Jewish Ethos: David Koigen's Contribution to the Sociology of Religion*. Berlin and Boston: De Gruyter.
Utley, Ebony A. 2012. *Rap and Religion: Understanding the Gangsta's God*. Santa Barbara, CA: Praeger
Vahanian, Gabriel. 1961. *The Death of God: The Culture of Our Post-Christian Era*. New York: George Braziller.
Van Buren, Paul M. 1963. *The Secular Meaning of the Gospel: Based on an Analysis of Its Language*. New York: Macmillan.
Vattimo, Gianni. 1999. *Belief*. Stanford, CA: Stanford University Press.
Voltaire. [1759] 1991. *Candide*. New York: Dover Publications.
Walker, David. [1829] 1995. *David Walker's Appeal: To the Coloured Citizens of the World, but in Particular and Very Expressly, to Those of the United States of America*. New York: Hill & Wang.
Washington, Joseph, Jr. 1970. *The Politics of God*. Boston: Beacon Press.
Watkins, S. Craig. 1998. *Representing: Hip Hop Culture and the Production of Black Cinema*. Chicago and London: University of Chicago Press.
Weaver, Harold. 2008. "Filmmakers Have a Great Responsibility to Our People." In *Ousmane Sembène: Interviews*, edited by Annett Busch and Max Annas, 24–35. Jackson: University Press of Mississippi.
Weber, Daniel. 2000. "Culture or Commerce? Symbolic Boundaries in French and American Book Publishing." In *Rethinking Comparative Cultural Studies: Repertoires of Evaluation in France and the United States*, edited by Michele Lamont and Laurent Thevenot, 127–147. Cambridge, UK, and New York: Cambridge University Press.
Weber, Max. [1920] 2009. *The Protestant Ethic and the Spirit of Capitalism*. New York and London: W. W. Norton & Company.
———. 1958a. "The Three Forms of Theodicy." In *From Max Weber: Essays in Sociology*, edited by H. H. Gerth and C. Wright Mills, 358–359. New York: Oxford University Press.
———. 1958b. "The Social Psychology of the World Religions." In *From Max Weber: Essays in Sociology*, edited by H. H. Gerth and C. Wright Mills, 267–301. New York: Oxford University Press.
———. 1978. *Economy and Society: An Outline of Interpretive Sociology*. Berkeley and London: University of California Press.

Weisenfeld, Judith. 2007. *Hollywood Be Thy Name: African American Religion in American Film, 1929–1949*. Berkeley and London: University of California Press.

West, Cornel. 1982. *Prophesy Deliverance! An Afro-American Revolutionary Christianity*. Philadelphia, PA: Westminster Press.

———. 1999. "Black Theology and Human Identity." In *Black Faith and Public Talk: Critical Essays on James H. Cone's Black Theology and Black Power*, edited by Dwight Hopkins, 11–19. Maryknoll, NY: Orbis Books.

———. 2011. "Prophetic Religion and the Future of Capitalist Civilization." In *The Power of Religion in the Public Sphere*, edited by Eduardo Mendieta and Jonathan VanAntwerpen, 92–100. New York: Columbia University Press.

White, Andrea C. 2014. "Screening God." In *Womanist and Black Feminist Responses to Tyler Perry's Productions*, edited by LeRhonda S. Manigault-Bryant, Tamura Lomax, and Carol Duncan, 73–88. New York: Palgrave Macmillan.

Whitted, Qiana. 2009. *"A God of Justice?": The Problem of Evil in Twentieth-Century Black Literature*. Charlottesville and London: University of Virginia Press.

Williams, Delores S. 1993. *Sisters in the Wilderness: The Challenge of Womanist God-Talk*. Maryknoll, NY: Orbis Books.

Wilmore, Gayraud S. 1962. *The Secular Relevance of the Church*. Philadelphia, PA: Westminster Press.

———. 1989. "Introduction to Part Three." In *African American Religious Studies: An Interdisciplinary Anthology*, edited by Gayraud Wilmore, 173–175. Durham, NC, and London: Duke University Press.

———. 1998. *Black Religion and Black Radicalism: An Interpretation of the Religious History of African Americans*. Maryknoll, NY: Orbis Books.

Wilson, Bryan. 1982. *Religion in Sociological Perspective*. Oxford, UK, and New York: Oxford University Press.

Winter, Gibson. 1963. *The New Creation a Metropolis*. New York: Macmillan.

Witt, Emily. 2017. *Nollywood: The Making of a Film Empire*. New York: Columbia Global Reports.

Woolfork, Lisa. 2009. *Embodying American Slavery in Contemporary Culture*. Urbana and Chicago: University of Illinois Press.

Wrong, Michela. 2001. *In the Footsteps of Mr. Kurtz: Living on the Brink of Disaster in Mobutu's Congo*. New York: HarperCollins.

Wuthnow, Robert. 2012. *The God Problem: Expressing Faith and Being Reasonable*. Berkeley and London: University of California Press.

Yannaras, Christos. 2005. *On the Absence and Unknowability of God: Heidegger and the Areopagite*. London and New York: T&T Clark International.

Yearwood, Gladstone L. 2000. *Black Film as Signifying Practice: Cinema, Narration and the African American Aesthetic Tradition*. Trenton, NJ: Africa World Press.

Young, Josiah, III. 2007. "'Wonder What God Had in Mind?' Leibniz's Theodicy and the Art of Toni Morrison." *Black Theology* 5: 63–80.

Zerubavel, Eviatar. 1997. *Social Mindscapes: An Invitation to Cognitive Sociology*. Cambridge, MA: Harvard University Press.

Zuckerman, Phil. 2008. *Society without God: What the Least Religious Nations Can Tell Us about Contentment*. New York and London: New York University Press.
———, Luke W. Galen, and Frank L. Pasquale. 2016. *The Nonreligious: Understanding Secular People and Societies.* New York: Oxford University Press.

Index

Abu-Lughod, Lila, 41–42
Adventures of Huckleberry Finn, 98–99; filmic adaptations, 98–102
Agyeman, Jaramogi, 60
Alexander, Jeffrey, 22
Ali, Ayaan Hirsi, 54
Allah Is Not Obliged, 9, 12
Amata, Jeta, 102, 105, 191
The Amazing Grace, 102–105
Amistad, 79–80
Ammerman, Nancy, 14, 21, 34–37, 39, 74
apartheid, 16, 182, 184–186, 174, 203–204
Asante, Molefi Kete, 111
Ashes and Embers, 170–171

Baker-Fletcher, Karen, 69–70, 72
Baldwin, James, 58
Bamako, 173–174
Band of Angels, 110
Barth, Karl, 42
Beat the Drum, 200–201
Becker, Ernest, 4, 23–25
Belly, 164–165
Berger, Peter, 26–29, 31, 33, 40, 45
Berkovits, Eliezer, 76–77
Best, Wallace, 43
Beyond the Gates, 176–180, 202

black liberation theology, 14, 57–58, 73–75. *See also* black theology, womanist theology
Black November, 191
black theology, 57–66, 72. *See also* black liberation theology
Blumenthal, David, 6, 76
Bonino, José Miguez, 51
Boyz N the Hood, 166
Braiterman, Zachary, 4
Brother to Brother, 56
Burke, Kenneth, 40
Burton, Tara, 4, 30–31

Call Me Kucho, 54–55
Cannon, Katie, 67
Casanova, José, 29
Children of God, 56
Civil Brand, 16, 156–158, 169
Clark, Jawanza, 64
Cohen, Arthur, 76
Coleman, Monica, 70, 72
Coleman, Will, 64
Cone, Cecil, 62
Cone, James, 49–50, 58–59, 62, 65
Copeland, M. Shawn, 67–68, 71
Cox, Harvey, 43, 75
Crawford, Elaine, 68
The Crime of Padre Amaro, 53–54

Crumpton, Stephanie, 68
Cry Freedom, 181–182, 204
Cry, the Beloved Country, 182–184

Day, Keri, 63
A Day Late and a Dollar Short, 168
Deeb, Lara, 42
Diawara, Manthia, 115–116
Dillon, Michele, 29, 32
Django Unchained, 108
Douglas, Kelly Brown, 63, 68
Durkheim, Emile, 22, 25, 28, 47
Dyson, Michael Eric, 10

Economy and Society, 1
Eve's Bayou, 16, 158–161

Fackenheim, Emil, 42, 76–77
Family, 55
Floyd-Thomas, Juan, 57
Floyd-Thomas, Stacey, 43–44, 67–68
Frederick, Marla, 44

Gangster Paradise: Jerusalema, 56–57, 63, 73
Glory, 37–39
God Grew Tired of Us, 199–200
God Loves Uganda, 54
Goodbye Uncle Tom, 15, 92–96
The Gospel, 166
Grant, Jacquelyn, 68
Guerrero, Andres, 51
Gutierrez, Gustavo, 51

Habermas, Jürgen, 32–33, 43, 140
Hardy, Clarence, 58
Harriet, 87–92
Harris, Fredrick, 44
Hart, David Bentley, 42
Hayes, Diana, 68
Heyward, Isabel Carter, 46
Hickman, Jared, 6
Higgins, Kathleen, 4
Hopkins, Dwight, 62–63
Hurley, Neil, 40–41

Isasi-Diaz, Ada Maria, 51

Jackson, Sherman, 64
Jakelic, Slavica, 30
Jakes, Bishop T. D., 161, 169
Jonas, Hans, 76–77
Jones, Major, 61–62
Jones, William R., 61–62, 64–66, 70, 76

Key, Andre, 65–66, 74
Kirk-Duggan, Cheryl, 67, 71

Lackawanna Blues, 37
The Last King of Scotland, 197
The Last Supper, 108–109
Lee, Spike, 15, 142, 151, 169–170
Leibniz, Gottfried, 2–3, 6–7, 22, 49
Lemmons, Kasi, 87, 89–90, 158
liberationist films, 52–56
liberation theology, 50–52, 72, 75
Life, Above All, 54
Lincoln, 109–110
Litch, Mary, 34
Living in Bondage, 187–189, 192
Living in Bondage: Breaking Free, 192–193
Lord Help Us, 166–167
Luckmann, Thomas, 29
Lumo, 194–196
Lumumba, 193

Mahmood, Saba, 41
Mandela: Long Walk to Freedom, 184–185, 203–204
Mandingo, 107–108
Mays, Benjamin, 44, 57
Medina, Nestor, 52
Menace II Society, 166
Metz, Johannes, 42–43
Micheaux, Oscar, 45
Mississippi Damned, 38–39
Moltmann, Jürgen, 43
Mooz-Lum, 54
Morris, Aldon, 44
Morrison, Toni, 5

Motherland, 185–186

Neal, Ronald, 44
Neiman, Susan, 6
Niebuhr, H. Richard, 41
Nietzsche, Friedrich, 4, 22, 25, 47
Nightjohn, 110
Nollywood, 16, 186–193, 202
The North Star, 121–122

Pariah, 56
Parsons, Talcott, 25, 28
Pattillo, Mary, 44
Perry, Tyler: *Daddy's Little Girls*, 15, 141, 148–151, 156, 168–170; *Diary of a Mad Black Woman*, 151, 159; *Madea's Big Happy Family*, 168; *Meet the Browns*, 15, 143–148, 151; Womanist critique of, 70–71
Pfaff, Francoise, 119, 120
Pinn, Anthony, 5, 10, 65–66, 77, 171
Plantinga, Alvin, 3, 7
The Prayer Circle, 167–168
Pray the Devil Back to Hell, 198–199
The Preacher's Wife, 164
Precious, 71–72

Race to Freedom: The Underground Railroad, 82–85
Raphael, Melissa, 77
Red Hook Summer, 15–16, 151–156, 169–170
The River Niger, 38
Roberts, J. Deotis, 5–6, 59–60
Rodriguez, Ruben, 51
Rome, Open City, 52
Romero, 53–54
Roots, 7–9, 10
Rorty, Richard, 46
Roth, John, 4, 6
Rubenstein, Richard, 76
Rwandan Genocide, 12, 16, 175–180, 202–203
Ryan, Judylyn, 5

Sankofa, 13, 15, 96–98, 170
Savage, Barbara, 45
Schmidt, Leigh, 45
Schweid, Eliezer, 76
Scott, Mark, 72
A Screaming Man, 38–39
Sembène, Ousmane, 15, 175; and Bergman, 113–114, 136–137; *Borom Sarret*, 114–118, 138; *Ceddo*, 114, 122–124; *Emitai*, 115, 120–122; 124; *Faat Kiné*, 131–136, 140; *Guelwaar*, 115, 124, 128–131, 138–139; *Mandabi*, 114, 118–120; and modern values, 125–128, 131–136, 139; *Moolaade*, 115, 125–128; 138
Submission, 54
Swinburne, Richard, 6

Taken from Me, 16, 165
Taylor, Charles, 6, 27–33
Taylor, Mark C., 41
Terrell, JoAnne, 68, 72
theodicy, 1, 3–7, 19, 23; boundary work, 6–7, 11–12, 19–25, 40; Job, 2, 3, 26; post-Holocaust Jewish thinkers, 4, 76–77; of sin, 74–75, 101, 196; survey of approaches, 3–7; theodical secularity, 14, 19–21, 27, 33–37, 45
Townes, Emilie, 4–5, 68
Tsotsi, 204
Tubman, Harriet, 84–92
Twain, Mark, 98–99

Ukadike, N. Frank, 115–116
Uncle Tom's Cabin, 105–107
Underground Railroad, 81–92
Utley, Ebony, 45

Vattimo, Gianni, 45–46

War Dance, 197–198
Washington, Joseph, 61
Weber, Max, 1, 3, 6, 19, 21–25, 32
Weisenfeld, Judith, 45
West, Cornel, 1, 41, 49–50

When the Levees Broke: A Requiem in Four Acts, 170
White, Andrea, 70–71, 145, 168
Wilmore, Gayraud, 31–32, 57
Winter, Gibson, 41
Within Our Gates, 45
Without the King, 174
A Woman Called Moses, 85–87
Womanist and Black Feminist Responses to Tyler Perry's Productions, 70
womanist theology, 67–72. *See also* black liberation theology
Woman Thou Art Loosed: On the 7th Day, 16, 161–163, 169
Wuthnow, Robert, 5–6, 14, 36–37, 39

Yannaras, Christos, 73
Yeelen, 200–201

Zuckerman, Phil, 45

About the Author

Shayne Lee earned his PhD in sociology from Northwestern University and is associate professor of sociology at the University of Houston. He is the author of several books. They include *Tyler Perry's America: Inside His Films*; *Erotic Revolutionaries: Black Women, Sexuality, and Popular Culture*; and *T. D. Jakes: America's New Preacher*. He is coauthor of *Holy Mavericks: Evangelical Innovators and the Spiritual Marketplace*. Lee has been a guest expert on CNN, ABC, Fox, and HuffPost Live, and has offered editorials and commentary in numerous periodicals and media outlets. His research interests include cinema, modernity, religion, sexuality, and culture.

www.ingramcontent.com/pod-product-compliance
Lightning Source LLC
Chambersburg PA
CBHW021547020526
44115CB00038B/853